Incredible Moments in Sport

The 101 Biggest Moments in Sport

IAN SLATTER

ISBN-13: 978-1539897989
ISBN-10: 1539897982

DEDICATION

For Tanya, Euan, Bethan and my parents.

CONTENTS

May

June

July

INTRODUCTION

Ian Botham smashes the Aussie bowlers to all four corners of Headingley.

Torvill and Dean fall to the ice at the end of their perfect Bolero routine.

The Crucible holds its breath as Dennis Taylor attempts to sink the black for the World Championship.

Gareth Edwards crosses in the corner to score the greatest try ever.

English nails are bitten to the quick as Johnny Wilkinson steps back to kick for rugby World Cup glory.

Geoff Hurst blasts into the top of the net to win the World Cup.

The unbelievable roar as Mo Farah sprints clear to claim 10,000 metre gold on Super Saturday.

Do you remember how you felt when you watched those magical events unfurl, if you were lucky enough to witness them at the time? The elation; the ecstasy; the joy?

Sometimes a sporting occasion can make the hairs on the back of your neck stand up just thinking about it. Be it a sublime achievement, snatching victory from the jaws of defeat (or vice versa), or an unforgettable misdemeanour, these are the moments that get the nation talking; the "did you watch?" moments that become "do you remember?" moments. They are the events that make the front pages as well as the back pages, sometimes for the right reasons, sometime the wrong ones.

Relive 101 of the best remembered, most talked about moments in British and world sport – the build-up, the aftermath, and of course, the incredible events themselves.

January

25th January 1995
Cantona's kung fu kick

All eyes at the start of the match were on Manchester United's new record signing Andy Cole. It was his strike partner Eric Cantona who made all the headlines however, and for all the wrong reasons.

Cole had just been signed from Newcastle United for an English record £7 million to play alongside Cantona, who had been an inspired signing by Alex Ferguson. Having been enticed away from reigning champions Leeds for a bargain £1.2 million in 1992, Cantona was a key figure in the Man Utd side that won two Premier League trophies in as many years, their first since 1967. His silky skills and spectacular goals had made him a huge favourite at Old Trafford, but his strutting style, trademark upturned collar and propensity to get himself sent off made him a regular target for opposing fans.

Chasing a third consecutive title in 1994/95, United found themselves battling with high spending Blackburn Rovers. Fired by the goals of their prolific striker Alan Shearer, Rovers had closed a sixteen point gap to trail only on goal difference the previous season before slipping away at the end to finish runners-up to United, eight points behind the champions. Owner Jack Walker had given manager Kenny Dalglish even more money to spend on players in the close season, and they had themselves broken the English transfer record to sign a strike partner for Shearer, Chris Sutton. The two gelled quickly and started scoring freely, propelling Blackburn to the top of the table.

With Cantona in fine form, United were not far behind, and when he scored his twelfth goal of the season to secure a 1-0 victory against the leaders at Old Trafford, heading in a Ryan Giggs cross at the back post, United were hot on the heels of Rovers. With Cole just having signed as well, it was looking ominous for Blackburn.

Three days after their victory over Blackburn, United were playing again, looking to claim another three points away at struggling Crystal Palace. The match had started uneventfully, with no goals in the first half. Cantona was kept quiet by Palace's man-to-man marking, carried out vigorously by Richard Shaw, and although United felt that the Frenchman wasn't being given enough protection from some heavy challenges, referee Alan Wilkie dismissed their protests. Ferguson had noticed that Cantona was becoming frustrated, and cautioned him at half time not to allow himself to be provoked, but his warning fell on deaf ears, and shortly after the restart Cantona kicked out at Shaw after another strong challenge. His offence was spotted by Wilkie, who had no hesitation in showing him the red card. Cantona had to walk the length of the pitch to get to the tunnel, and as he walked along the touchline he was subjected to taunts and abuse from the home fans.

One Palace fan, named later as Matthew Simmons, ran down the steps from his seat in the stand to yell abuse at the Frenchman from just behind the advertising hoardings. Something he said made Cantona stop and turn. He started to run at Simmons, before leaping at him feet first and kicking him in the chest and, as he landed, punching him on top of his head. United kit-man Norman Davies pulled him back before he could launch another assault, but the damage was done. As other nearby fans stood open-mouthed, no-one watching at the stadium or on TV could quite believe what they had just witnessed. Then the United players reacted, angrily rushing over to confront the supporters, thinking that it was their team-mate who had been attacked.

Cantona was eventually led away from the pitch and back to the dressing room by Davies, goalkeeper Peter Schmeichel and two policemen, where he sat in silence, contemplating what he had just done. The club solicitor was quickly summoned, and at the end of the match, which almost irrelevantly ended 1-1, Ferguson was understandably furious, although he tried to play down the incident in his post-match interview.

Speculation soon mounted as to what Cantona's punishment would be, with some even calling for a lifetime ban. The club itself imposed a four month suspension on their player, and fined him £20,000. An FA hearing later imposed an unprecedented nine month ban on him, plus a further £10,000 fine. Many still thought he'd got off lightly. Cantona also faced criminal charges, and was initially sentenced to two weeks imprisonment by East Croydon Magistrates Court for common assault, although this was reduced to 120 hours of community service on appeal. Following his sentence, United and Cantona gave a press conference during which he uttered just one sentence, his now famous line *"When the seagulls follow the trawler, it's because they think sardines will be thrown into the sea."*

Cantona served his sentence by running coaching sessions for children, but wasn't allowed to return to the pitch until the following season, with United in his absence having to settle for second place, one point behind Blackburn. Frustratingly for them they would have claimed the title if they had won their final match, with Blackburn having lost their last game against Liverpool, but they could only manage a draw against West Ham. Inevitably, Cantona scored on his return, equalising from the penalty spot to secure a 2-2 draw for United's old rivals Liverpool. They went on the win the league and cup double.

27th January 1973
Barbarians score "That try"

The Barbarians invitational rugby side had always had a reputation for daring and attacking rugby, but one moment in their revered history stands out for its skill, flair and brilliance, to such an extent that it has become known in rugby circles simply as "that try".

The 1970s was a golden era for Welsh rugby. With six Five Nations titles, including three Grand Slams, the side boasted a string of names that have gone down in Welsh folklore. However, they hadn't beaten New Zealand since 1953, despite coming agonisingly close in December 1972. What looked like a try by Welsh full-back JPR Williams had been denied by the referee, who thought that Williams had failed to ground the ball fairly, despite having awarded a Keith Murdoch try for the All Blacks in similar circumstances. Wales were trailing 19-16 with a minute to go but had a chance to snatch a draw when they were awarded a penalty. Phil Bennett's kick hit the post though, and New Zealand held on for their fifth straight win against the Welsh.

Just over a month later, a Baa Baas side featuring seven Welsh stars, plus the cream of English, Scottish and Irish talent, playing at the home of Welsh rugby, Cardiff Arms Park, gave the Welsh supporters a chance for revenge. To give the match extra spice, many of the Barbarians players had successfully toured New Zealand in 1971 with the British and Irish Lions, winning their first ever series against the All Blacks. With TV coverage being nothing like it is today, few people had witnessed the win, and this was their chance to hopefully see a repeat performance.

A raucous Arms Park crowd was expecting something special, and they didn't have long to wait. With just four frantic minutes played New Zealand wing Bryan Williams sent a kick deep into the Barbarians' half. Outside half Bennett turned, waited for the ball to stop bouncing, then picked it up ten yards from his own try line. A quick glance over his shoulder revealed All Blacks flanker Alistair Scown bearing down on him with murderous intent. With his team-mates and most of the crowd expecting him to kick the ball to safety, Bennett had other ideas, and he turned and deftly sidestepped the onrushing Scown. Behind Scown were more chasers though, Peter Whiting and Ian Kirkpatrick, and he sidestepped them too. 50,000 supporters roared at his audacity, and he set off towards the New Zealand half.

Bennett sent a raking pass out to his compatriot, JPR Williams. The All Black defence was on top of him as he took the ball, but he managed to get it away to England captain John Pullin a split second before he was clattered by a high tackle from Bryan Williams. Referee Georges Domercq could have awarded a penalty, but he favoured allowing the game to flow and played the advantage. That allowed Pullin to pass to John Dawes, who looked as if he would pass to the outside before finding Tom David in support on his inside as the crowd rose to its feet as one.

David hared forward, into the New Zealand half, before being tackled by Geoff Whiting, but he got his pass away one-handed as he fell to ground. With the All Blacks defence outnumbered, Derek Quinnell brilliantly took the ball from David's offload from off his toes to keep the move going. Outside him Gareth Edwards was coming at pace, and he screamed for the ball. With perfect timing, Quinnell drew the tackle and fed Edwards, who had forty yards between himself and glory. He took the ball at speed, put his head back and made for the line. Joe Karam came across to attempt a tap tackle, getting got a hand to him, and Grant Batty desperately tried to stop him as he closed in on the line, but it was too little too late. With the noise in the stadium by now deafening, Edwards launched himself at the line, flying over in the corner to complete an incredible score of unparalleled skill.

Commentator Cliff Morgan's description of the "perfect try" has become almost as famous as the try itself:

"Kirkpatrick to Williams. This is great stuff! Phil Bennett covering chased by Alistair Scown. Brilliant, oh, that's brilliant! John Williams, Bryan Williams. Pullin. John Dawes, great dummy. To David, Tom David, the half-way line! Brilliant by Quinnell! This is Gareth Edwards! A dramatic start! What a score!!.....Oh that fellow Edwards....If the greatest writer of the written word would've written that story no one would have believed it. That really was something."

Edwards was unable to add the conversion, so the Baa Baas led 4-0. The match continued in a similar vein, although never quite reaching the heights of that wonder try. David Duckham was bundled into touch a yard short of the tryline at the end of move started by a scything break by Gerald Davies inside his own 22, then another breathtaking Davies break started a move that saw John Dawes touch down, only for play to be called back for a forward pass.

When the Barbarians did score again it was a scrappy affair, a mistake in a defensive New Zealand scrum allowing Fergus Slattery to pick up the ball and score. Then another turnover gave possession to the Barbarians inside the All

Blacks half and quick passing gave Duckham the chance to show his strength to cross for the third try of the match, making it 17-0 at half time.

The start of the second half saw a New Zealand comeback, a Karam penalty getting the on the board, then a Williams break put Grant Batty into space for a fine try of their own. Batty soon scored his second try of the game, running onto a chip kick before himself kicking over Williams and gathering the loose ball to score.

That made the score 17-11, with the All Blacks within a converted try of the Barbarians, but the Baa Baas had one final flourish with which to make the win safe. Duckham started the move, picking up a clearance kick just inside the All Black half and beating four tackles before being held. He offloaded to Quinnell, who fed Dawes, who passed to Williams. Williams found Gibson outside him, who slipped away from two tackles and slipped the ball to Slattery. Slattery got the ball away to Williams as he was tackled, and the fullback stepped outside Karam to cross in the corner. Bennett added the conversion to make the score 23-11, and that was how the match ended.

It was a game full of great enterprise and attacking play from both sides, but it was the opening try that is still remembered as a piece of rugby perfection that has yet to be bettered.

February

14th February 1984
Torvill and Dean's Bolero perfection

British medals at the Winter Olympics had been few and far between. Great Britain had not won a single medal for eight years before John Curry in 1976 and Robin Cousins in 1980 won men's figure skating golds. With just two medals in four Olympics, and only six since the Second World War, British hopes at the 1984 Games in Sarajevo rested once again on the ice, with Jayne Torvill and Christopher Dean.

Torvill and Dean were already three time ice dancing World Champions by 1984, but had finished outside the medals in fifth place in the previous Olympics at Lake Placid. As reigning World Champions they were understandably favourites for gold, but would face stiff competition from talented Russian pairs Natalia Bestemianova and Andrei Bukin, the World Championship silver medallists, and exciting youngsters Marina Klimova and Sergei Ponomarenk.

The pair had learned from their previous Olympic disappointment, and had both given up their jobs to concentrate on their skating full-time, with funding being provided by Nottingham Council, the city where they lived and trained. They recruited actor and West End star Michael Crawford to work with them and their coach Betty Callaway to create standout routines and to teach them to deliver their performances as an actor would. They had also begun to experiment with the idea of building themes into their routines, interpreting the music and choosing their costumes to complement it in a way not seen before.

For their free dance routine in Sarajevo the pair had chosen to skate to a piece of music called Bolero by French composer Joseph-Maurice Ravel, but faced the problem that it was significantly longer than the four minutes and ten seconds that was the maximum time allowed for an Olympic performance of. A musical arranger was called in, who managed to cut it down to four minutes twenty eight, but it couldn't be reduced any further without losing its integrity, and was still eighteen seconds too long. However, a close study of the rules revealed that they would be timed from the point when their skates first touched the ice, so ingeniously they created an opening sequence that didn't involve skating at all for the first eighteen seconds.

When they time came they took to the ice in flowing purple and violet costumes to great anticipation, and twenty four million viewers in the UK held their breath. Chris and Jayne knelt in their starting positions, keeping their skates off the ice to prevent the clock from starting. The music started, gently at first, and they began their routine swaying their torsos gracefully around each other like swans.

Gradually the music picked up pace, and Torvill and Dean followed suit, captivating the crowd with the emotion and passion of their performance. With balletic lifts and perfectly synchronised skating they told a story that held the spectators and the global audience in awe.

As the music reached a crescendo, Chris spun Jayne around in the air, then they descended to the ice together the instant the last note ended, and there they lay, visibly panting, their routine complete. The crowd knew they had witnessed something special and rose to their feet, the first standing ovation of the night.

As the cheers continued the world awaited the scores. Surely they had done enough for gold. The technical merit scores were outstanding – three 6.0s and six 5.9s – but as they were leaving the ice laden down with flowers and union jacks a gasp went up as the artistic merit scores were revealed - 6.0, 6.0, 6.0, 6.0, 6.0, 6.0, 6.0, 6.0, 6.0. It was the first, and still the only, perfect score in Olympic history.

Their achievement wasn't universally celebrated however. As well as the circumventing of the timing rules there were also complaints that didn't use multiple pieces of music during their performance, again stipulated in the rules. The judges accepted however that Bolero had different rhythms and pacing throughout, and this was sufficient. The rules were changed soon afterwards however, making it unlikely that a performance like theirs will ever be seen again.

The pair decided that they needed to start making money from their talents following the Olympics, and turned professional. They created a highly successful ice-show that they toured in the UK, Europe, Australia and the US, but their professional status meant that they were no longer eligible to take part in Olympic competitions. However, the rules changed prior to the 1994 Olympics in Lillehammer, and they started to plan their comeback. They made a triumphant return to competition at the European championships at the beginning of 1994, with a routine based around the song "Let's Face the Music and Dance". It was, once again, a routine that pushed the limits of the rules, but was well received as they claimed the European Championship gold. However, when it came to the Olympics one of their lifts was deemed to be illegal and their score was marked down, to the dismay of the crowd who booed when their scores were announced. Torvill and Dean finished third, taking a disappointing bronze medal, and they returned their attentions to their highly popular tours.

14th February 1988
Eddie the Eagle

Figure skating, bobsleigh, downhill skiing, curling. British athletes had competed in all of those sports at the Winter Olympics, but never in ski jumping. That was, however, until Eddie "The Eagle" Edwards came along. Although never likely to win a medal, his efforts won the hearts of the nation and the world and he became a national hero anyway.

Michael Edwards, known as Eddie, dreamt of competing at the Olympics. A talented downhill skier, he had narrowly missed out on selection for the GB team for the 1984 Games in Sarajevo. He was also one of the best speed skiers in the world, but unfortunately for him that wasn't an Olympic sport. In a bid to make it to the 1988 Calgary Games he made the decision to switch to ski jumping. The UK had never had a representative in that event, and he would face little, if any, competition to become the best in Britain.

With no financial backing and having to fund his own training, he found himself a coach in Lake Placid in the USA, and, borrowing kit to begin with, he began his quest to become a world class ski jumper. This wasn't an easy task however. He had to wear multiple pairs of socks to make the borrowed boots fit and his first helmet was held on with string. He was heavier than most ski jumpers, and his poor eyesight meant that he had to wear his glasses under his goggles, which often steamed up and stopped him from seeing where he was going. He also had to work in his spare time to survive, taking on whatever part time jobs he could find, and was living on the breadline, at one point paying about £1 a day to stay at a Finnish mental hospital. At least he wasn't afraid of heights, as some rumours had suggested.

Eddie's first international competition was in the World Championships in 1987. He finished 55th, but that was enough to give him a world ranking and make him eligible for Olympic selection. He was duly selected to compete for Great Britain, and Eddie the Eagle, as he was later nicknamed by the Canadian press, was set to realise his Olympic dream. Edwards was delighted, but the news wasn't universally welcomed, with some believing that his inclusion in the GB team was an embarrassment with his performances so far behind the other competitors. Many did support him though, admiring the sacrifices he had made to achieve his goal.

Nevertheless, he was on the plane to Canada. His first event in Calgary was the Normal Hill, a terrifying 70 metre long descent at speeds up to 60mph before the jumper launches himself into the air. The nation held its breath as Edwards edged himself out onto the bar at the top of the slope. He adjusted his goggles over his glasses, then he was away. He reached the end of the slope and was airborne. Could he land it safely, or would his Olympics end in immediate disaster? He landed without mishap, and punched the air with both hands in delight. His distance was 55 metres, over 30 metres less than the eventual winner, Finland's Matti Nykanen, and 16 metres down on his closest rival. His second jump was exactly the same distance, giving him a total points score based on distance and form of 69.2, 71 behind his closest rival and 159 points behind Nykanen. That left him in 58th and last place, but he had completed his two jumps successfully, could now call himself an Olympic athlete, and a star had well and truly been born.

Nine days later he was in action again, competing in the 90 metre Large Hill event. The result was the same, with Edwards finishing last of the 55 competitors, with distances 90m less than the winner, again Nykanen, and well behind the jumps of the 54th place competitor, but he did break the British record with his first jump of 71 metres. Again Eddie the Eagle split public opinion, with some commentators and fellow competitors believing he was making a mockery of the sport whilst others believed he was the epitome of the Olympic ideal that it's not about the winning, it's about the taking part.

He had undoubtedly become one of the stars of the Games, and even received a personal mention in the closing ceremony for his efforts. He found himself giving interviews and appearing on talk shows around the world including the renowned The Today Show in the US. An estimated 10,000 fans greeted him when he returned home at Heathrow airport. His legacy even led to a change in Olympic rules. Two years later the International Olympic Committee brought in a rule dubbed the Eddie the Eagle rule, which stated that athletes had to be in the top fifty competitors in the world in order to be considered for selection by their country. Unfortunately Edwards fell foul of this change himself, and he failed to qualify for the 1992, 1994 and 1998 Winter Olympics.

He never competed at the Olympics again, although he was chosen to be a torch bearer for the 2010 Games in Vancouver, and his achievements were brought to a whole new audience in 2016 with the global release of a film based on his life starring Taron Egerton, Hugh Jackman and Christopher Walken – "Eddie the Eagle".

21st February 2002
Rhona Martin wins gold with The Stone of Destiny

Curling could never lay claim to the title of Britain's favourite sport, but when six million people in the UK stayed up past midnight to watch Rhona Martin lead her team in a bid to secure the country's first Winter Olympic gold since Torvill and Dean in 1984, you'd have struggled to find a sport more talked about.

It had been a long hard road to the final for the all-Scottish quartet of Martin, Debbie Knox, Fiona MacDonald and Janice Rankin. They had narrowly missed out on a medal at the World Championships in 2000, losing the bronze medal match to finish fourth, but that result had announced them on the world stage and had suggested that they were serious contenders for a medal at Salt Lake City two years later.

Martin herself was almost out of the competition before it had even started, just recovering from a stomach condition in time. The problem didn't seem to affect her or the team's performance, and they made a strong start to the round robin stage, winning five of their first seven matches. However, successive defeats against USA, by one point after an extra end, and Germany left them with a final tally of five wins and four defeats. That left them with an anxious wait, as Germany could have secured a place in the semi-finals ahead of them had they beaten Switzerland in their last match, but fortunately for GB the Swiss came out comfortably on top.

That meant that Great Britain, Sweden and Germany all finished with identical records, and each would have to play each other in a series of tie-break matches. They managed to win both of those, beating Sweden 6-4 and Germany 9-5, and secured their place in the semi-final where they would face Canada, the team that had beaten them in the World Championship semi-final and which had finished top of the round robin table with just one defeat.

Canada moved into an early 1-0 lead in the first end, but Martin put them back on level terms in the third. GB kept the momentum and moved two ahead in the next, but Canada slowly pulled back to 3-3 with singles in the fifth and sixth. Another good end then put GB in sight of the final at 5-3, but again Canadian skip Kelley Law kept her nerve and used her experience to claw them back to parity with singles in the next two ends. With the score going into the final frame 5-5 and the tension mounting, Martin kept her cool to see her team home, winning the match and a place in the final with a well-placed stone to win 6-5.

Guaranteed at least a silver medal, but hungry for gold, the British team faced a Swiss team led by Luzia Ebnother which had beaten the USA 9-4 in their semi final. A tight and nervy start to the match saw neither side score for the first three ends, before Switzerland edged 1-0 ahead in the fourth. GB hit straight back in the fifth to move 2-1 up, then added another point in the seventh to stretch their lead to 3-1. Could the gold medal be heading their way? Ebnother was doing her best to prevent that, and scored in the eighth and ninth to level the scores at 3-3 with the final end of the competition to play.

Significantly, Martin "had the hammer" in the final end, which meant that she would deliver the very last stone. When it came to that last stone the Swiss were holding shot, with their red stone fractionally closer to the button than the best GB stone. It would take something special from Martin to turn silver into gold. A picture of intense concentration, Martin prepared to deliver her yellow stone. The cheers started to get louder and louder as it made its way steadily up the ice, closing in on the head. As it started to slow it approached the Swiss stone, then nudged it out of way before nestling on the edge of the button. Martin had done it, winning gold in dramatic fashion with the final stone of the competition, a shot later dubbed "the Stone of Destiny".

Never before had curling been so popular in the UK. Martin was awarded an MBE for her achievement, and the yellow stone that she won the gold medal with can now be found in the Scottish Sports Hall of Fame. She led a changed team to the 2006 Winter Olympics in Turin, but their record of five wins and four defeats wasn't quite good enough to see them through to the semi final. The following year she switched to coaching, and in 2014, now known as Rhona Howie, she helped another all-Scottish four, skipped by Eve Muirhead, to Olympic bronze at Sochi. She then decided to take on a new challenge, becoming high performance coach for Scottish lawn bowls.

25th February 1989
Bruno v Tyson

With his instantly recognisable laugh and catchphrase "you know what I mean 'Arry", heavyweight boxer Frank Bruno was one of the biggest names in British sport in the 1980s in more ways than one. With an impressive record in the ring, with just two defeats, one of them a world title fight against Tim Witherspoon, he was just as popular for his out-of-the-ring activities, laughing and joking in interviews and whenever he met members of the public, as he was as a boxer.

That said, he had never been able to call himself World Champion. Now though he had a chance to change that, albeit against a formidable opponent. "Iron" Mike Tyson was arguably one of the heavyweight fighters of all time. With 35 wins and no defeats going into the fight, he had become the youngest man to win the WBC, WBA and IBF world titles. He had won his first nineteen professional fights by knockout, twelve of those in the first round. It was billed as a Britain versus America contest, and the nation was backing their man to topple the champion and bring the belt home.

The fight had almost not happened though. Originally scheduled for 8th October 1988 at Wembley Stadium, the bout had to be postponed after Tyson broke his hand in a street fight, pushing it back to 22nd October. He was then knocked unconscious in a car crash, before hearing that his wife was filing for divorce and claiming $125 million for defamation. The Wembley encounter was shelved, with a January 1989 match-up at the Las Vegas Hilton set to replace it. A row between Tyson's manager and agent delayed matters further, but finally a date of 25th February was agreed on.

As the date drew nearer the media frenzy began. Bruno was everywhere – on TV, radio and on the front as well as the back pages of the papers. He was a national treasure, and the nation had its fingers crossed, hoping both that he could win and that he come through the bout unscathed.

When they finally got under way, the fight got off to a flier. Right from the bell both men came out with attacking intent, trading punches in the centre of the ring. As many expected though, the World Champion quickly started to get the better of their exchanges, and he caught Bruno with a right hook that knocked him backwards, almost causing him to stumble out of the ring. Given a standing count of four, it was an ominous start for the challenger. He continued undaunted though, and tried to counter Tyson's attacks with shots of his own, but was also having to hold on to avoid further punishment and was penalised by the referee. Then, out of the blue, Bruno unleashed a powerful left hook that landed on Tyson that rocked the champion for almost the first time in his career. The 5,000 British fans who had made the trip to Las Vegas roared, and commentator Harry Carpenter excitedly exclaimed "He's hurt Tyson! He's hurt Tyson and Tyson knows it and is going for him.'

Could the British challenger cause a famous upset? "He knows he can hurt him now. Get in there Frank!" said Carpenter, but unfortunately Bruno was unable to find a way through Tyson's defences in round two. Then Tyson caught Bruno with a right hand that knocked him into the ropes, before cornering him with a ferocious attack. Bruno was able to hold on and made it to the end of the round, but the danger signs were there.

The next three rounds continued in the same vein, and it seemed that, barring a miracle, the writing was on the wall for Bruno. The referee eventually stepped in to stop the punishment at the end of the fifth round, with Bruno again stuck on the ropes and Tyson hammering him with a barrage of punches. Tyson had retained his title with a technical knockout, but Bruno's brave performance reaffirmed him as a national hero and for a few moments his supporters had dared to believe that he was really going to do it.

Tyson unexpectedly lost the title the following year to James "Buster" Douglas, and his hopes of regaining his crown were thwarted when he was convicted of rape in 1992. Bruno lost a second world title fight in 1993, an all-British encounter with Lennox Lewis, but he finally achieved his goal of becoming World Champion, beating Oliver McCall on points at Wembley in 1995. A rematch was arranged upon Tyson's release in that same year, which Tyson again won, this time with a stoppage in the third round.

Bruno retired on medical advice shortly after that fight, having suffered an eye injury, but continued to be a popular figure, making regular appearances on the BBC Sports Personality of the Year show and other TV shows, until he was diagnosed with bipolar disorder in 2003. In 2016 he announced that he wanted to make a comeback to the ring at the age of fifty-four, more than twenty years after his last fight, but his application for a boxing licence was turned down.

Tyson lost his title to Evander Holyfield in 1996, then shamed himself in the rematch the following year as he was disqualified for biting off part of Holyfield's ear. His only other world title fight was against Lewis in 2002, but he lost to an eighth round knockout, and he retired from the ring in 2005.

March

16th March 2012
Sachin Tendulkar scores hundredth international hundred

When Indian batsman Sachin Tendulkar scored his ninety-ninth international hundred on 12th March 2011, the world of cricket expected him to be celebrating his hundredth soon afterwards. No-one thought it would take more than a year of anticipation, disappointments and near-misses before he would achieve that unprecedented landmark.

Tendulkar was practically worshipped by Indian cricket lovers. Some fans even adopted the mantra "Cricket is my religion and Sachin is my God". Having scored his first test century in 1990 at the age of seventeen he went on to score more runs in test matches than anyone else - 15,921- as well as 18,426 in one-day internationals. He is the only player to score over 30,000 runs in all forms of international cricket, and he helped his country win the 2011 World Cup. No wonder the Indian fans loved him.

However, the record of a hundred hundreds still eluded him. Twice he had come close, falling agonisingly short with scores in the nineties. Other innings had ended further short. In total he had had thirty two innings during which he had failed to reach three figures. People started to wonder whether he would miss out on the record. How long could he keep trying? Had his powers waned? How much longer would India keep picking him if his form didn't improve? Comparisons were being made with the great Don Bradman, who had missed out on a record right at the end of his career, just failing to average over 100 in tests. Surely Tendulkar wouldn't be denied in similar style. Even opposition supporters were willing him to score a century, as long as their side still beat India.

His thirty-third attempt came against Bangladesh in a one day international in the Asia Cup, at the Shere Bangla stadium in Mirpur, Bangladesh. Tendulkar, opening the batting, started steadily, building his innings and picking up the runs without much of the swashbuckling style that had been his trademark for much of his career.

When he reached fifty the stadium began to fill up as the word got out that the record might be on the cards. The atmosphere started to build, with the crowd bouncing and chanting, sub-continent style, and noisy Mexican waves making their way around the ground.

As he made it into the nineties the nerves appeared to set in, and twice he was nearly run-out trying to force runs that really weren't there, just getting back to safety in time. Then a mistimed drive landed just short of the fielder. The Bangladeshis, roared on by their fans, sensed they had a great chance of taking a wicket and did their best to put the pressure on, with seven fielders in the circle. Surely the "Little Master" wouldn't fall in the nineties yet again?

Tendulkar survived though, and by the 44th over he was on 99, just needing one more precious run. The crowd, now wanting to witness a piece of history, rose to its feet and began to cheer him on. Shakib Al Hassan ran in to bowl, and Tendulkar carefully guided the ball to square leg for a single to finally reach three figures in an international for the hundredth time. The noise in the stadium rose to a crescendo as the crowd hailed a truly great moment. Tendulkar took off his helmet and raised his bat to the crowd, then looked up to the heavens before acknowledging his team mates in the dressing room. The Bangladeshi players joined in the congratulations, before the game had to carry on. His hundred had come of 138 balls, and he carried on to make 114, but it wasn't enough to stop Bangladesh from achieving what for them was a famous but widely overshadowed victory.

Fittingly, the score also completed his full set of centuries in both test matches and one day internationals against every test playing nation. He retired from cricket in November 2013 after playing in his two hundredth test match. As well as being the only man to play in two hundred test matches and to score one hundred international centuries, he had set records for the most one day international hundreds and the most one day international runs. He is the only man to have scored 15,000 ODI runs as well as taking one hundred wickets and catches, and set the record for the most runs in a calendar year, as well as countless other records.

After his final innings at his home stadium in Mumbai he left the field in tears before making an emotional speech to the crowd, who chanted "Sachin, Sachin" in response. He was carried on a lap of honour by his team-mates, before touching the pitch, then his eyes and forehead as a symbol of reverence for one of the pitches that had witnessed his incredible career.

22nd March 2015
The Six Nations' Super Saturday

The final round of matches of the 2015 Six Nations couldn't have been better poised. England, Ireland and Wales were all going into their final match level on points, with three wins and one defeat in their earlier matches giving them six points apiece. England had beaten Wales, Ireland had beaten England and Wales had beaten Ireland, but England held the advantage thanks to their superior points difference – plus 37 compared with Ireland's plus 33 and Wales' plus 12.

Wales kicked the afternoon off in Rome against Italy, knowing that only a big win would put them in contention for the title, but it was Italy, smarting from a 29-0 defeat at the hands of France the previous week, who made the better start, a penalty putting them 3-0 up within a minute. Wales struggled to take control of the game, and although Jamie Roberts did cross for Wales' first try of the afternoon, Italy soon responded through Giovanbattista Vendetti, and Wales were only 14-13 ahead at the break, nowhere near enough to make up the points difference.

However, the second half proved to be a very different story. Rhys Webb took a quick penalty that saw Liam Williams score, and soon afterwards Williams turned provider to help George North touch down. Italy were soon down to 14 men when Andrea Masi was sin-binned, and Wales capitalised with two further tries from North and one from Webb. Then came the pick of the lot, a superb 80 metre move seeing captain Sam Warburton get his name on the scoresheet, before Scott Williams added Wales' seventh try of the half and eighth of the match. By this time the Welsh had scored 47 unanswered points and had not only secured the win but also improved their points difference to +60, and although Italy had the last word with a late try by Leonardo Sarto, a final score of 61-20 and a difference of +53 meant that Ireland would have to beat Scotland by 21 points to move ahead of them.

The Irish, attempting to win back-to-back titles for the first time in 66 years, were facing a Scotland side in Edinburgh who were staring down the barrel of a winless Six Nations and the wooden spoon, but although they were without a win, their previous defeats had only been by 7, 3, 3 and 12 points, so a 21 point victory looked like it could be a challenge. An early try by captain Paul O'Connell gave them hope though, and midway through the first half they crossed again, with Sean O'Brien bursting through some weak tackles, giving Ireland a 17-3 lead. The Scots did get a try back through Finn Russell, but the relentless penalty kicking of Johnny

Sexton and a Jared Payne try early in the second half kept them at bay, and Ireland began to stretch their lead towards the magic 21 point mark with the score at 30-10.

Another Johnny Sexton penalty saw Ireland edge ahead of Wales, and when O'Brien crossed for his second try of the afternoon the Irish were 40-10 up with a points difference of 63. A late Scottish effort was ruled out as Stuart Hogg was ruled not to have grounded the ball, leaving Ireland on top of the table with just England v France to come.

Playing last, at Twickenham against a thus far disappointing French side, England had the advantage of knowing what they had to do. Only a win by 26 points would see them take the title from Ireland, and they started the match with all guns blazing, Ben Youngs finishing off a swift move to score after just two minutes. A missed penalty meant that England couldn't build on their early lead though, and it was France who scored next, Sebastien Tillous-Borde latching onto an English error and racing clear to put France ahead. It got worse for England four minutes later when they again lost possession and Noa Nakaitaci finished off the counter attack to put France 15-7 ahead. The win now looked doubtful for England, let alone overcoming the points deficit which had now gone up to 34, but they hit back on the half hour mark through Anthony Watson, and Youngs added his second try following a stunning Jamie Joseph break and England finished the half 27-15 up, needing another 14 points to overtake Ireland.

Disaster struck at the start of the second half though, with another French try, this time from Maxime Mermoz. It only took England four minutes to get back on track however, George Ford scoring England's fourth try of an increasingly frantic match. The two sides traded tries in a breathless twelve minute period – Jack Nowell going over for England, Vincent Debaty for France, Billy Vunipola for England and Benjamin Kayser for France – leaving England needing thirteen points in the last fourteen minutes to do it. With just five minutes on the clock Nowell scored again, and the English needed just one converted try to pinch the crown. Attacking desperately, England made it to within a foot of the French line, but a penalty to the French dashed their hopes, and although France gave Irish fans a scare by attempting the run the ball from under their own posts with the 80 minutes already up, they finally kicked the ball out to end an astonishing afternoon of rugby.

England's 55-35 win was their biggest ever score against France, but it left them an agonising six points behind champions Ireland. The incredible finale had seen an unbelievable 27 tries scored, the most ever scored in one day, and the 221 points scored by the six teams was the most in one weekend. It was only the second time a side had scored 30 points in a match and lost, and Ireland's biggest ever score in the championship away from home, whilst Wales' seven tries in one half was also a Six Nations record.

24th March 1956
Devon Loch almost wins the Grand National

The Queen Mother, a lifelong fan of horseracing, was the owner of Devon Loch, the horse tipped by many to be in with a chance of winning National Hunt racing's most prestigious race – the Grand National.

She had become hooked on the sport seven years earlier, when a friend had persuaded her to purchase her first steeple-chaser. She bought a horse called Monaveen, which won its first race, her first of 457 winners that she enjoyed during her long association with racing. At a time when national hunt racing was lagging in popularity behind flat racing, the Queen Mum's interest did wonders for restoring its appeal, especially when her horses began to win grade one races, such as in 1950 when Manicou won the King George VI Chase.

She was yet to win any of the really big races though, but in Devon Loch it was thought that she was in with a chance of landing the Grand National. Although not the favourite as he was up against two former winners, he was still well backed having produced a fine performance to finish third at Cheltenham earlier in the year as well as winning two other races that season. On board was accomplished jockey Dick Francis, who had been Champion Jockey in the 1953-54 season.

Devon Loch started to look like a good bet as the race began, with the pre-race favourite Must and one of the two former winners Early Mist both falling at the first fence. Devon Loch was travelling well, jumping comfortably on the first circuit and only looking in any danger when a horse fell in front of him and Francis was forced to swerve.

As the horses came around for the second time the field started to thin with fallers and refusals, and Devon Loch was still well-placed. Just ten horses were still running at the last, and Devon Loch jumped clear. Looking strong and fresh he started to pull away, and was five lengths clear when disaster struck. With just fifty yards to go and the crowd, and the Queen Mother, getting ready to celebrate, the horse suddenly leapt into the air and landed on his stomach for no apparent reason. With the chasing pack closing he struggled to his feet, and Francis desperately urged him to continue, but he was unable to carry on, seemingly injured or exhausted. The other horses surged past the distraught Francis, with the race eventually won by ESB.

No definitive explanation was ever found for Devon Loch's unexpected actions that day, but many theories have been put forward. Francis himself thought that the roar from the crowd may have startled his mount; others suggested that he may have been trying to jump a dark wet patch or a shadow on the ground and become confused. The physical condition of the horse has also been put forward as a reason – perhaps cramp in his hindquarters or even that he suffered a heart attack, although his subsequent quick recovery seems to rule that theory out.

Francis, who was never to win the race but who went on to become a best-selling writer of horse-racing related thrillers, was inconsolable after the race as his big chance to win racing's biggest prize was cruelly snatched from his grasp. He wrote of the moments before the incident in his autobiography: "Never had I felt such power in reserve, such confidence in my mount, such calm in my mind." The Queen Mother was also desperately disappointed, but is quoted as having magnanimously told the winning trainer and jockey "Oh, that's racing."

Although Francis retied the following year, the Queen Mother's horses continued to compete and win races for her. In 1964-65 she was the third most successful owner of the season, then in 1984 Special Cargo won the Whitbread Gold Cup for her in a thrilling photo finish. She always cared deeply for the jockeys as well as the horses, and she became the patron of the Injured Jockeys Fund, playing an active part and often visiting injured jockeys herself.

Indeed, it was the Queen Mother herself who had urged Francis to retire, concerned for his welfare after a series of heavy falls. In doing so she unwittingly set in motion a stellar writing career that include forty two novels that sold more than sixty million copies. The two continued their friendship, and Francis always sent the Queen Mother a first edition of his books.

The Grand National hadn't seen the back of Francis though, as he was drafted in to help the Jockey Club raise the millions of pounds it needed to save Aintree and the race. The race was saved, and it continues to be one of the highlights of the British sporting calendar, but no-one has come as agonisingly close to victory only to be denied in such dramatic style as Dick Francis and Devon Loch.

29th March 1981
First London Marathon finishes hand in hand

In 1979 Chris Brasher, former Olympic steeplechase champion and one of the men who helped Roger Bannister achieve the first four minute mile, ran the New York Marathon along with fellow athlete John Disley. It was to be an experience that had a profound effect on him, and which led to him creating one of the biggest annual sporting events in the world.

The New York City Marathon had been first staged in 1970 and had established itself as a popular and important event in the city by the late 70s. Brasher wrote of his experience "11,532 men and women from 40 countries in the world, assisted by over a million black, white and yellow people, laughed, cheered and suffered during the greatest folk festival the world has seen." He was hooked, and started to formulate the idea of staging a similar event in London.

London already had a strong marathon tradition. The distance of all modern marathons had been established in London, when the 1908 Olympic marathon had been extended by 385 yards to ensure that the start was at Windsor Castle and the finish in front of the royal box. The extra distance was too much for Italian runner Dorando Pietri, who led the way into the stadium before collapsing and having to be helped over the line, leading to his disqualification. The following year, as a result of the huge interest Pietri's efforts had created, The Sporting Life newspaper had offered a trophy for a annual marathon event. A running club called Polytechnic Harriers organised one, and it became a regular event known as the Poly Marathon which ran for many years until its popularity declined in the 1970s.

Brasher and Disley returned with a plan to create a new event in London that would achieve six main aims, amongst them to prove that Britain is best at organising major events, to raise money, to improve British marathon running, to boost tourism and to show that mankind, on occasions, can be united. Before long they had signed their first contract with a sponsor, the Greater London Council and City of London were on board, and even the Metropolitan Police had been persuaded to close a major chunk of London's roads for the day. The first ever London Marathon was on the way to becoming a reality.

At 9am on Sunday 29th March 1981 a twenty five pound cannon was fired in Greenwich Park and 6,747 runners began their twenty six mile journey, the successful of the 20,000 applicants who had applied to take part. Thousands of spectators turned out on London's streets to cheer the runners on despite the poor weather, whilst millions watched at home on the BBC. 1,000 volunteers lined the route, along with 500 special constables and 300 St John's Ambulance helpers.

Two hours eleven minutes later the first ever finishers crossed the line in a dead heat. Dick Beardsley of America and Norway's Inge Simonsen decided not to compete with each other for the outright win as they approached the Constitution Hill finish, and joined hands to finish the race together, a fittingly symbolic end to the race that Brasher had hoped could help to unite the city and the world. The first woman to finish was British athlete Joyce Smith, eighteen minutes behind the men. 6,255 of the participants finished the race that year, and the last to finish also joined hands as they crossed the line – Marie Dominique de Groot and David Gaiman – who finished in a time of seven hours.

The nation took the event to its heart, and the London Marathon is now firmly established as one of the highlights of the British sporting calendar, with millions flocking to London to watch and cheer every year. Attracting a high class field of elite athletes to compete each year, it is also one of the world's leading marathon events, as well as growing in size to allow almost 40,000 amateur runners to compete alongside the Olympians. A wheelchair event was added in 1983, and a shorter race for children, the Mini Marathon, is also staged on the same day, which was won three times in a row by a young Mo Farah. Between 1981 and 2015 more than £450 million was raised for charitable causes, and in 2016 the one million millionth runner completed the course. The event is now shown on TV in almost two hundred countries around the world, and continues to be oversubscribed with runners wanted to take part.

Chris Brasher died in 2003, but his legacy lives on. He once said "You must believe that the human race can be one joyous family, working together, laughing together, achieving the impossible," and for at least one day a year, when the streets of London are taken over by the Marathon, it's possible to believe just that.

April

2nd April 1977
Red Rum wins third National

If animals were eligible for the BBC's Sports Personality of the Year award, Red Rum would have almost certainly have won, probably more than once. Loved by the public, not so much by the bookies, Red Rum achieved legendary status as the most successful horse ever to have graced the Aintree turf. Not only did he win it three times, he also finished second twice. It was an unbelievable record over the formidable Grand National fences, but Red Rum treated the course like a second home.

Bred in County Kilkenny in Ireland, the horse showed little sign of his future greatness in his early days, not helped by a bone disease that affected his feet. When Ginger McCain took over his training he managed to sort out his foot problems, legend has it by getting him to run on the beach and swim in the sea off Southport, and he had made enough progress to be entered into the 1973 Grand National. He duly won a thrilling race, overhauling a fifteen length deficit from long time leader and fellow joint favourite Crisp in the run-in to win by three quarters of a length, smashing the course record in the process.

Victorious jockey Brian Fletcher teamed up with Red Rum again the following year, and the partnership triumphed once more, beating L'Escargot into second and becoming the first horse since 1936 to win back-to-back Nationals. They fell just short in 1975, finishing second, the same position that Tommy Stack achieved when he took over as Red Rum's rider in 1976 after Fletcher had been forced to retire following a head injury.

By 1977 Red Rum was twelve years old, and considered by many as too old to be a serious contender for the National. His form at the start of the season was far from convincing, but he slowly showed signs of getting back to his best, and was entered for a fifth attempt at the Aintree circuit. Despite his age, only having won one of his seven races that season, and the fact that his previous record meant he would be carrying extra weight as a handicap, his popularity ensured that he started the race at odds of 9-1, still one of the most fancied horses. Would the nation's favourite, ridden again by Stack, find his best form for the track he knew so well?

The race got off to a dramatic start, as seven horses fell at the first fence. Twelve more had fallen by the end of the first circuit, leaving Boom Docker with a big lead going into the second lap. He refused at the seventeenth though, with the favourite Andy Pandy taking over at the front until he fell at Becher's Brook. That left Red Rum in the lead, and to the delight of the Aintree crowd he used all of his experience to steadily pull away from the field. Only Churchtown Boy showed any signs of sticking with him, apart from a couple of rider-less horses that could have caused him problems if they had got in his way, but he never got closer than a couple of lengths away. Red Rum looked comfortable over each jump and strong in between, whereas his nearest rival was starting to fade, and he eventually came home twenty five lengths clear of Churchtown Boy. Sir Peter O'Sullevan described it for the BBC: "He's coming up to the line to win it like a fresh horse, in great style. It's hats off and a tremendous reception – you've never heard one like it at Liverpool."

Red Rum was entered into the 1978 National as well, and would have been bidding for a fourth victory but for a hairline fracture that forced him out of the race. Instead the great horse was retired, but became no less busy, taking on a celebrity lifestyle of public appearances and event opening. It was often noted how at ease with large crowds he was, and he seemed to revel in the attention and adulation. He returned to his beloved Aintree many times in the following years, and it became a tradition that the races greatest ever participant led out the parade of contenders for each year's race. Although he never won it, he was also a studio guest at the Sports Personality of the Year awards.

His success and popularity is also credited with helping the save the Grand National, which was in real danger of disappearing from the sporting calendar, and Aintree itself, which was run-down and dated in the 1970s and threatened with closure. The revived public interest in the event helped to galvanise the race's importance, and Aintree was eventually purchased and given to the Jockey Club to look after.

Red Rum died in October 1995, at the age of thirty. The news made the front pages of all of the national press, and the national mourned the loss of a hero. He was fittingly buried at the scene of his past glories, at the winning post at Aintree. His epitaph reads "Respect this place, this hallowed ground, a legend here, his rest has found, his feet would fly, our spirits soar, he earned our love for evermore."

3rd April 1993
"The race that never was"

The 1993 Grand National had run into problems before the race had even begun, with the start having to be delayed to allow a dozen or so animal rights protesters who had made their way to the first fence to be taken away from the course. When the course was clear and the race got under way, some of the most chaotic scenes ever witnessed at a major British sporting event were about to unfold.

The start of a large national hunt race is rarely the smoothest of processes, and as the thirty nine competitors began to "line up", circling and jockeying for position, some of the horses got too close to the long piece of elastic that stretches across the course to mark the start. As the elastic was raised to signal the start of the race it became caught around the necks of a couple of the horses, and official starter Keith Brown, overseeing his last National before he retired, declared a false start. He waved a red flag to alert another official, Ken Evans, who in turn waved his flag to warn the jockeys to turn back before the first fence.

The system worked perfectly the first time, but the problems started when the runners and riders lined up for a second attempt. Again the horses were too close to the tape, and when Brown tried to start the race it became wrapped around jockey Richard Dunwoody, onboard Won't Be Gone Long's neck. Brown attempted to call them back again, but for some reason, some have said because Brown's flag didn't unfurl, Evans didn't spot the false start in time. As a result, thirty of the thirty nine horses set off on the four and a half mile circuit, unaware that a false start had been called.

Panic started to set in all around Aintree, as officials and trainers scrambled to the course to try to alert the jockeys, largely to no avail. Some of the jockeys explained afterwards that they were unsure whether the race was actually being stopped or whether protesters were still trying to disrupt the race, and they had kept going so as not to forfeit their chance if there was no real reason to stop. The commentators seemed equally bemused as they continued to commentate on a race where the result would not count. In the words of the BBC's Peter O'Sullevan it was "the National that surely isn't."

The remaining horses continued around the first circuit. One or two fell, but mercifully there were no serious injuries to horses or riders, avoiding the potential tragedy of a fatality during a void race. A number of the jockeys did realise what was happening at the end of the first circuit and pulled up at the water jump, leaving fourteen horses still running at the start of the second lap. Sure Metal and Howe Street were clear of the rest, but they both fell at fence twenty, leaving second favourite Romany King, ridden by Adrian Maguire, in front.

One by one horses were falling or refusing, leaving just seven horses to complete the race, and it was a four horse race coming off the final fence, with Romany King, The Committee, Esha Ness and Cahervillahow all vying to finish first. Esha Ness, ridden by John White, got the edge on his rivals, pulling away at the elbow to cross the line first, but his joy was short-lived as the news was broken to him that the race was void. The greatest moment of his career had been cruelly snatched from him, and his image as he realised the truth featured on almost every back page the next day.

Brown had suggested that the race could be re-run that day with just the nine horses that hadn't raced at all competing, but that idea was quickly quashed, and the Jockey Club officially declared the race void.

The recriminations immediately began. White was understandably distraught, and other jockeys and trainers of horses that had been pulled up but believed that the race had been their one and only chance for glory were furious. Bookies had to refund an estimated £75 million to punters, including to some who had backed Esha Ness at 50 to 1. The Jockey Club initiated an inquiry to discover what had gone wrong and how a similar occurrence could be avoided.

The report eventually blamed Brown for allowing the horses to get too close to the tape, but also Evans for not waving his flag to stop the race for a second time, although he claimed that he had. Changes were recommended, including a more robust starting tape, a narrower start area, two officials before the first fence with fluorescent flags in radio contact with the starter, and a third further up the track to alert any jockeys who hadn't spotted the first two officials.

Grand National starts haven't always been perfect since 1993, for example in 2012 the race had to be restarted twice and in 2014 jockeys were threatened with fines for again getting too close to the tape, but there has been nothing to compare with the debacle of the Race that Never Was, as it later became known.

4th April 1981
Bob Champion beats cancer to win the National

It was miraculous that they were both still alive, let alone competing, let alone winning the Grand National, but Bob Champion and Aldaniti both managed to cheat death to win Britain's biggest horse race in a remarkable tale of triumph over adversity.

Champion was a highly successful jump jockey in the late 70s, having won his first race at the age of fifteen. He won the Hennessy Gold Cup on Approaching in 1978, and rode a series of winners for trainer Josh Gifford. He had never won the Grand National though in his eight attempts, and had set his sight on winning the race. However, in the middle of 1979 he was given the devastating news that he had testicular cancer that had also spread to his lymph nodes. Despite initially refusing to believe the diagnosis he was given six to eight to months to live, or a 40% chance of surviving if he embarked on a newly available chemotherapy programme. The treatment was so new that if he had developed the disease eighteen months earlier he would almost certainly have died. It was an arduous process that didn't always go smoothly, and he was almost killed by septicaemia at one point.

Eventually he made it through the treatment though, and the cancer had gone from his body. He was still in a bad way however, as the treatment had taken its toll on him. His lungs had been damaged and he found he was struggling to breathe, so he moved to South Carolina where the warm weather helped his recovery. When he made his comeback it was in flat racing in the US, and he struggled to cope when he first tried his hand over the jumps, but eventually, by the end of 1980, he had got his career back on track.

Meanwhile, Aldaniti was also having a tough time of it. Having suffered two serious tendon injuries and a fractured leg, the vet had recommended he be put down, but his owner Nick Embiricos refused, and after a long rehabilitation process and lots of work with trainer Gifford he was ready to race again. An impressive performance at Ascot convinced his team that he was ready for the National, something that Champion had always believed he was capable of.

Despite their history they started the race as second favourites, behind Spartan Missile, ridden by fifty four year old amateur John Thorne, but their race almost ended at the very first fence. Perhaps a little too excited, he overjumped the fence and nosed the turf, almost unseating Champion, but he was able to recover and they continued on to the second. It was a shaky jump there as well, but from there on they settled into a rhythm. They steadily moved through from the back of the field, and took the lead for the first time at the eleventh, sharing it with Rubstick and Royal Stuart until well into the second circuit.

Aldaniti started to pull clear at the eighteenth, and only Royal Mail looked capable of staying with him, until a mistake two fences from home ended his challenge. Aldaniti was two lengths clear over the final fence, and only the fast-finishing favourite Spartan Missile looked like making a challenge in the run-in, but the lead was unassailable, and Aldaniti and Champion crossed the line four lengths ahead of Spartan Missile to complete an incredible comeback. No-one at Aintree or watching around the world could begrudge them their victory, and there were few dry eyes around the winners enclosure as they came in to celebrate.

They were awarded the BBC Sports Personality of the Year Team of the Year award later that year, but they were unable to defend their crown the following year, as the horse made the same mistake at the first and this time Champion couldn't stay on. Aldaniti was retired from racing after the race, but Champion continued to race until 1983, when he made the switch from jockey to trainer. He continued training horses until 1999.

There was a bond though between the defiant pair that lasted for the next sixteen years, until Aldaniti died of a heart attack in 1997. They attended numerous events together, many of them in aid of the cancer trust that Champion set up, for which they raised an estimated £6 million together, and Aldaniti was given a hero's welcome when he returned to the course on Grand National day in 1987 at the end of a 250 mile walk for the charity. Champion himself survived two heart attacks, attributed to damage caused by his chemotherapy treatment. He also wrote a book about his experiences, which was turned into a successful film called *Champions*, starring John Hurt as Champion and Aldaniti as himself.

8th April 1967
Foinavon

It's surely a sign of true fame when part of the arena that saw your sporting triumph is named after you, and every year when the Grand National contenders jump the Foinavon fence, racegoers and viewers are reminded of the remarkable win of a 100 to 1 outsider in 1967.

Not only was Foinavon a rank outsider with the bookmakers, but his owner Cyril Watkins hadn't even travelled to Aintree to watch his horse compete, thinking that he was just there to make up the numbers. Neither was his trainer there, as he was also a jockey and, failing to make the required weight to ride Foinavon, went to ride in a race in Worcester instead, where he did at least ride a winner of his own, 5 to 1 shot Three Dons. Perhaps Foinavon's 100 to 1 odds were a little generous, given that he had competed in the Gold Cup and had finished fourth in the King George, but he was still given little chance for the race.

Ridden by replacement jockey John Buckingham, who was riding in his first Grand National, Foinavon had made it look as though the bookies had got it right, as he lost ground on the pack over the first circuit. He was still in the race though, unlike the sixteen horses that had fallen by the time the race reached the twenty third fence. The smallest fence on the course at four foot six, it should have posed few problems, but it was one of the horses that had fallen that changed that, and racing history, forever. Popham Down, who was still running despite having unseated his rider at the first fence, decided that he didn't want to jump the twenty third, and instead changed direction to run in front of the fence. The leading horses were all either obstructed or spooked, and none of them were able to jump. Jockeys were unseated, some of them being thrown over and through the fence, and the horses behind them were unable to get to the fence due to the melee of horses and riders in front of them.

Foinavon, however, had been so far behind the pack that Buckingham had time to steer around the carnage, and after avoiding the favourite Honey End as his jockey Josh Gifford tried to turn him round for another attempt, he calmly jumped the fence to take the lead. Commentator Michael O'Hehir was unflustered despite the astonishing scenes he was describing, and was able to identify the surprise leader despite a last minute change of the jockey's colours. As Foinavon ran on to the next fence, jockeys were frantically trying to retrieve their horses to remount and continue the race, one even running down the course in pursuit of his horse and others remounting but heading off in the wrong direction. The lead was stretching however, and as he reached the Canal Turn he was thirty lengths clear. Surely, if he could just keep going, he would be the winner.

Seventeen of the jockeys managed to get going again to continue the race, some of them, including Honey End, needing three attempts to clear the fence, and set off in pursuit of the leader, but the gap was too great for them to gain enough ground. Fence after fence came and went, and the crowd held its breath as Foinavon safely cleared them all. He crossed the line still twenty lengths clear of Gifford and Honey End in second place.

After the race O'Hehir suggested that the fence might be named after the winner, and his prediction came true in 1984 when the fence was officially named the Foinavon fence. Foinavon attempted to retain his crown the following year in 1968, ridden by Phil Harvey as Buckingham had broken his arm, but was brought down at the Water Jump.

Although the most famous incident of its kind, this wasn't the first time something like this had happened, as in 1928 a horse called Easter Hero caused chaos as he fell at the Canal Turn. Only seven horses escaped, one of them being eventual winner Tipperary Tim, also a 100 to 1 shot before the race, who was one of only two horses to complete the race and the only one to do so without his jockey having to remount. There was trouble at the Canal Turn in 2001 as well, a loose horse named Paddy's Return having taken many of the runners out to leave only about a dozen horses running. In terrible conditions there were only two horses left in contention by the end, with Red Marauder winning by a distance from Smarty, with only two other horses finishing well behind.

Buckingham struggled to repeat the success he had in the National that year however, and rode just one winner during the 1970-71 season. He retired from racing that year, but took a job as a jockey's valet, building a successful business along with his brother Tom, looking after fourteen Grand National winning jockeys over the years until his death in 2016. None of them won the race in quite the manner that he had though.

14th April 1996
Nick Faldo overhauls Greg Norman to win The Masters

Six shots clear of the field coming into the final round at the US Masters at Augusta, it looked like it would be a battle for second place behind two time major winner and world number one Greg Norman. Leading the chasing pack was Nick Faldo, who himself had won the title twice before, as well as the Open three times, but he was coming to terms with the breakdown of his marriage, and wasn't expected by many to be a contender.

Australian Norman had got off to a flier on the first day, carding a course record equalling 63, nine under par and two shots clear. Bidding for his first Masters title after two near misses in the past – in 1986 he had bogied the 18th on the final day to allow Jack Nicklaus to win, and 1987 he had lost out to Larry Mize in a playoff – it was the perfect platform for another attempt. His momentum continued into the second round, as he shot 69 and extended his lead to four shots, with Faldo moving up into second on the leaderboard. A third round 71, with Faldo only managing 73, saw him move to six clear, and it could have been even more if the Englishman hadn't managed a birdie at the end of his round.

That late birdie meant that he was paired with the leader for the final round, which may have been crucial in enabling the Englishman to put pressure on the favourite, and Norman, unfortunately, had a reputation for failing to win majors having led going into the final round. Ten times in the past he had led a major after three rounds, but only once had he managed to complete the job and win the title. Surely this time though his lead was unassailable.

It wasn't a promising start for the Aussie though. A hooked drive into the trees at the first saw him instantly drop a shot, and that set the tone for the round. Further bogies were to follow at the fourth and eighth. Despite one bogey of his own, Faldo was starting to look as though he might be able to take advantage, with a birdie at the sixth and a twenty foot putt for another birdie on the eighth. Suddenly Norman's lead was down to three, and the memories of previous slip-ups meant that the pressure was on.

On the ninth he left his chip short and had to watch the ball dribble back down the green towards him, meaning that he dropped another shot. On the tenth he dropped another, overcompensating for his error on the previous hole and chipping past the hole. His six shot lead was now down to just one, and the mood on the course started to change, with fellow competitors and spectators starting to sense the devastating change in fortunes that was unfolding. Faldo meanwhile had shot a steady 34 on the outward nine holes, two under par, which, with Norman's score going the wrong way, was precisely what he needed to do.

It looked like Norman might have got his game together just in time on the eleventh though, with great approach play leaving him a ten foot putt for a very welcome birdie. The putt lipped out though, and unbelievably, he missed the resulting three-footer for par. That left him level with Faldo, his six stroke lead wiped out in eleven catastrophic holes.

The pair moved on to the tricky twelfth hole, where the small, fast green is protected by the infamous Rae's Creek. Faldo managed to find the green, as initially did Norman, until he saw the sickening sight of his ball rolling slowly back into the water. He double-bogied, and Faldo now led the tournament by two shots. Norman had now conceded six shots to his rival in five holes, and it looked as though his opportunity had gone. The course went quiet. None of the players wanted to see a fellow professional suffering as Norman was, and the crowd almost looked embarrassed to be there.

To his credit, Norman did then steady the ship, with long overdue birdies at the thirteenth and fifteenth either side of a par at fourteen. Unfortunately for him though, Faldo matched him stroke-for-stroke, and Norman's frustration started to show on the fifteenth when he was inches from a stunning eagle. He sank to his knees, and the crowd groaned, sensing that that could have been his last chance.

Desperate to salvage his round and his chances, Norman needed to find some birdies in the last three holes, but it still wasn't his day. He found more water on the sixteenth for his second double-bogey of the day, leaving Faldo four up with two to play. He ended his final round of 78, six over par, five shots behind Faldo, who capped his extraordinary day sinking a fifteen foot putt for birdie on the eighteenth. The champion, not noted for showing emotion on the golf course, hugged his adversary in commiseration, and it looked like they were both in tears. He had shot a highly creditable five under par 67, an excellent final round score under pressure.

The presentation of the famous Green Jacket to champion Faldo was a strangely muted affair. Outgoing champion Ben Crenshaw said "Our sincerest feelings go out to Greg" as he put the jacket on Faldo, and Faldo himself said "I do feel sorry for Greg." So did golf fans all around the world.

The 1996 Masters was Faldo's last major title, and Norman was also unable to add to his tally of major wins.

14th April 1999
Ryan Giggs scores FA Cup wonder goal

The 1998/99 season will long live in the memory of Manchester United supporters as their greatest ever season, but one goal in particular stands out, both because of its individual brilliance, the fact that it won a match that United looked like losing, and because it helped set the tone for the glories that lay ahead in the weeks to come.

United had come into the match locked together with Arsenal at the top of the Premier League, and now they had been drawn against each other in the FA Cup semi-final. Whichever team made it to the final would have the chance at completing the league and cup double. United were also still in the Champions League, and were eyeing an unprecedented treble.

The teams were replaying the tie, just three days after the two sides had played out a largely uneventful 0-0 draw at the first time of asking. It was an extra match that United in particular could have done without, with the second leg of their Champions League semi final away against Juventus just days away. Welshman Ryan Giggs had scored an injury time equaliser in the first leg at Old Trafford, but United knew that they would have to go to Turin and win to keep their hopes of a treble alive. With this in mind, United manager Alex Ferguson decided to rest some of his key players, including Giggs, who was replaced by Jesper Blomqvist, and also Dwight Yorke and Andy Cole, picking Ole Gunnar Solskjaer and Teddy Sheringham instead.

The changes didn't seem to have upset United one bit, and they started the match brightly, asking questions of the Arsenal defence. A goal was on the cards, and David Beckham duly delivered it after seventeen minutes, receiving the ball from Teddy Sheringham and curling home a long range strike that David Seaman in the Arsenal goal could do nothing about. It was the first goal that Arsenal had conceded in more than seven hours of play. There were few other chances in the rest of the half, and United went in at half time 1-0 up.

United pushed for a second goal to give themselves a cushion at the start of the second half, and only two fantastic saves from Seaman kept them out, the first a block when Solksjaer was through one on one and the second a reflex save from a Blomqvist strike. His efforts gave his side renewed hope, and they gradually took the ascendency, and they were finally back on level terms in the sixty ninth minute courtesy of Dennis Bergkamp, whose shot from outside the box took a slight deflection off Jaap Stam and flew past Peter Schmeichel into the United net.

Arsenal thought they had taken the lead moments later, when Schmeichel failed to hold onto Bergkamp's shot and Nicolas Anelka was perfectly placed to poke the ball home. The flag was up for offside against the Frenchman though, and the goal didn't count. The Gunners were definitely looking the more likely winners though, and United captain Roy Keane made things even tougher for his side when he picked up a yellow card for a foul on Marc Overmars. It was his second booking of the match, and United would have to play out the rest of the game with ten men.

Arsenal looked to take advantage of their extra man, launching attack after attack on the United goal, but couldn't find a breakthrough. Then, in the second minute of injury time Ray Parlour was brought down in the penalty area by Phil Neville. It was a chance for Arsenal to inflict the killer blow. Goalscorer Bergkamp stepped up to take the spot kick, only to see Schmeichel anticipate his strike and fling himself to his left to parry the ball clear. United fans celebrated, but Arsenal were still favourites to progress against United's tiring ten men.

Arsenal continued to create the majority of the chances as extra time began, and Schmeichel was called upon to save from Bergkamp yet again. United seemed to be hanging on in the hope that they could get through on penalties. Just as everyone was readying themselves for spot kicks though, Patrick Vieira gave away possession and Giggs, who had come on as sub mid way through the second half, picked up possession just inside the United half. He set off towards the Arsenal goal, first beating Vieira as he tried to make amends for his mistake, then going around Lee Dixon. As he closed in on the Arsenal box he squeezed between Martin Keown and the recovering Dixon, and evaded Tony Adams' desperate lunge before unleashing a fierce shot. Seaman was unable to react in time, and the ball powered past him into the roof of the net. As Giggs sprinted off to celebrate he tore his shirt off and whirled it around his head in triumph before his team-mates caught up with him.

With ten minutes on the clock the Gunners pushed for a second equaliser, and Adams and Anelka both had chances that they were unable to take, but they were unable to find the goal they needed, and United were into the final. They proceeded to beat Newcastle United 2-0 in the final, finished one point ahead of Arsenal to claim the Premier League title and scored two very late goals against Bayern Munich to win the Champions League to complete the treble.

Giggs' goal was chosen as the best ever scored on Match of the Day by BBC viewers in 2015.

27th April 1974
Denis Law backheels Man Utd down

Few players have made the switch from red to blue or blue to red in Manchester, but Denis Law did both during his career, and his divided loyalties were brought into conflict in dramatic style in a match between his old and new clubs at the end of the 1973/74 season.

He played for Manchester City first, when they signed him from Huddersfield Town for a British record £55,000 in 1960 despite United's attempt to lure him to Old Trafford. He was there for just one season though before securing a move to Torino, but he struggled to come to terms with the defensive style of play in Italy and returned to Manchester the following season, this time signing for United.

His time at United is remembered as one the club's golden eras. Playing alongside fellow club greats George Best and Bobby Charlton, the "United Trinity" helped the club to the FA Cup in 1963, First Division title in 1965 and 1967, and also the European Cup in 1968, although Law missed the final through injury. He won the UEFA Ballon d'Or award for the best player in Europe in 1964, and in his eleven seasons at the club scored a total of 237 goals in 404 matches, including 46 in one season, a club record.

By the early 70s things were in decline at Old Trafford however. Inspirational manager Sir Matt Busby had resigned and the team were struggling under new boss Wilf McGuinness. McGuinness departed after the side only finished eighth, and was replaced by Frank O'Farrell, but their form was still erratic, and Law was also regularly missing matches through injury. He was finally offered on a free transfer by new boss Tommy Docherty in 1973, and made the decision to move back for a second spell at Manchester City.

City had a reasonable season, finishing 14th in the league and reaching the League Cup final, but United were continuing to struggle. Threatened by relegation heading into the penultimate match of the season, United desperately needed a win to stand any chance of surviving. That match was, at fate would have it, at home against Man City and Law.

Law received a warm reception from the Old Trafford crowd, testament to the high esteem they held him in despite his move to their rivals. A disappointing game remained scoreless, with United creating the majority of the few chances and forcing a couple of goal-line clearances, but with time running out the home side still hoped for a late winner to seal the vital points. With nine minutes to go though City attacked, and a Frannie Lee ball fell to Law in the United box. With his back to goal he back-heeled the ball through the legs of Alex Stepney and into the net, giving his side a 1-0 lead but seemingly condemning the club he enjoyed eleven seasons with to relegation to the second flight. He refused to celebrate the goal, standing frozen to the spot as his team-mates mobbed him, and he was substituted off soon afterwards looking shell-shocked. A few minutes later disgruntled United fans, unhappy with their team's first relegation in 37 years, invaded the pitch, forcing the match to be abandoned.

The result stood though, and it turned out that Birmingham City's win over Norwich City United meant that would have gone down even if Law hadn't scored, but he was still left with the feeling that he had relegated them. He was quoted as saying "I have seldom felt so depressed in my life as I did that weekend. After 19 years of giving everything I had to score goals, I have finally scored one which I almost wished I hadn't." He retired from competitive football after the World Cup that summer, making that fateful backheel his final touch in domestic football.

United fans didn't have long to wait for a return to the top flight though, as Docherty led them to the Second Division title and promotion at the first attempt, whilst City finished eighth in Division One. They kept their momentum, and made a fine return to top division by finishing third in 1975-76, with City against eighth. Although Docherty departed the following season after an affair with the club physiotherapist, United had established themselves in Division One, and they haven't been relegated since, winning thirteen titles after the league was replaced by the Premier League. City in contrast were relegated after the 1982-83 season, and spent the next two decades bouncing between the top two divisions, even suffering a season in the third tier of English football in 1998-99. In 2002 they returned to the Premier League though, and have remained there since. In 2011-12 they won the Premier League, beating United to the title on the final day of the season in dramatic style, before adding a further title in 2012-13.

29th April 1985
The "Black Ball Final"

Steve Davis was set to become world snooker champion for the fourth time in five years. That was the view of most people watching the final, at the Crucible Theatre in Sheffield, in 1985. Davis, not always popular with snooker fans due to his cautious playing style and perceived lack of personality, had been world number for the past two years, and was up against Northern Ireland's Dennis Taylor, who was more famous for his oversize glasses than his success at the snooker table. Surely Taylor, whose best previous performance was when he was runner-up six years before, wouldn't be able to challenge the defending champion.

Taylor had qualified for the final comfortably enough though, beating former champion Cliff Thorburn and two time finalist Eddie Charlton along the way before a straightforward 16-5 victory over Tony Knowles in the semi-final. Davis had won his semi-final against Ray Reardon by the same margin, and had also come through the rounds without too much trouble aside from his 10-8 victory against Neal Foulds in the first round.

Davis got off to a flyer in the best of thirty five frame final, winning all of the seven frames played in the first session on Saturday afternoon. He then took the opening frame of the evening session too to take a commanding 8-0 lead. It looked like the final would be over in double-quick time. Taylor dug deep though, and managed to take the ninth frame after Davis missed a green that would have taken that frame as well. From there he Ulsterman started to battle back into the match to the delight of his fans and the neutrals, and he was just 9-7 behind by the end of the day's play.

Taylor continued his recovery when play resumed on the Sunday, and got back on level terms at 11-11, only to see Davis edge ahead again to lead 17-15, leaving the defending champion needing just one more frame for victory. Taylor again resisted though, and won the next two to make it 17-17 and take it to a deciding frame.

By now the epic final had gripped the nation, and 18.5 million people were watching on TV, despite it being past 11pm. The two players shook hands before the deciding frame. Davis got in first, but could only make 4. With the balls in unfavourable positions it was a while before either player managed to score again, and Davis could only make 5 in his next break. Taylor potted a red but couldn't follow it with a colour, then minutes later did the same again to trail 9-2. The tension was getting unbearable, with both players knowing that a single error could let their opponent in for the decisive clearance. Time ticked on, but eventually Davis made a mistake. Taylor built a small break of 22, but couldn't go any further. It was the first time in the entire match he had been ahead. Davis couldn't take advantage though, and the two traded small breaks, with every miss met with gasps from the crowd, as the clock ticked past midnight. By now the frame was more than forty five minutes old, and the world championship was still up for grabs.

Davis managed to edge ahead 62-44, and had a chance on the brown that would have left Taylor needing snookers with just three balls on the table, but the ball rattled in the jaws of the pocket and stayed out with Taylor unable to look. Taylor missed the brown himself, then Davis missed it again before Taylor made a fantastic cut to give himself a lifeline. He added the blue and the pink to trail 62-59. If he could sink the black he would be world champion, but his brave attempt to double it in failed. Davis wasn't able to take it on though, and played safe. Taylor tried again and missed, then Davis also tried without success. Taylor missed again, this time an easier chance as the pressure mounted, but again Davis failed to take his chance. Taylor came back to the table, lined up the top right pocket, and finally the black disappeared from view, sixty eight minutes after the frame began.

The Ulsterman raised his cue above his head, shook hands with Davis and the referee, then put his cue down on the table. He wagged a finger at a friend in the crowd to say "I told you so", walked over to the trophy and gave it a kiss. He had won the most incredible of finals and had realised his dream – he was the world champion.

He crashed out in the first round the following year as defending champion however, shocked 10-6 by Mike Hallett, whilst Davis again lost in the final, this time to Joe Johnson in far less dramatic style. Taylor never got further than the quarter finals in future appearances until his final world championships in 1994, one of those quarter finals being against Davis, which the Englishman won 13-7. Davis got revenge over Johnson as well in the 1987 final, and claimed the title the following two years as well to become a six-time world champion.

May

2nd May 1953
The Matthews Cup Final

Outside of Bolton, most of the country was rooting for Blackpool to win the FA Cup Final in 1953, not because they had anything against Bolton Wanderers, but because it would mean that national hero Stanley Matthews would win a long-awaited medal.

In a glittering career that had seen him entertain football fans at home and abroad with his unparalleled skills, Matthews, nicknamed the Wizard of Dribble, had failed twice to win the FA Cup. In 1948 Blackpool, bidding for their first ever FA Cup title, had lost to Matt Busby's Manchester United despite having led twice, and in 1951 they had also lost out, this time to two Jackie Milburn goals for Newcastle United. Now in a third final at the age of thirty eight, it would probably be Matthews' last chance at winning some silverware. A thigh strain a few days before the final threatened to thwart him, but a pain-killing injection ensured that he was fit to play.

Blackpool had started their road to Wembley beating Sheffield Wednesday and Huddersfield Town before needing a replay to get past Southampton. They then saw off Arsenal before beating Spurs in the semi final to reach their third final in five years. Their opponents, Bolton Wanderers, had also needed a replay along the way, against Notts County, as well as beating Fulham, Luton Town, Gateshead and Everton.

With many British households buying or renting televisions for the first time that year in anticipation of the Queen's coronation the following month, the final was set to be watched by the largest ever home audience in addition to the 100,000 inside Wembley stadium, and they witnessed Bolton get off to a dream start when Nat Lofthouse scored in just the second minute, his long range shot bouncing awkwardly in front of keeper George Farm and finding its way into the net. Lofthouse almost doubled his tally quarter of an hour later, beating Farm to a through ball, but this time his shot rebounded off the post and Blackpool somehow kept the ball out in the ensuing goalmouth scramble.

It was all Bolton at that point, but Blackpool somehow got back on level terms in the thirty fifth minute when Stan Mortensen broke clear and aimed a powerful shot at goal that found the net with a slight suspicion of a deflection off Harold Hassall. Bolton were soon back in front though, Willie Moir beating Farm to Bobby Langton's lobbed cross to head home and make it 2-1 six minutes before half time.

Blackpool found themselves with a mountain to climb ten minutes after the break when Eric Bell, despite having injured his hamstring, out-jumped the Tangerines defence to head home Doug Holden's cross to put Wanderers 3-1 up. It looked as though Blackpool and Matthews would be denied again, but Matthews had other ideas. Playing with renewed purpose he started to torment the Bolton defence, taking advantage of the space being left because of Bell's injury, and his side were given a lifeline with just over twenty minutes to go when his dangerous cross was fumbled by Stan Hanson and the ball fell to Mortensen, who squeezed it home to make it 3-2.

Blackpool were back in the game but time was running out, and Bolton held onto their lead despite Matthews' efforts until the very last minute. Bill Perry and Jackie Mudie both missed chances to equalise, and Mortensen was denied by a brilliant Hanson save, and it looked as though it wasn't going to be Blackpool's day. Then, with just two minutes of normal time left, Mudie was fouled just outside the Bolton box and the referee awarded a free kick. Two goal man Mortensen took responsibility for what could have been their last chance, and his powerful shot beat the Bolton wall to nestle in the back of the net without the goalie moving, a stunning strike to equalise and complete the first ever Cup Final hat-trick.

Although extra-time was beckoning, Blackpool weren't finished yet. Deep into injury time Matthews again found space on the right wing and cut back a teasing cross into the six yard box. Mortensen couldn't quite latch on to it this time, but behind him was Perry, whose shot flew in at the near post. Blackpool, inspired by thirty eight year old Matthews, had sealed a storybook victory that would live in the memory forever, and he finally had himself an FA Cup Winners medal. Perhaps the biggest cheer of the day was when he climbed the famous Wembley steps to receive his prize.

The match became known as the Matthews Final, but Matthews himself, who was later knighted, modestly said that it should be called the Mortensen final. To this day it is still the only hat-trick ever to be scored in an FA Cup Final. Matthews continued to play top class football until he was fifty, and played his last competitive match at the age of seventy. He died in 2000 at the age of eighty five, but is still revered as one of the most talented players England has ever produced, and a statue of him takes pride of place outside Stoke City's Britannia Stadium, the club he started and ended his career at. A statue of Mortensen stands outside Blackpool's Bloomfield Road ground.

5000-1 shots win Premier League

2nd May 2016

With just a handful of games left in the 2014-15 Premier League season, Leicester City looked doomed to be relegated. In their first season back in the top flight after winning the Championship the previous year they had been rooted to the bottom of the table since the end of November, but a remarkable run of seven wins in their final nine matches saw them climb away from danger to finish fourteenth. However, the manager who had masterminded their great escape, Nigel Pearson, had had a volatile relationship with the media and opposition players, and was sacked by their owner Vichai Srivaddhanaprabha at the end of the season.

He was replaced by Italian coach Claudio Ranieri, an appointment that wasn't universally welcomed, as although he had previously guided Chelsea to second place in the Premier League and the semi-finals of the Champions League, his last role as manager of the Greek national side had ended when they had lost to international minnows the Faroe Islands. The bookies agreed with them, making them 5,000-1 outsiders to win the Premier League and were as short as 1-20 to be relegated. The favourites were the usual suspects, the rich, big boys who had spent big and who had dominated the Premier League since its inception in 1992. Aside from Blackburn Rovers in 1994-95, only Manchester United, Arsenal, Chelsea and Manchester City had won the title, and few thought 2015-16 would be any different.

However, they made a fine start to the season, with two wins and a draw that put them top of the table. Everyone thought it would be a flash in the pan, but Leicester hung in there, and although a home defeat at the hands of the Gunners saw them slip to sixth, four straight wins in October and November saw them surprisingly climb back to top spot. Although Chelsea were having an unexpectedly poor season, Man City and Arsenal were both mounting a challenge, and Manchester United were also back at the top of the table after a couple of disappointing seasons. Those teams were still the favourites for the title, but Leicester's odds had been slashed to 500-1.

The following week their striker Jamie Vardy broke Manchester United's Ruud van Nistelrooy's record for scoring in consecutive Premier League matches, scoring in his eleventh match in a row in a 1-1 draw against, fittingly, United. It was his fourteenth goal of the season, a remarkable story for a player who was playing non-league football before he signed for Leicester in 2012. His goals had been crucial in firing Leicester to the top of the table, but when he wasn't scoring, Algerian winger Riyad Mahrez was, and he scored six goals as they won their next three games. A run of three matches without a win at the turn of the year made many think that would be the start of their expected slide down the table, but again they defied the odds and posted five wins in eight matches during January and February to remain top. That run included a 1-0 victory over Norwich City, when Leonardo Ulloa's last minute winner caused such a reaction in the King Power stadium that scientists detected a minor earthquake on their seismometers.

Arsenal and Man City were both failing to maintain a serious challenge, and it was another outsider, Tottenham Hotspur, who were two points behind the leaders and looking like they would be the ones who could overhaul Leicester. Still no-one believed that the Premier League minnows could maintain a challenge.

Leicester were still only third favourites for the title behind Arsenal and Spurs, with the pressure now expected to start to take its toll on them. They were proving to be able to win the crucial matches though, and they strung together four 1-0 wins in a row as they edged closer to the title. It looked like the tension had finally got to them though as they trailed West Ham United 2-1 late on, having had Vardy sent off for two yellow cards, but a slightly fortunate penalty converted by Ulloa five minutes into injury time salvaged a vital point. Vardy was given a two match ban, and Spurs beat Stoke City emphatically 4-0 to cut Leicester's lead to five points and keep the title race alive.

Leicester bounced back though with a 4-0 win of their own against Swansea City, even without Vardy, and when Spurs could only draw 1-1 with West Bromwich Albion they were on the brink of achieving the unbelievable, and their odds had tumbled to 1-16. A victory at Old Trafford would have won them the title, but they could only draw 1-1, leaving Spurs needing to beat Chelsea to stay in the hunt. It looked like they would do just that as they led 2-0 at half time, leaving the thousands of Leicester fans watching in pubs and clubs expecting the anxious wait to go on to their next match, but a spirited fightback by Chelsea earned them a 2-2 draw to deny their London rivals and give their former boss the unlikeliest of achievements.

Their accomplishment was hailed as the greatest in the history of football by many commentators and pundits. It was soon pointed out that Man Utd had spent more on players in the last two years than Leicester had in their entire 132 year history. Instead of a nail-biting attempt to secure the final points they needed, their last home game of the season turned into a celebration, and the Leicester players responded to their rapturous reception, beating Everton 3-1 before being presented with the Premier League trophy. Leicester city centre then enjoyed the biggest party it had ever seen. Not joining in the celebrations however were the bookies, who lost an estimated £10 million as a result of Leicester's win.

Spurs lost their final two matches to slip back to third, with Arsenal finishing in the runner up spot, ten points behind the champions. Leicester hadn't just won, they had won comfortably. As well their memorable victory, their success brought them Champions League football for the first time in their history. They were immediately given odds of 25-1 to defend their title, a far cry from the 5000-1 they had begun the previous season at, but amazingly the same as the odds to see them relegated. Whatever the odds, it seems unlikely that Leicester's amazing achievement will ever be repeated again.

6th May 1954
The four minute mile

On a cold and windy day at a running track in Oxfordshire, British medical student Roger Bannister contemplated whether to go ahead with his attempt to break the world record for the mile, and the coveted four minute mark, or to wait for another day when conditions were more favourable.

The world record had been edging steadily closer to four minutes throughout the 1940s, with Swedish athletes Gunder Hagg and Arne Andersson pushing each other and the record down to 4:01.4. By 1954 that time had stood for nine years though, and Bannister and his Australian rival John Landy were both threatening the beat that time, and to possibly run below four minutes for the first time. The time had become something of a psychological barrier akin to climbing Everest, which Sir Edmund Hillary and Sherpa Tenzing Norgay had achieved the previous year, and the world awaited a hero to conquer it.

Bannister, spurred on by the disappointment of failing to win a medal at the 1952 Helsinki Olympics despite being favourite for the 1,500 metres, was determined to beat Landy to the milestone, and set about planning his attempt. He had tried once in 1953, but had fallen short with a time of 4:03.6, so went back to the drawing board.

Bannister decided that four things were needed if he was going to succeed: a good track, absence of wind, warm weather and even-paced running. On that morning he would have just two of those things, with two pacemakers, Chris Chataway and Chris Brasher, lined up to help him through the race at the Iffley Road track. The plan designed by the trio was for Brasher to set the early pace, pulling Bannister and Chataway along with him for the first two laps. Chataway would take over at that point, leaving Bannister to attack the record on his own on the final lap. The cold wind was a big concern however, as it was strong enough to slow him down considerably each lap, but he felt that mentally and physically he was in peak condition, and that he might never be as ready as he was that day if he delayed his attempt.

With just half an hour to go before the race, Brasher and Chataway pushed Bannister for a decision. He decided to give it a go. As the athletes lined up they were rewarded with a bit of luck as the wind started to drop, the sky cleared and a rainbow even appeared. The starter's gun fired, only for the tension to mount further as they were called back for a false start caused by an over-keen Brasher.

They were away at the second attempt, and as planned Brasher took the lead, with Bannister tucked in behind. At one point he thought Brasher was going too slowly and told him to speed up, but his friend was a master at setting the pace and ignored him.

They completed the first lap in 57.7 seconds, then put in a 60.6 second second lap to pass the half-mile point in 1:58.3, on schedule for the record, and Brasher pulled away for Chataway to come through to take the lead. The third lap was a little slower, and with one lap to go the time read 3:0.7. A sub-sixty second lap would secure the record, but what did Bannister have left in reserve?

Chataway pulled Bannister along for the first part of the lap, but Bannister moved past him with 240 yards to go. The 3,000 strong crowd lining the outside of the track willed him on. Closer and closer he got to the line as the clock ticked on towards 4 minutes, straining every sinew and gasping for air. With a final effort he threw himself at the line and collapsed, barely conscious, into the waiting arms of his good friend the Reverend Nicholas Stacey.

As Bannister recovered he, his team and everyone else waited anxiously for news of his time. Timekeeper Norris McWhirter built the tension further, taking his time over his announcement: "Result of Event Eight: One mile. First, R. G. Bannister of Exeter and Merton Colleges, in a time which, subject to ratification, is a new Track Record, British Native Record, British All-Comers Record, European Record, Commonwealth Record and World Record… Three minutes…". He got no further as cheers erupted around the track. Bannister had done it, and claimed the accolade so many had sought to achieve. His time was 3:59.4, half a second under four minutes, but a half second that would immortalise him.

Although Bannister had broken a record that had stood for nine years, his own record was only to stand for forty six days, as his rival Landy broke the barrier himself at a meeting in Finland with a time of 3:58.0. There could only be one man who was the first to achieve the magic mark though. The two went head to head later that year at the Empire Games in Vancouver in a race that came to be called The Miracle Mile. Landy led for most of the race, but lost sight of Bannister as he looked for him over his left shoulder whilst the Englishman passed him on his right, and Bannister won the gold in the first race where two men finished in under four minutes.

Despite his achievements, it was Chataway rather than Bannister who won the inaugural BBC Sports Personality of the Year award in 1954, having won gold in the three miles at the Empire Games and silver in the European Championships

5,000 metres. Brasher went on to co-found the London Marathon, whilst Bannister himself retired from athletics to continue his medical career and in time became an esteemed neurologist.

8th May 1999
Last minute Jimmy Glass goal keeps Carlisle in the League

Many footballers have written themselves into the folklore of their clubs, but only one has managed to do it after playing only three matches for them.

Goalkeeper Jimmy Glass was the epitome of a journeyman footballer. Having started his career at Crystal Palace, where he spent seven years without playing a first team match, he spent time being loaned out to various lower division and non-league clubs before signing for Bournemouth in 1996. He spent two seasons at the Cherries, playing regularly for them, but was sold to Swindon Town in 1998 where he struggled to get into the side after a falling out with manager Jimmy Quinn.

Carlisle United were having a terrible 1998-99 season, struggling at the bottom of Division Three and facing the possibility of relegation to the Football Conference. Their problems deepened when, with only a handful of matches left they found themselves without a goalkeeper, with their regular goalie Tony Caig having been sold to Blackpool and their on-loan replacement Richard Knight having returned to his club following an injury. Carlisle were allowed an emergency loan, and brought in Glass from Swindon.

Glass was set to play in Carlisle's final three games of the season, but his new side were unable to pull themselves away from the danger zone. Their nearest rivals, Scarborough, had secured a win in their mid-week fixture against Carlisle's final opponents Plymouth Argyle to ensure that Carlisle would start the last day propping up the Football League and needing Scarborough to slip up to stand any chance of survival.

Carlisle were at home for what could have been their last ever League game, and 7,500 vociferous fans packed the aging stands of Brunton Park. The first roar of the afternoon came as news came through that Peterborough had taken the lead against Scarborough. If that score stayed the same then a 0-0 draw would be enough to see Carlisle survive, but their lead was short-lived and Scarborough were soon back on level terms.

It was 0-0 at half time at Brunton Park, and 1-1 at Scarborough. Carlisle would need to score or hope that Peterborough would do them a huge favour if their afternoon wasn't to end in tears, but their hopes became even fainter four minutes after half time, when Lee Phillips put the visitors in front. It was looking bleak and the ground fell silent as fans faced the prospect of seventy one years of league history coming to an end. They received a lifeline though with just under half an hour to play, as a speculative shot was only half cleared and the ball fell to David Brightwell, whose first time shot bounced awkwardly in front of the Plymouth keeper and went in. That gave the crowd renewed hope, and a mini pitch invasion was evidence that the atmosphere was well and truly back.

Carlisle started to believe again, and started creating chances, but apart from a Scott Dobie shot that flew just wide they weren't seriously threatening the Argyle goal, and with time ticking down some fans could bear it no longer and left the ground.

When ninety nail-biting minutes were up the fourth official held up a board with the number four on it - four desperate minutes for United to find a goal - and the crowd began one last effort to spur their team on. Time was already up at the McCain Stadium, and the Scarborough fans were celebrating on the pitch in the knowledge that Carlisle were only drawing, thinking that their point was enough. With three and a half minutes of injury time played the ball ricocheted off a Plymouth defender, and Carlisle were awarded a corner. This would surely be their last throw of the dice, and manager Nigel Pearson waved Glass forward. The corner was played in, and found Dobie in space, but his header was parried by the Plymouth keeper, only to fall perfectly into the path of Glass just inside 6 yard box. His half volley swept into the beckoning net, and pandemonium followed. He was mobbed by team mates, and fans emerged from all four sides of the pitch to pile on top. Even the referee was jumped on.

Eventually the pitch was cleared, but there was barely time to kick off before the final whistle was blown, sparking another pitch invasion even bigger than the last. Glass was carried from the pitch on the shoulders of the ecstatic supporters. Carlisle had grabbed a vital win, just their eleventh of the season, to finish one precious point above Scarborough and remain in the Football League by the narrowest of margins.

Despite achieving hero status, cash-strapped Carlisle were unable to secure Glass' services on a permanent basis and he never played for them again. He went on to play for a number of other clubs before slipping into non-league football himself, and retired from the game in 2004.

Carlisle continued to struggle to avoid relegation to the Conference, and finally succumbed in 2003-04. However, a play-off win the following season saw them bounce straight back, and they have remained in the Football League ever since.

11th May 1968
Don Fox misses last minute conversion

The scene was set for the highlight of the Rugby League season – the Challenge Cup Final. The teams, Wakefield Trinity and Leeds, had battled hard to reach the final, the fans were ready, the media was waiting. The only fly in the ointment was the weather. An hour long thunderstorm before kick-off had left the Wembley pitch saturated. In hindsight the game should have been called off, but Rugby League isn't known for letting a bit of rain stand in its way, and it would have been a brave man who told 87,000 fans that they would have to go home. One man however was left wishing that the match had never been played that day.

Don Fox was one the best rugby league players of the 1950s and 60s, playing a total of 485 games for Featherstone Rovers and Wakefield Trinity. His 162 tries for Featherstone broke their try-scoring record, and he won two Championship titles with Wakefield. He also played for England and Great Britain, but unfortunately he will be remembered mostly for one fateful conversion attempt.

With the pitch immediately starting to cut up despite the sun making a brief appearance, the two sides traded early penalties, firstly Bev Risman for Leeds to give them an early lead. Fox, who was only on kicking duty because his brother Neil, the side's usual goal kicker, had suffered a groin injury the previous week as the brothers helped their team to the Championship against Hull Kingston Rovers, replied for Wakefield, then Risman struck again to put Leeds 4-2 ahead.

The opening try came when Fox launched a kick up field from just inside his own half. The ball looked like it would either be picked up by Leeds defender John Atkinson or bounce into touch, but Atkinson slipped, and the ball stayed in play. Ken Hirst hacked the ball past him and over the line, diving on the ball for the first try of the match. Fox converted to make it 7-4 to Wakefield at half time.

Unfortunately the rain returned, and another heavy shower made playing conditions in some parts of the pitch almost impossible as the second half started. The teams battled through the mud and the puddles, every tackle throwing up sheets of water and giving the match its subsequent nickname, the Watersplash Final. It was hard for either team to build a serious attacking move, but with ten minutes left on the clock referee John Hebblethwaite awarded a controversial penalty try to Leeds. A through ball stopped dead in a large puddle, the closest Wakefield defender slipped, and Atkinson kicked it on, pursuing the ball towards the Wakefield line. There was a scramble for the ball on the try line, and Gert

Coetzer was adjudged to have obstructed Atkinson as defenders skidded around on the pitch. Risman kicked the conversion, and suddenly Leeds were in front, 9-7 with just minutes to go.

As Wakefield tried in vain to battle back, their task was made even tougher as Leeds were awarded a penalty, which Risman again slotted home to make it 11-7. Leeds were now crucially four points clear, meaning that Wakefield needed a converted try with only seconds left. The smiles on the faces of the Leeds players were plain to see – they thought they had done enough to become champions.

Wakefield hadn't given up hope though, and in a final desperate throw of the dice faked to kick the restart to the left, before Fox kicked the ball low to his right instead. The ploy worked, as the ball stuck in the mud and caught out the Leeds players. Bernard Watson tried to trap the ball with his feet, but the ball slid past him. Hirst reacted quickest, and hacked the ball once, then a second time as Leeds players slipped as they frantically tried to get their hands on the ball. Just as the ball seemed like it was going to cross the dead ball line Hirst dived head-long, and touched the ball down just in time for a momentous score under the posts.

That left Wakefield one point behind, with a simple-looking two point conversion to come. With eighty minutes on the clock it would be the last kick of the match. Up stepped Fox, who had already been chosen to receive the Lance Todd Trophy for man-of-the-match. Surely Wakefield's star man would win the trophy for his side, although as commentator Eddie Waring pointed out "It's always a hard shot when the match depends on it." The Leeds players were unable to watch as the title they thought was theirs was about to slip from their grasp. But disaster struck for Fox. As he approached the ball, his leading foot slipped slightly on the soft ground and his kick sailed to the right of the posts. Fox dropped to his knees and pounded the wet ground in desperation, as the Leeds players around him celebrated before turning to console the distraught Fox. "He's missed it, he's missed it... he's in tears is the poor lad" said Waring memorably.

Fox continued to play for Wakefield until 1970, but it has been reported that he never managed to get over that day up until his death in 2008.

13th May 2012
Man City score twice in injury time to clinch Premier League title

Leading the Premier League on goal difference from local rivals Manchester United, Manchester City were on the verge of claiming their first title for forty four years as they headed into the final game of the season.

The two Manchester clubs had exchanged the lead a few times over the course of the season, with United, who were the defending champions and had won twelve titles since the Premier League had started in 1992-93, ahead for the first couple of months before City overhauled them in October. A 6-1 victory at Old Trafford for the sky blues saw them move five points clear, but United clawed them back and were eight points ahead and seemingly on course for their fifth title in six years with just six matches to go. However, United's form then deserted them, and City fought their way back into contention, moving back to the top of the table on goal difference with another win against their rivals, this time with a much tighter 1-0 scoreline.

Playing at home against relegation-threatened Queen's Park Rangers, all City had to do was match United's result at Sunderland to take the crown, but it was to be far from plain sailing on an afternoon of high drama.

City made a slow start to their match, and it was United who gained the early initiative, with Wayne Rooney finding the net mid way through the first half to put them in front and two points clear if the results stayed that way. Silence filled the Etihad as the news came through to the City supporters, but the nerves were soon forgotten as Pablo Zabaleta found the net to restore City's lead at the top six minutes before half time, QPR keeper Paddy Kenny only able to parry the ball which ballooned over his head, onto the post and across the line despite his despairing effort to scoop the ball clear.

However, the second half started disastrously for City as QPR equalised three minutes after the restart when Djibril Cisse latched on to a misplaced backheader by Joleon Lescott to thump the ball past Joe Hart. City would have to score again or hope that Sunderland equalised against United if they were to take the title. Things got even worse just after the hour mark though, as QPR, despite going down to ten men when former City player Joey Barton was sent off for an off the ball incident with Carlos Tevez, did the unthinkable and took the lead through Jamie Mackie's headed goal. City's Premier League dreams were now in tatters.

They had just twenty four minutes to score twice, or hope that Sunderland could do them a huge favour.

Time was running out, and with City launching attack after attack on the QPR goal, the visitors' keeper Paddy Kenny was having the game of his life as he kept the home side at bay.

As the clock hit ninety minutes and with United still ahead in their match the tears started to flow in the stands as the home supporters saw their dream disappear in front of their eyes. But then, two minutes into stoppage time, striker Edin Dzeko found space in the box to head an equaliser from David Silva's corner. The stadium erupted, but they still needed another. Surely there wasn't enough time for a winner.

Meanwhile, at the Stadium of Light in Sunderland, the Man Utd players and coaches were starting to celebrate. The final whistle had sealed their three points, and they had heard that City were drawing with seconds to go. But they were still playing at the Etihad, and City were still attacking. Suddenly, with five minutes of injury time already played, Sergio Aguero found space in the QPR box, and the crowd held its breath. He kept his head, shot, and the stadium went wild as the ball flew past Kenny and into the net. The final whistle sounded moments later and City had finally done it. The celebrations began in Manchester and ended abruptly in Sunderland. Jubilant manager Roberto Mancini ran onto the Etihad pitch to celebrate bringing the championship home for the first time since 1968, whilst at the Stadium of Light Alex Ferguson led his United team mournfully back to the dressing room.

City had won the title by the narrowest of margins – a better goal difference of eight, helped in no small measure by that 6-1 victory at Old Trafford. It was the tightest finish to a top flight season since Arsenal had beaten Liverpool to the Division One crown in 1989, also with an injury time goal. The two teams then had finished level on goal difference, Arsenal finishing ahead as they had scored more goals.

Despite their defeat, QPR survived by one point as Bolton Wanderers only drew with Stoke City, a late penalty denying them the win that would have seen them survive. They finished bottom the following season however and were relegated. United bounced back to become champions in 2013 in Alex Ferguson's final season as manager, whilst City added another Premier League title of their own in 2014.

14th May 1988
"The Crazy Gang have beaten the Culture Club"

Having played for most of their history in non-league football, Wimbledon FC had only been promoted to the Football League in 1977. Amazingly they had made it to the top division by 1986, and had put together their best ever cup run during the 1987-88 season to reach the FA Cup final.

In stark contrast, their opponents, Liverpool, had been League Champions ten times in the 1970s and 80s, including that season, had won the FA Cup twice in that period as well as the League Cup four times and had been Champions of Europe four times. It was hard to think of a match-up that could be better described as a "David and Goliath" contest.

Liverpool had however started their cup campaign a little shakily, needing a replay to overcome second division Stoke City, then saw off Aston Villa, local rivals Everton and Manchester City before two John Aldridge goals, one from the penalty spot, helped them win their semi-final against Nottingham Forest. Wimbledon, starting out as 33-1 outsiders, had won all of their previous round ties at the first time of asking, beating West Brom, Mansfield, Newcastle, Watford and Luton to reach Wembley.

It looked as though the match would be true to form in the opening encounters, with the 98,000 strong crowd witnessing Liverpool, seeking the double having secured the League title, start the brighter, and Alan Cork was forced to head away a John Barnes cross with Aldridge waiting dangerously behind him.

Liverpool came close to taking the lead when Dave Beasant pulled off a stunning point-blank save to deny Aldridge following great work by Peter Beardsley and a cross from Ray Houghton. As the rebound drifted towards the waiting John Barnes and the empty net beckoning, Beasant, despite lying flat on his back, somehow managed to reach up and push the ball away from the winger, with Vinnie Jones on hand to complete the clearance.

Wimbledon were mounting some attacks of their own however, and John Fashanu gave the favourites a warning as his first time shot from just inside the area flew inches wide. The Dons did require a huge stroke of luck in the 35th minute to stay on level terms though, when Peter Beardsley rode a foul by Andy Thorn, ran into the Wimbledon box and chipped the ball over Beasant and into the net, only to see the goal ruled out as the whistle had already gone for the foul. It was starting to look like it wouldn't be Liverpool's day.

Two minutes later they took full advantage of their good fortune. Terry Phelan won a free kick for his side close to the corner flag on the Liverpool right. Dennis Wise curled in the free-kick, and Lawrie Sanchez rose unchallenged on the edge of the six yard box to head the ball into the net for a highly unexpected lead.

Liverpool tried to hit back immediately, and almost did so, Beasant making a save with his feet to deny Liverpool captain Alan Hansen after a neat one-two, and that was enough the see the underdogs reach the break 1-0 up.

As the second half began Liverpool looked purposeful as Beardsley and Barnes in particular tried to conjure up a goal, but clear-cut chances were few and far between.

They were however given a golden opportunity to finally break through the stubborn Wimbledon defence and get back on level terms just after the hour mark. Aldridge went down in the box under a sliding tackle by Clive Goodyear, and referee Brian Hill pointed to the spot. Wimbledon players instantly surrounded him, claiming that Goodyear had won the ball, a claim that replays showed to be correct, but the decision stood. Aldridge, whose semi-final spot-kick had helped his side to reach the final and who had scored eleven penalties in a row, stepped up to take the penalty himself. Beasant had however been studying Aldridge's previous penalties, and his homework paid off. Aldridge hit it to Beasant's left, the same way he had struck his semi-final penalty, and the big goalie guessed correctly and brilliantly pushed to ball around the post to make the first ever penalty save in a Wembley FA Cup Final. Aldridge was substituted soon afterwards.

The Reds did their best to find an equaliser, but failed to break down a defence that was playing as if their lives depended on it. Defender Steve Nicol came closest to scoring, heading over the bar from a long throw from second-half substitute Jan Molby, but Wimbledon almost made the win secure through Eric Young as he drew a sharp save from Bruce Grobbelaar following a corner.

Wild scenes on the pitch greeted the final whistle, as Wimbledon celebrated the unlikeliest of victories. The BBC's John Motson commented "The Crazy Gang have beaten the Culture Club." Liverpool supporters sportingly saluted the victors as they received the trophy from Princess Diana, Beasant achieving another first as he became the first goalkeeper to receive the Cup as captain.

14th May 1981
Ricky Villa scores the best ever FA Cup Final goal

Tottenham Hotspur's FA Cup Final song in 1981, recorded with the band *Chas and Dave*, had been called *Ossie's Dream* in tribute to their Argentine midfielder Ossie Ardiles, but it was their other Argentine international, Ricky Villa, who stole the headlines with a goal that it still widely considered to be the greatest Cup Final ever scored.

Tottenham faced Manchester City in the Final, which was the one hundredth FA Cup Final. They had needed a replay to beat Wolverhampton Wanderers in their semi-final, as they had against Queens Park Rangers in the third round. Their opponents had had no such problems on their route to the final, and had been free-scoring too, knocking in fifteen goals in the five previous rounds.

The final was played on 9th May, but unfortunately wasn't the spectacle that the fans were hoping for. The first half was short on quality, although there were a few chances at either end. Graham Roberts drew a sharp save from Joe Corrigan in the City goal with a header, and Tony Galvin ran on to a Chris Hughton pass to force Corrigan into action again. It was City who broke the deadlock though, Tommy Hutchison putting them in front on the half hour mark, powerfully heading home Ray Ransom's cross after some determined play from Dave Bennett for a 1-0 half time lead.

At the start of the second half Ardiles was through on goal but Bobby McDonald recovered to thwart him. Then came perhaps the best move of the match, Steve MacKenzie playing a couple of one-twos with Reeves, taking the ball past Milija Alexsic in the Spurs goal but hitting the post.

With twenty minutes to go and Spurs still seeking an equaliser they took off Villa, who had been anonymous for most of the match, replacing him with Garry Brooke. The Argentine left the pitch clearly upset with his performance.

The turning point came ten minutes later, as Hutchison was to go from hero to villain. Glenn Hoddle's free-kick deflected off the Scot's shoulder, leaving Corrigan completely stranded and unable to keep out the deflection. Spurs were back on level terms, and Hutchison was left with the unfortunate distinction of being the first player to score for both sides in an FA Cup Final since 1946.

With the scores level at 1-1 extra time followed, but it was half an hour of little incident, and it became only the tenth FA Cup Final ever to finish level, and the first since 1970.

Just five days later the teams and their supporters were back at Wembley for the replay, the first to be staged at the famous stadium. In a much more open and entertaining encounter it took only eight minutes for Villa make amends for his below par performance first time round by opening the scoring for Spurs, following up Steve Archibald's shot that Corrigan was only able to block.

Spurs were only in front for three minutes though. Ransom took a free kick which Spurs could only half clear, Hutchison cleverly headed it to MacKenzie and the nineteen year old brilliantly volleyed the dropping ball from the edge of the D into the top corner. Tottenham came close to retaking the lead, Hoddle hitting the post with a free kick and Villa's long range effort being beaten away by Corrigan, but the half ended 1-1.

City had their noses in front for the first time on the night four minutes after the restart courtesy of the penalty spot. Bennett was bundled over in the box by Paul Miller, and referee Keith Hackett awarded the first FA Cup Final penalty since 1962. Kevin Reeves beat Aleksic to his left and it was 2-1 to City.

Spurs had a penalty appeal of their own turned down, as a cross hit Tommy Caton's arm, but they were level again with twenty minutes to go when Archibald brought down Hoddle's brilliant chip and the ball fell into the path of Crooks to stab home.

Just as it was starting to look like it would be extra time again, Roberts won a strong challenge on the edge of his own box. He played the ball out to Galvin on the Spurs left and he raced forwards, over the half way line, then checked as he ran out of space and played it inside to Villa. Villa took the ball into the City penalty area, outside Ransom and Caton, then inside Caton as the defender tried to recover, and shot past Corrigan as he came off his line. "Villa… and still Ricky Villa… what a fantastic run… he's scored! Amazing goal" described John Motson. It was a wondrous goal of skill, control and vision, and Man City were unable to find a reply. The man who had been taken off in tears in the first match had won the FA Cup with a truly magnificent goal, and Tottenham had become the winners of the one hundredth FA Cup Final.

Villa's goal has been replayed over and over again, and was voted as the Wembley Goal of the Century in 2001. Tottenham went on to defend their crown the following year, again following a replay, but Villa was absent from the match, feeling that it was inappropriate for him to play in the match as the UK and Argentina were then at war over the disputed Falklands Islands. He later called his autobiography *Still Ricky Villa* after John Motson's famous commentary.

14th May 1983
David Pleat celebrates Luton's great escape

With six teams threatened by relegation going into the last match of the season, and a last-gasp goal saving the team that had started the day as favourites for the drop, it was always going to be a day to remember, but it was the celebration of the jubilant manager that became more famous than the result itself.

David Pleat had taken over as manager of Second Division Luton Town in 1978, and had led them to promotion to Division One as Second Division champions in 1982, a fine achievement for a small club. They started the season in exciting style, including a 3-3 draw at Anfield against champions Liverpool, and scored twenty four goals in their first nine matches. They conceded twenty one as well however, and their leaky defence was to prove costly as the season progressed, as a series of heavy defeats stalled their momentum and saw they start to drop down the table.

Four defeats in a row in March saw them slip into the bottom three for the first time, before a run of six games unbeaten helped them pull away from the danger zone. Two more heavy defeats pushed them back down the table though, and they found themselves twentieth out of twenty-two with just one match to go – the final relegation spot with Brighton and Hove Albion and Swansea City already doomed.

One place and one point above them was Manchester City, the team they would face on the final day and coincidentally the team they had faced the last time they had been relegated from Division One. Also in the danger zone were Sunderland, Notts County, Coventry City and Birmingham City, with three points separating all six teams, although because of their goal difference it looked like either Luton or Man City would be the one to go down.

It was a simple equation for Luton as they travelled to Maine Road – win and they would survive, draw or lose and they would be down. For City a draw would be enough, but a defeat would leave them hoping that Birmingham suffered a heavy defeat. Desperate for the three points, Pleat took a risk and picked top scorer Brian Stein, despite him only having played once in the previous five months following a foot injury.

Unsurprisingly both teams made an anxious start to the match, and neither created many chances, the best opportunity of the half coming late on when City's

Kevin Reeves latched on to a long ball from Ray Ransom only to pull his shot wide of the Luton goal.

The Hatters, knowing that they had to win, started the second half on the front foot, and they nearly made their pressure count as a deflection off Kevin Bond drifted just wide of his own goal. From the corner that followed Alex Williams was forced to save sharply from Paul Walsh. Luton were starting to dominate, but couldn't get the ball into the net.

In an attempt to change that Pleat brought on Yugoslav international Raddy Antic, but City started to come more into the game as the match began to open up. Luton hearts were soon in their mouths as their goalie Tony Godden failed to claim a cross and needed his defenders' help to get the ball clear. It was played straight back into the box and Dennis Tueart's effort was just about kept out. At the other end Kirk Stephens' shot was saved, then Nicky Reid's follow up effort hit the bar.

With five minutes on the clock and time running out for Luton, Stein fired a cross into the City penalty area. Williams came out to punch the ball clear, but only to the edge of the box, straight to the waiting Antic. He hit the ball on the volley, past Williams who had fallen to the ground and could only get his fingertips to it, and in between two defenders on the goal line into the back of the net. The Luton supporters packed into Maine Road erupted in excitement and relief, but Pleat knew they weren't safe yet and frantically signalled to his players to calm down.

The tables had now turned, and it was now Man City who desperately needed to find a goal as Birmingham were winning their match. Throwing everyone forward, it was Luton's turn to hold on. Godden managed to thwart Asa Hartford as he tried to create an opening, then the keeper was forced to push a cross out for a corner. He failed to claim the ball from the resulting corner, but Steve Kinsey's shot was blocked.

That would prove to be City's last chance. As the final whistle sounded an elated Pleat rushed onto the pitch, skipping his way towards his players, punching the air and trying for some reason to button up the jacket of his light brown suit. There had probably never been a more joyful reaction from a manager, and there probably hasn't been one since.

Luton continued to battle for First Division survival for the next few seasons, but then found their feet and managed top ten finishes between 1986 and 1988. They finished ninth in 1986, Pleat's final season at the club. He had also led them to the FA Cup Semi Final in 1985, and they went on to win the League Cup in

1988 before returning to relegation dogfights. They eventually lost their place in the top flight at the end of the 1991-92 season. Hero of the hour Antic went on to have a successful managerial career, including spells in charge of Barcelona, Real and Atletico Madrid and the Serbian national side.

25th May 1967
The Lisbon Lions

Who was the first British team to win the European Cup? Many sports fans might guess at Liverpool or Manchester United, but in fact it was a Scottish side consisting almost entirely of local boys that defied the odds to achieve that accolade.

Celtic had finished just ahead of their Glasgow rivals Rangers to claim the Scottish title the previous season, finishing just two points ahead of their Old Firm neighbours to qualify for Europe. In the first round they had had a comfortable 5-0 aggregate win against FC Zurich, then beat Nantes 6-2 over two legs, a clear indication of their favoured attacking style. Their quarter-final was a tighter affair, and it took a ninetieth minute goal in the second leg from captain Billy McNeill to overcome Vojvodina Novi Sad 2-0 having lost the first leg 1-0. A 3-1 victory in the semi final first leg against against Dukla Prague was enough to secure them a place in the final in Lisbon, the second leg finishing goalless.

Their opponents in the final were Internazionale, better known as Inter Milan, the Italian Champions who had already been European Champions in 1964 and '65. After a tight 1-0 aggregate win against Torpedo Moscow in the first round they had overcome Vasas 4-1 in the second round before knocking out defending champions Read Madrid 3-0 over two legs in the quarter final. Two 1-1 draws against Bulgarians CSKA Red Flag in their semi final meant a replay on a neutral ground, which Inter went on to win 1-0.

Celtic manager Jock Stein told his players in his pre-final team-talk to "go out and enjoy yourselves", but with their European pedigree and having beaten Real Madrid along the way, Inter were runaway favourites for the title. It looked as though the tie would run true to form when Sandro Mazzola's downward header from a Renato Cappellini cross was kept out by Celtic goalie Ronnie Simpson's knees after just a couple of minutes. It didn't take them long to find a way past Simpson though. Jim Craig brought down Cappellini in the box and Mazzola calmly rolled the spot kick to Simpson's right to make it 1-0 with just seven minutes on the clock.

With Inter's defence famed for its tightness, employing a tactic known as Catenaccio, *the chain*, that meant that they often took a 1-0 lead then defended it for the rest of the match, it looked like it would be tough for Celtic to get back on level terms, despite their own attacking prowess. The Scots battled away, but were largely restricted to long range efforts for the remainder of the first half and the beginning of the second. Nevertheless they kept Giuliano Sarti busy in the Inter goal, Jimmy "Jinky" Johnstone forcing him to tip a header over the crossbar and Tommy Gemmell forcing a save with a deflected free kick. Sarti was on fine form, but Inter were also receiving plenty of help from the woodwork, with both Bertie Auld and Gemmell hitting the crossbar.

Early in the second half Celtic were awarded an indirect free kick in the Inter box, but the resulting shot was blocked by a sea of black and blue shirts. From the follow up a deflected shot was stopped on the line by Sarti. Celtic claimed the ball had crossed the line but the referee waved away their protests. It was starting to look as if the Inter defence would keep the Bhoys at bay.

The breakthrough finally came though just after an hour. Craig made amends for conceding the penalty with a cut-back that picked out Gemmell and he let fly from the edge of the box, thumping his shot passed the helpless Sarti and into the net to make it 1-1.

With half an hour still to play Inter could no longer afford to pull everyone back behind the ball if they wanted to win the match, but it was still Celtic who were creating the better chances. Sarti kept pulling off great saves though to keep his side in it, but with six minutes to go his resistance finally succumbed, Stevie Chalmers diverting Bobby Murdoch's shot from outside the box past him to put Celtic in front.

Inter were unable to respond, and at the final whistle thousands of joyous Celtic fans poured onto the pitch to celebrate. Bobby Lennox had to sprint to the Celtic goal where he had left his false teeth before anyone claimed them as a souvenir, and many of his teammates weren't so lucky with their shirts. The trophy presentation had to be moved from the middle of the pitch to the edge of the stand, and armed guards had to help McNeill make his way to receive the cup.

Celtic's performance was hailed throughout Europe as a victory for attacking football, and the team became nicknamed "The Lisbon Lions". That every one of them had been born within thirty miles of Glasgow made their triumph even more poignant for their fans.

Their defence ended in the first round the following season at the hands of Dynamo Kiev, although they continued to dominate domestically, winning the Scottish League that season and for the following six seasons.

25th May 2005
The Miracle of Istanbul

No-one was surprised to see Milan in the Champions League final. The winners from 2003, Milan had qualified for the competition as Italian champions and were chasing a seventh European Champions title. Their squad boasted Paolo Maldini, who had won the trophy four times with Milan before, and Clarence Seedorf, who had won it three times with three different clubs. Their opponents Liverpool in contrast, although they had won the trophy four times before, were making their first final appearance since 1985, after which they had been banned from European competitions following the Heysel Stadium disaster. They had qualified by finishing fourth in the Premier League the previous season, and an inconsistent season had seen then finish only fifth that year.

Liverpool's best form had been saved for Europe however, and they had come through a qualifying round comfortably to qualify from their group ahead of Olympiacos and Deportivo la Coruna. They then thumped Bayer Leverkusen 6-2 on aggregate, beat Juventus 2-1 in the quarter final and won a tight all-English semi-final against Chelsea 1-0 to reach the final.

If Liverpool supporters were surprised they were in the final, there was a further shock in store for them when they went 1-0 down in the first minute, Maldini putting his side into the lead with a volley from Andrea Pirlo's free kick. Liverpool responded well however, and almost levelled soon afterwards, Sami Hyppia drawing a smart save from Dida with a header. Milan continued to cause problems for Liverpool's defence though, with Luis Garcia forced to clear a Hernan Crespo header off the line and only the offside flag preventing Andriy Shevchenko from doubling their lead. Liverpool thought they should have had a penalty, but instead Milan counter-attacked through Kaka, who slipped the ball to Shevchenko, and his cross found Crespo on the edge of the six yard box to make it 2-0. It wasn't long until it was 3-0, with Kaka again involved, finding Crespo whose calm chip over Jerzy Dudek found the back of the net a minute before half time.

Liverpool were shell-shocked. They had gone into the match as underdogs, but Milan were threatening to turn it into a rout. Surely there was no way back for Liverpool, and the second half would be a case of damage limitation.

Liverpool captain Steven Gerrard had other ideas though. A born-and-bred scouser, he wasn't going to let the club he had grown up supporting bow out with a whimper. Xabi Alonso set the tone for the half, shooting just wide from distance, and nine minutes after the restart Gerrard himself got one back, guiding in a well placed header from John Arne Riise's cross to give the Reds a glimmer of hope. Gerrard egged on his team to do more, and two minutes later they were well and truly back in the match, first half substitute Vladimar Smicer striking a ferocious shot from distance to make it 3-2. Just four further minutes passed before Liverpool unbelievably had a chance to level at 3-3. Gerrard was brought down in the box by Gennaro Gattuso, and although Alonso's penalty was initially saved by Dida the rebound fell kindly for him to thump his follow up shot into the roof of the net. It was a remarkable six minutes that had turned the match on its head.

Milan were stunned, but regained enough composure to almost regain the lead, with Jimi Traore managing to clear off the line after Dudek had failed to deal with a cross. Both sides had chances to win it in normal time, but full time ended with the score 3-3 and the game moved into extra time.

Fatigue started to affect the players in the humid Istanbul atmosphere, with several of the Liverpool players in particular suffering after their second half efforts. Liverpool created early pressure but couldn't capitalise, and Dudek was forced to make a stunning double save from point blank range as Milan pressed late on, and no further goals meant that the title would be decided on penalties.

Milan went first, but Serginho blasted high and wide. Dietmar Hamann made no mistake with his strike, despite a broken toe, then Dudek guessed right to save Pirlo's penalty. Djibril Cisse scored his to put Liverpool 2-0 ahead, before Jon-Dahl Tomasson finally got one on the board for Milan. Riise saw his penalty saved by Dida to give Milan hope, making it 2-1 to Liverpool after three penalties each. Kaka beat Dudek to level at 2-2, but Smicer scored Liverpool's fourth to restore their advantage. Shevchenko, who had scored the winning penalty in Milan's win two years before, had to score to keep his side in it. He hit his shot straight at the middle of the goal, but although Dudek was diving to his right he stuck out a hand and kept the ball out. As the rest of the team sprinted to celebrate with their goalie, Liverpool were, against all the odds, Champions of Europe once again.

As it was their fifth victory Liverpool were allowed to keep the trophy, and more than a million fans lined the streets of Merseyside for their celebratory open-top bus tour. Their win also changed Champions League rules, as their failure to qualify for the following season's competition through the Premier League meant that they wouldn't have been able to defend their title if UEFA hadn't allowed England an extra place to accommodate Liverpool. All champions since then have had the right to defend their title, regardless of whether they would have qualified through their domestic league. Liverpool's defence ended at the last sixteen stage though, beaten 3-0 over two legs by Portuguese champions Benfica.

26th May 1989
Arsenal pinch title from Liverpool with final kick of the season

The First Division title had come down to the final match of the season, but few people gave Arsenal a chance in the deciding game. Three points behind Liverpool and with an inferior goal difference, the Gunners needed to beat the reigning champions by two clear goals in order to match them on points and goal difference but beat them on goals scored. It was a tall order for a side that was without a title win for eighteen years and which hadn't won at Liverpool's Anfield ground for fifteen, against a team that had won eight league titles in the previous thirteen years.

Arsenal fans would have argued that the season shouldn't have gone down to the final match anyway. Their team had been nineteen points clear of Liverpool at one point, but a twenty four match unbeaten run had seen Liverpool close the gap then edge ahead. Whilst Liverpool were on a roll, Arsenal's form had started to slip, and they were going into the match on the back of a defeat and a draw. Liverpool were also chasing the Double, having beaten Everton in the FA Cup Final.

The match also had emotional significance for Liverpool, coming little more than a month after ninety six of their supporters had lost their lives in the Hillsborough stadium disaster, and this match had been postponed as it had been scheduled to be played the weekend after the tragedy, which was why it was being played after the season had already finished for everyone else. Arsenal players presented flowers to home supporters in memory of those who had died before kick-off.

Arsenal manager George Graham's tactics were an immediate surprise as the match kicked off. Despite the fact that they needed to win by two goals, he selected an extra defender, playing David O'Leary as a sweeper alongside the infamous Arsenal back four. The plan was successful in stifling the home side's attacking capabilities in the first half, and also allowed their full backs Lee Dixon and Nigel Winterburn more freedom to push forward. However, they created few chances in the first half, and their task looked to be beyond them with the half-time score 0-0.

The visitors were back in the hunt soon after the restart though. Seven minutes into the second half, Arsenal were awarded an indirect free-kick on the edge of the box. Winterburn played it into the box and Alan Smith got the faintest of touches with his head to help the ball past Bruce Grobbelaar and into the net. Liverpool protested that Smith hadn't touched it and therefore the goal shouldn't stand as it wasn't a direct free kick, but after consulting his linesman referee David Hutchinson awarded the goal.

Now just one goal from claiming the title, the Gunners pushed forward, and the home fans began to feel the tension. The game started to open up at last, helped by Arsenal switching to a 4-4-2 formation. Michael Thomas had a chance for Arsenal but his shot was saved, and Ray Houghton missed a chance to seal it for Liverpool. The home fans thought it was all over when John Aldridge put the ball in the net, but their celebrations were cut short by the offside flag.

Time was running out for Arsenal. Normal time was up and injury time was being played. Steve McMahon could be seen telling his team-mates they just had to hold on for one more minute, and Liverpool had the ball through John Barnes, but when he lost possession Arsenal launched one more attack. Goalie John Lukic threw the ball out to Dixon, he hit it up field to Smith, and his flick-on found Michael Thomas on the edge of the box. "It's up for grabs now" exclaimed ITV commentator Brian Moore. Thomas held off the challenge of Steve Nicol, the ball taking a touch off the Liverpool defender but falling back into his path. He took one more touch to steady himself, then guided the ball past Grobbelaar.

Liverpool had just about time to kick off, but the whistle blew to leave the Arsenal players jubilant and Liverpool shell-shocked. It was an incredible result that sealed the league title against the odds by the narrowest of margins – the teams had finished level of points and goal difference, but Arsenal had scored eight goals more over the season. The very last one would of course be the most memorable.

Liverpool comfortably reclaimed their title the following season, with Arsenal back in fourth, but they haven't won the title since, and Arsenal were champions again in the 1990-91 season. Remarkably, Thomas moved from Arsenal to Liverpool two years after breaking his dramatic winner, and became a favourite with the fans whose hearts he had broken on that famous night.

26th May 1999
Man Utd score twice in injury time to win the Champions League

Despite already winning five Premier League titles, four FA Cups, a League Cup and a Cup Winners Cup since taking over as Manchester United manager, Alex Ferguson's holy grail was a Champions League title. Not since 1968, under the great Sir Matt Busby, had United been able to call themselves champions of Europe. Fergie was determined to change that, and they had qualified for the final.

It had been a long journey to the final for United and their opponents Bayern Munich. As neither side had won their domestic championship the previous year they had both had to go through a qualifying round. They were then drawn together in the group stage, sharing a 2-2 draw in Germany and drawing 1-1 at Old Trafford. Their results against Danish side Brondby and Barcelona ensured that both teams progressed though, Bayern as group winners.

United faced Inter in the quarter final, and overcame their Italian opponents 3-1 on aggregate. Meanwhile, Bayern comfortably won an all-German tie against Kaiserslauten 6-0 over the two legs. Fergie's side journeyed to Italy again for their semi-final, rescuing a 1-1 draw in their home leg against Juventus with an injury time Ryan Giggs strike and coming from two goals down in Turin thanks to Roy Keane and Dwight Yorke before Andy Cole clinched the win with a late goal. Bayern were drawn against Dynamo Kiev, also coming from behind to draw 3-3 in Ukraine, then winning their home leg 1-0 to take a 4-3 victory.

That set up an England v Germany final, which always invoked the greatest of footballing passions, and to add extra spice, both teams were chasing the treble having just won their domestic league and cup titles. United had selection problems for the final, played in front of 90,000 fans in Barcelona's Nou Camp stadium, with both captain Roy Keane and Paul Scholes missing through suspension and Henning Berg out through injury.

Ferguson's dream was under threat almost straight away however. With just six minutes on the clock Carsten Jancker won a free kick for Bayern on the edge of the box. Up stepped Mario Basler, and his low free kick swerved its way around the United wall and past Peter Schmeichel to put the Germans 1-0 up. That lead allowed Bayern to sit back and try to hit United on the break, and although United dominated possession they created nothing in the first half to trouble Oliver Kahn in the Bayern goal.

Bayern looked intent on increasing their lead after the break, with Schmeichel having to save from Jancker within a minute. United huffed and puffed throughout the second half, but created little. With still little sign of an equaliser coming, Ferguson threw on another striker, Teddy Sheringham, but it was Bayern who were creating the better chances, Stefan Effenberg shooting wide and then forcing another save from Schmeichel before Mehmet Scholl's chip hit the post with the Danish keeper beaten. With ten minutes to go United were getting desperate. Ferguson rolled the dice one more time and threw on Ole Gunnar Solksjaer up front. His impact was immediate, Kahn having to push away his header. Bayern nearly sealed the win moments later though, hitting the woodwork again via Jancker's overhead kick. Subs Sheringham and Solksjaer kept working hard however, keeping Kahn busy in the Bayern goal as the game finally came to life.

As the match moved into injury time, Bayern knew they had to keep United out for just another three minutes as the fourth official's board went up. Celebratory flares were let off by their fans, and their ribbons were attached to the trophy. United won a corner, and Schmeichel left his goal in a desperate attempt to grab an equaliser. David Beckham took the corner, which Bayern failed to clear. Giggs mis-hit a shot that fell perfectly for Sheringham who guided it into the net for a dramatic equaliser. Bayern appealed for offside in vain, whilst United celebrated, mightily relieved, and extra time beckoned.

But, there were still two minutes of injury time to play, and United won another corner. Schmeichel stayed back this time, not wanting to risk conceding a late winner. Beckham took it again, picking out Sheringham, whose header down found Solskjaer in space, and he pounced to poke the ball home. He slid across the turf in celebration and was covered by teammates, subs and coaches, whilst Schmeichel cartwheeled at the other end of the pitch.

There was barely time to kick-off, and referee Pierluigi Collina had to help the distraught Bayern players back onto their feet to do so. He blew his whistle moments later, and Manchester United were finally champions of Europe. The Bayern players found their loss hard to bear, sinking to the ground in despair. Sammy Kuffour broke down in tears and pounded the ground in anguish.

UEFA president Lennart Johansson had left his seat at the beginning of injury time to make his way through the inside of the stadium to the pitch to make the presentation. He missed both of United's goals, and was amazed to see the scenes that greeted him when he emerged onto the pitch. "I can't believe it" he is quoted as saying, "The winners are crying and the losers are dancing." Schmeichel, standing in as captain in the absence of Keane and playing his last ever match for United, received the trophy from Johansson with Ferguson, who had at last achieved his aim of winning the Champions League, as well as securing the treble.

Both sides were knocked out by eventual winners Real Madrid the following season, United in the quarter final and Bayern in the semis, but the Germans finally got their hands on the trophy in 2001, beating Valencia on penalties in the final. In 2008 United won it again, winning an all English final against Chelsea on penalties, and Bayern won an all German final in 2013 against Borussia Dortmund.

30th May 1984
Grobbelaar's crazy legs help Liverpool win the European Cup

AS Roma were hoping that the unusual benefit of home advantage would help them as they sought to overcome their opponents' formidable record in European Cup finals. English champions Liverpool had reached three finals in the previous seven years - 1977, '78 and '81 – and had won them all. In contrast, it was Roma's first final, but with their Stadio Olimpico ground having been chosen as the venue for the final at the start of the season it would feel like a home game to them. Liverpool also had fond memories of the stadium however, having beaten Borussia Mönchengladbach there in 1977 to claim their first title.

Liverpool had had a comfortable passage to the final, thrashing Odense 6-0 on aggregate in the first round before a tighter second round encounter against Athletic Bilbao which required a single Ian Rush goal in the second leg to see them through. They then saw off Benfica 5-1 in the quarter final and Dinamo Bucharest 3-1 in a feisty semi final that saw Graeme Souness break Dinamo's Lica Movila's jaw to make it to the final.

Roma's matches had also seen plenty of goals, as they beat Gothenburg 4-2, CSKA Sofia 2-0 and Dynamo Berlin 4-2 before facing Dundee United in their semi final. Their Scottish opponents won the first leg 2-0, meaning that the Italian champions would need a seemingly unlikely 3-0 victory in the return to progress. In an incredibly hostile atmosphere, with United players having objects thrown at them from the stands, Roma managed an incredible comeback, with two goals from Roberto Pruzzo and a hotly disputed penalty by Agostino Di Bartolomei giving them the 3-0 victory they required. The result however has been marred by later admissions that Roma's president attempted to bribe the referee that night.

The Roma supporters created a similarly intimidating atmosphere for the final, and Liverpool seemed happy at first to keep possession and wait for things to quieten down. They almost became unstuck though as they failed to deal with a through ball and their eccentric Zimbabwean goalkeeper Bruce Grobbelaar had to come out quickly to gather the ball off the toes off Francesco Graziani.

It was an error in the Roma defence that led to the opening goal however, along with a large slice of luck. Sammy Lee fed the ball to Craig Johnston on the Liverpool right, who sent in a high, hanging cross. There seemed to be little danger, but Franco Tancredi collided with Ronnie Whelan as he tried to catch the ball and dropped it. Michele Nappi headed the ball down and tried to turn and clear it, but the ball hit Tancredi on the head and ricocheted straight into the path of Phil Neal who stabbed it home from the six yard line, making it 1-0 after thirteen minutes.

Liverpool almost doubled their lead moments later when Souness put the ball in the net, but his strike was ruled out for offside. Grobbelaar was again called into action just before the half hour mark, making a great save low to his right from the onrushing Graziani. Liverpool were looking fairly comfortable defending their lead, but a moment of brilliance from Roma midfielder Bruno Conti shortly before half time unlocked their defence. Battling for the ball on the Roma left against Neal and Mark Lawrenson he half-volleyed in a cross, picking out Pruzzo, whose flicked header looped over Grobelaar's head and into the net, making it 1-1 at half time.

Roma looked to build some momentum at the start of the second half, but found it difficult to create anything against the well organised Liverpool defence, and their best chance was a long range effort from Falcao. Kenny Dalglish drew a sharp save from Tancredi at the other end, and was involved again as Liverpool nearly won it at the death, picking out Steve Nicol in the Roma box, but his shot was straight at the keeper.

With normal time ending with the scores level, both sides seemed reluctant to commit men forward in extra time for fear of conceding what might have been a killer blow, and the extra thirty minutes passed with little goalmouth action and no further scoring. The title would have to be decided by penalties.

It was a disastrous start to the shoot-out for the English champions, with Nicol firing his penalty over the bar. Graziani stepped up to take the first kick for Roma, but Di Bartolomei followed him up to the spot, took the ball from him and promptly scored to give the Italians the early advantage. Neal made no mistake with Liverpool's second however, and when Conti's strike also flew over the bar they were back on level terms. Souness hit his penalty into the top corner, and Ubaldo Righetti also scored to make it 2-2. Liverpool top scorer Rush sent Tancredi the wrong way to put Liverpool 3-2 up, then Graziani stepped up for the second time for Roma. As he placed the ball on the spot Grobbelaar wandered about on the goal-line, wobbling his legs as if they had turned to jelly with the pressure. Whether or not he put the Italian off or not remains to be seen, but his penalty became the third to be blasted over.

That left Alan Kennedy with the opportunity to win the Cup – if he scored Liverpool would win the shoot-out 4-2. He placed the ball, stepped back, ran forward, and stroked the ball left footed past Tancredi and into the goal. Liverpool were European Champions for the fourth time in dramatic style.

Liverpool came close to defending their title the following year, losing 1-0 to Juventus in a final remembered more for the deaths of thirty nine fans in the Heysel Stadium disaster than for the match itself. Liverpool and all other English clubs were banned from European competition for the next five seasons as a result.

June

3rd June 1978
Referee Clive Thomas disallows very late Brazilian goal

Welsh football referee Clive Thomas was no stranger to controversy. One of the youngest Football League referees ever when he began his career, he progressed to officiate English First Division matches and was then selected for international duty, refereeing in both the 1974 and 1978 World Cups as well as the 1976 European Championships.

Nicknamed "The Book" for his strict adherence to the rules, he had hit the headlines for mistakenly disallowing an Ipswich goal for offside against West Ham in the 1975 FA Cup semi final, then for missing a foul on Johan Cruyff in the semi final of the 1976 European Championships that allowed Czechoslovakia to score the winning goal. During that match he had sent off three players and at one point threatened to have the match abandoned as the players lost their discipline in extra time. In yet another semi final encounter he disallowed an Everton goal for no obvious reason that would have seen them beat Liverpool to reach the final.

Those incidents were dwarfed however by the storm that was created by a decision he made at the 1978 World Cup in Argentina. Brazil were playing Sweden in their opening match of the group stage. Thomas Sjoberg had given Sweden the lead after thirty seven minutes, finishing off a crisp passing move that Brazil themselves would have been proud of. Bo Larsson almost doubled their lead, but his header from a well-worked free kick came back off the bar, and instead Brazil were soon back on level terms, Reinaldo equalising when he got to a Toninho Cerezo cross first and clipped the ball past Ronnie Helstrum.

In the second half Rivelino forced a good save from Helstrum when his deflected half volley almost flew into the top corner, and Leao had to save acrobatically from Benny Wendt's well hit shot after he had beaten the Brazilian offside trap, but neither side was able to find the net.

With just seconds left Brazil won a corner. Nelinho placed the ball and was about to take it when the linesman told him the ball needed to be moved back into the corner quadrant. The extra few seconds that that took up proved to be costly. With the linesman now happy he took the corner just as the clock ticked past ninety minutes, firing the ball into the box and picking out Zico, who moved from the penalty spot to the six yard box unopposed to head the ball into the net.

The Brazilians started to celebrate what they thought was the winning goal, until they realised that Thomas had blown his whistle with the ball in mid-air, just before Zico had headed it. According to "The Book" it was full time before the goal was scored and therefore he was correct to disallow it, and despite Brazil's protests the match had finished as a 1-1 draw.

Brazil went on to draw their next game as well, 0-0 with Spain, so needed to beat Austria in the final group match to progress. They managed to do so 1-0, a Roberto Dinamite goal five minutes before half time the difference between the sides, but still only finished second behind the Austrians on goals scored.

That put them in a second round group with the hosts, Peru and Poland. Brazil started well with a 3-0 victory over Poland with two goals from Dirceu and a Zico penalty, but the two South American giants then drew 0-0 in a violent encounter that left the outcome of the group hanging on the results of their final matches. Brazil won their game against Poland 3-1, Nelinho opening the scoring before two more goals from Dinamite, but with Argentina playing later they knew what they needed to do to progress – to win by four goals. They duly achieved that and more, thrashing Peru 6-0 to reach the final on goal difference, which they went on to win. If Brazil's "winner" against Austria had stood they would have been in the other group, and it could have been Brazil and not the Netherlands who went on to meet Argentina in the final.

Thomas' decision was by no means the only controversy of the World Cup however. Many thought that Argentina should not be hosting the tournament at all, with the country being run by a regime that had come to power via a military coup just two years before and which had faced accusations of brutality and oppression. Argentina had also been accused of bribing the Peru side that they thrashed 6-0 in their final second round match, enabling them to overtake Brazil on goal difference, although nothing was ever proved. Beaten finalists the Netherlands were also unhappy with the circumstances of the final, believing that Argentina had used gamesmanship to delay the start of the match by questioning the legality of a plaster-cast on Rene van de Kerkhof's arm. The referee also ignored a number of clear offsides and handballs by Argentine players during the course of the final, which they won 3-1 after extra time. As a result the Dutch refused to attend the post-match ceremony.

4th June 1993
The "Ball of the Century"

There was nothing to suggest it was going to be anything other than just another Ashes debut. Twenty three year old Aussie leg spinner Shane Warne was about to bowl his first ever ball in Ashes cricket. It was his twelfth test match, and he had thirty one test wickets under his belt, but he had failed to trouble the radar of the English press in the build-up to the series.

It was the first test of a six match series between the two old rivals. Australia had easily won the Ashes back on their previous tour of England in 1989, taking the series 4-0, and had defended them back in Australia equally comfortably with a 3-0 win. England had also lost a three match series in India 3-0 over the winter, and English cricket fans were desperate for a change in fortune.

On an Old Trafford pitch that was expected to give some help to spinners the tourists had only selected their inexperienced new spinner Warne, whilst England had gone with two spinners, Phil Tufnell and Peter Such. England won the toss and chose to bowl, a decision that seemed to be a right one when Australia were all out for a modest 289, despite Mark Taylor's 124. The fact that Such had taken six wickets and Tufnell two suggested that the Aussie bowling attack might be light on spinners, and England looked very much on the front foot.

In reply, England had looked like building on their advantage, Graeme Gooch and Mike Atherton putting on 71 before Atherton was dismissed by Merv Hughes. Mike Gatting came in at three and continued to take the attack to Australia, and with the score 80 for 1 Allan Border threw the ball to his young spinner, despite Gatting being acknowledged as a fine player of spin. Warne, lips and nose plastered in white zinc cream and with a shock of bleach-blonde hair, carefully set his field, took one final look at Gatting, then started his run-up. The ball started straight, then drifted away from the batsman's legs and pitched just outside leg stump. Gatting, knowing that he couldn't be given out LBW, pushed bat and pad towards the ball, but the ball suddenly jagged back ferociously, passing bat and pad and clipping off-stump.

As the bails spiralled away and the jubilant bowler punched the air, Gatting remained rooted to the spot, unable to believe what had just happened, before trudging disconsolately back to the dressing room with a shake of the head. Warne had announced himself with a bang as a world-class spinner with a dismissal that was later described as The Ball of the Century. The spin he had generated was phenomenal, and it was anything but a fluke. He went on to dismiss Robin Smith in similar style soon afterwards, and ended the innings with 4 for 51 as England struggled to 210 all out.

The Australian batsmen found their form to build on their first innings lead, with Ian Healey leading the way with 102 not out, and Border set England an unlikely 512 to win, declaring their second innings on 432 for 5. Despite Gooch making 133 before being unusually given out for handling the ball, England could only manage 332, with Chris Lewis the only other batsman to get past 30. Warne took a further four wickets to end with match figures of 8 for 137 and claimed the man of the match award.

His form continued throughout the series, as his thirty four wickets, including figures of 5 for 82 in the second innings of the fifth test at Edgbaston, helped his side to a 4-1 series win to retain the Ashes, and he was named Australia's man of the series.

It was a taste of things to come for England, and Warne continued to be their nemesis for the next thirteen years, taking 195 English test wickets and helping Australia hold on to the Ashes until England finally reclaimed them in a dramatic series in 2005, before winning them back again in his final Ashes series in 2006-07. It wasn't just England he tormented either: he also became the first bowler to take 700 test wickets, ending his career with a total of 708, in the process making leg spin popular once again. He was the first bowler to take more than 1,000 test and one day international wickets, and contributed many valuable lower order runs for his country over the years, finishing with more than 3,000 test runs at an average of 17, and over 1,000 one day runs.

In 1999 Warne was man of the match in the Cricket World Cup final, taking four wickets as Australia beat Pakistan by eight wickets. He missed their successful defence of their title in 2003 though, as he was sent home and banned from cricket for a year for having taken a prohibited diuretic.

After his retirement from international cricket he embarked on a successful career in 20-20 cricket, both in the Indian Premier League and the Australian Big Bash, before retiring from all forms of the game in 2013.

His most famous wicket will always be however The Ball of the Century.

6th June 1994
Brian Lara scores 501

A century is the prime goal of any batsman. A double century is something special. A few batsmen achieve a rare triple century. But only one man has ever scored more than 500 runs in one innings in first class cricket.

Brian Lara was certainly used to producing big scores. Prolific in youth cricket both for his native Trinidad and Tobago and for the West Indies, he made his test debut in 1990, and soon cemented his place in the side with his first international century, 277 against Australia in Sydney. The left hander had continued to cause problems for bowlers around the world, and in April 1994 he broke Gary Sobers' world record for the highest individual test score by scoring 375 against England at St John's in Antigua, a record that had stood for thirty-six years.

In the summer of 1994 he agreed to play for Warwickshire in the English County Championship, a signing that helped the county to their best season ever, and perhaps the best by any county in the history of English cricket. It was a golden summer for Warwickshire, as they won the County Championship, the one day Sunday League and the Benson and Hedges Cup. They almost made it a clean sweep, narrowly losing to Worcestershire in the final of the Natwest Trophy. Lara himself had shone with the bat, especially in the four day games of the County Championship, and he finished the season having scored nine centuries and over 2,000 runs, with an impressive average of 89. Amazingly, 500 of those were scored in one innings.

Warwickshire were playing at their Edgbaston home against Durham, who had batted first and posted a highly creditable 556, including 204 by John Morris, a score that would have won the man-of-the-match award in most games. In reply on the second day, Warwickshire had lost opener Dominic Ostler early on for 8, bringing Lara to the crease. On a pitch that clearly had runs in it, The Prince as some called him must have fancied his chances of yet another big score, but it was almost not to be, as he was reprieved after being bowled off a no-ball whilst still on 10, then dropped by Durham wicketkeeper Chris Scott on 16. Those missed chances were to prove costly for the visitors, as Lara demonstrated his batting prowess to reach 111 not out by the end of the day in the company of Roger Twose, who was out for 51, then Trevor Penney.

Rain in Birmingham meant that no play was possible on day three, and with just one day of the four day match remaining Warwickshire captain Dermot Reeve spoke to his opposite number Phil Bainbridge to see if an agreement could be reached whereby the teams traded declarations to try to bring about a positive result. Luckily for Lara no consensus could be reached, and so Reeve decided that they should just bat on.

It took Lara a while to get going again, adding just 27 to his overnight score from the first 41 balls he faced, but all of a sudden he decided to turn on the style. He hit 147 off his next 78 balls to reach 285 at lunch, the only moment of danger a half chance he gave to the fielding side on 238. He continued the onslaught after lunch, adding another 133 between lunch and tea to take his total to 418, despite a scare when he could have been caught on 413. Now he was just 82 runs short of 500, a landmark which would see him surpass Hanif Mohammad's record first class total of 499 scored in 1959. Many other records had already tumbled during his innings – Warwickshire's highest score, the highest score in England, most boundaries in an innings and most runs in a day – but it was Hanif's landmark and becoming the first man ever to score 500 that he had set his sights on.

By now the word had got around that Lara was on the verge of history, and Edgbaston was starting to fill up rapidly with cricket fans anxious to witness it. As Lara came back out to bat for the final session of the match, alongside Keith Piper who had now joined him and was well on the way to a century of his own, it was Piper who found himself taking most of the strike. Lara was still scoring quickly when he was facing however, and his score edged steadily upwards, past 450 and on towards 500.

As he closed in on the record it looked as though the only thing that could deny him was the clock. After he defended the first three balls of a Morris over, then was hit on the helmet by a bouncer, Piper pointed out to Lara that they were probably in the final over of the match. With his score on 497 he was in danger in falling agonisingly short of 500, as Hanif had himself when he was run out on 499. With two balls to go, Lara stepped back across his stumps and carved the ball to the ropes for the seventy second boundary of his innings, but this one was perhaps the most important of the lot as it brought up his 500th run. Piper embraced his record-breaking team-mate, and the umpires sensibly brought the match to an end.

Lara had scored 501 not out in 474 minutes from 427 balls, including 62 fours and 10 sixes. That the match ended in a draw was neither here nor there.

He left Warwickshire in 1998, going on to reclaim the highest test score record that Australia's Matthew Hayden had briefly taken from him with a score of 400 not out, again versus England, at St John's in 2004. He retired from cricket in 2007, although he has made a few short comebacks since then. In his career he made more than 22,000 first class runs, including 65 centuries, at an average of 51. He also scored nine double centuries in tests, with only Donald Bradman having scored more.

7th June 1970
The greatest ever save and the perfectly timed tackle

World Champions England's preparations for the defence of their title in the Mexico world cup got off to a decidedly shaky start when their captain Bobby Moore was arrested after a warm up match in Colombia. Moore had been accused of stealing a bracelet from a gift shop at the team's hotel in Bogota, and was detained and questioned before eventually being released without charge. The incident was generally thought to be either an attempt to extort money from the England team or to unsettle them, but it was a distraction that the team could do without, especially as they faced a tough group that included two time winners Brazil.

Despite the incident however, the team started well, winning their opening game against Romania 1-0 thanks to a goal from 1966 hat-trick hero Geoff Hurst. Brazil also won their opener, 4-1 against Czechoslovakia, setting up an encounter with England that would more than likely decide the winner of the group.

Fielding six members of the team that won the final in 1966, the defending champions faced a Brazil side including greats such as Pele, Rivelino and Carlos Alberto, and which was determined to win its third World Cup in four tournaments, and it didn't take them long to demonstrate their attacking prowess. With just ten minutes gone, Jairzinho was put through on the Brazil right. He skipped past Terry Cooper's challenge and just managed to wrap his foot around the ball as it looked as though it would go out of play to float in a pin-point cross that found Pele waiting to pounce near the penalty spot. Pele rose above Tommy Wright and powerfully headed the ball down. He was so sure that he was going to score that he reportedly shouted "goal" as the ball left his head, but Gordon Banks had other ideas. Throwing himself down and to his right he parried the ball clear and over the bar for a corner in an incredible display of athleticism. Many people believe to this day that it was the greatest save ever seen on a football pitch.

England had chances of their own in the first half, with Franny Lee coming close with a diving header, but Brazil always looked dangerous and were giving the English defence a stern test. England held firm though, and the teams went in level at the break.

Fourteen minutes into the second half though, Brazil created the moment of brilliance that was to give them the lead. Tostao had been probing at the English defence on the left hand side of the pitch, but was pushed wide by Moore and Wright. Suddenly he spun around and delivered the ball in to the waiting Pele, who calmly controlled the ball before rolling it into the path of the advancing Jairzinho. He took one touch, then thumped the ball past the helpless Banks and into the net to make it 1-0 to Brazil.

A few minutes later Brazil were on the attack again. Moore was showing no adverse effects from his incident in Colombia, and had been a rock in the heart of the England defence, snuffing out Brazilian attack after attack with brilliant positioning and well-timed tackles, but it was his tackle on Jairzinho that has been replayed time and again. With the goal scorer running towards the England penalty area at pace, Moore tracked back with him every step of the way, never taking his eyes off the ball. As he ran into the box Moore picked his moment, stuck out his right leg as Jairzinho tried to go around his left, the wrong leg to be tackling with really, but his timing was superb and he came away with the ball as his opponent was sent tumbling.

From that tackle England attacked, moving into the Brazilian half where Cooper played a high ball into the box. Everaldo misjudged the flight badly and miskicked his clearance, and the ball fell to second half substitute and debutant Jeff Astle who only had goalkeeper Felix to beat, but he dragged his shot across the face of the goal and wide, and England's golden opportunity to draw level went begging.

At the final whistle Pele and Moore embraced and swapped shirts, the two true greats creating an iconic image. Football fans around the world expected the two to be taking each other on again in the World Cup final a few weeks later.

England had work to do to qualify yet though. Needing to win their final group match against Czechoslovakia to secure a place in the quarter final, England laboured to a 1-0 win courtesy of an Allan Clarke penalty, but with Brazil beating Romania to top the group they had to settle for second place. This matched them up with West Germany, who would be out for revenge having been beaten by England in the previous final.

England started strongly and were 2-0 up shortly after half time, but the Germans fought back to level the scores by full time, then went on to score a winner in extra time to end England's defence of their title. Brazil meanwhile beat Peru in their quarter final before seeing off Uruguay in the semi final, scoring seven goals in the process, to set up a final with Italy, where they kept up their free scoring attacking style to reclaim the title 4-1. As the first team to become World Champions three times they were allowed to keep the Jules Rimet trophy permanently.

The 1970 Brazil team is still considered by many to be the greatest ever to grace the World Cup stage, but their toughest match of the tournament was undoubtedly their encounter with England.

11th June 1978
Archie Gemmill scores stunner against Holland

Scotland qualified for the 1978 World Cup in Argentina in dramatic style, and went out almost as famously.

Scotland were in the same qualifying group as Wales, and faced the Welsh at Anfield with Wales needing a victory to qualify for their first major championship since 1958, with a win also enough to see the Scots through. The game turned on a refereeing decision though, with Wales defender David Jones adjudged to have handled the ball in the box despite replays clearing showing it was Scotland's Joe Jordan who punched the ball. Photographs taken just after the incident showed him kissing his fist, although he has always denied any wrongdoing. The penalty was awarded to Scotland however, and was promptly dispatched by Don Masson. Kenny Dalglish sealed the win late on as Wales desperately threw men forward, and Scotland were on their way to Argentina, with Wales left to rue one of the many near misses that haunted them for so long.

Hopes were high for a successful Scottish World Cup campaign under coach Ally MacLeod, who told supporters that his side would return with "at least a medal". Their official World Cup song, *Ally's Tartan Army*, recorded with comedian Andy Cameron claimed "We'll really shake them up, when we win the World Cup", and the Scottish public seemed to genuinely believe they were in with a chance of at least reaching the later stages as crowds flocked to the airport to wish their side well as they flew off to South America.

Scotland looked anything but a side likely to win the World Cup though as their first two group matches were both disastrous. Despite taking the lead against Peru courtesy of a Jordan goal they missed a penalty and slipped to a 3-1 defeat. Then, needing to beat lowly Iran to get their campaign back on track they could only manage a disappointing 1-1 draw, Scotland again failing to hold on to a 1-0 lead gifted to them by an own goal.

They were down, but not completely out, as a victory in their final match could still see them through. Unfortunately for them that match was against the Netherlands, one of the pre-tournament favourites and the runners up from the previous World Cup. Not only did Scotland need to beat them, they also had to win by three goals to go through.

It looked like an impossible task, and although Scotland started brightly, Bruce Rioch hitting the bar with a header and a Dalglish strike being disallowed for a foul inside the first fifteen minutes, it got even tougher when Stuart Kennedy was penalised for bringing down Johnny Rep whilst trying to win back the ball having been caught in possession. Rob Resenbrink converted the resulting penalty to put the Dutch 1-0 up. Scottish heads didn't go down though, and Dalglish put them back on level terms ten minutes later, thumping the ball home from a Jordan knock-down. Scotland still needed to find three more goals from somewhere though if they were going to cause an upset.

They were given hope right at the start of the second half, midfielder Archie Gemmill scoring from the spot after Graeme Sounness had been bundled over to put Scotland 2-1 ahead. Two more goals and they would be going through. With just over twenty minutes to go Gemmill picked the ball up on the right hand side, just outside the Dutch box after Dalglish had been dispossessed. He skipped inside the sliding challenge of Wim Jansen, changed direction and went outside Ruud Krol, and headed into the box. Jan Poortvliet hurled himself at him on the edge of the box but Gemmill slipped the ball past him. With only goalkeeper Jan Jongbloed to beat he waited for the keeper to commit himself, then calmly lifted the ball over him and into the net. It was a superb goal of solo skill, still considered to be one of the best ever scored in the World Cup finals.

With just one more goal required Scottish tails were up, and the Netherlands were under pressure. Like all great sides though, they were able to find a little bit extra when they needed it, and three minutes later Johnny Rep broke Scottish hearts with a screamer from thirty yards that gave Alan Rough in the Scotland goal no chance.

Neither side was able to find the net again, and the match finished 3-2 to Scotland, a famous World Cup victory but not quite enough to see them through to the second round. The Netherlands went all the way to the final, missing out 3-1 to the hosts Argentina in extra time to become runners up for the second World Cup in a row. It is Gemmill's goal that has gone down in Scottish folklore however, revered as one of their greatest moments and referenced regularly, for example in the film Trainspotting, when Ewan McGregor's character Renton declares "I haven't felt that good since Archie Gemmill scored against Holland in 1978."

11th June 1986
Gary Lineker's World Cup hat-trick

After crashing out of the 1982 World Cup despite not losing a match, England, now managed by Bobby Robson who had taken over two days after England had been knocked out, had failed to qualify for the 1984 European Championships. Robson had offered his resignation, but it wasn't accepted by the Football Association. It looked like they had been right to give him more time as his side qualified for the 1986 World Cup in Mexico unbeaten.

Their start to the tournament was far from impressive though, in stark contrast to the previous competition where they had opened the scoring in their opening match within thirty seconds. They lost their opener to Portugal, 1-0, to a Carlos Manuel goal fifteen minutes from time. With the pressure on in their second match, although they did secure a valuable point with a 0-0 draw against Morocco, the game was possibly even more disastrous than the first as within minutes they first lost captain Bryan Robson then vice-captain Ray Wilkins. Robson had fallen heavily challenging for the ball in the Moroccan penalty area shortly before half time, aggravating a shoulder injury and putting him out of the game and the tournament. Moments later a frustrated Wilkins threw the ball towards the referee, hitting him on the leg and picking up his second yellow card of the game. England would have to play the second half with ten men and without two of their key players. They managed to draw, but with just one point and no goals from their first two matches, only a win in their final group game against Poland would be enough to prevent them from flying home early.

With performances disappointing and Robson out and Wilkins banned, even the most optimistic of England supporters were expecting their side to be on their way home, but the team hadn't given up hope just yet, and they looked a different side against Poland, although acting captain Peter Shilton still had to make two sharp saves in the opening few minutes. It was England who took the lead though, with nine minutes on the clock. In a move that literally ran from one end of the pitch to the other, England won the ball on their own goal-line and Glenn Hoddle sent the ball up to Gary Lineker on the half way line. His header found Peter Beardsley infield, who played it back to Lineker in space on the left. He found Trevor Steven just outside the box, who held the ball up and rolled it into the path of the quickly arriving Gary Stevens, and his cross was turned in by Lineker sliding in on the edge of the six yard box. It had taken England more than three hours to score a goal, but what it goal it was.

Lineker, distinctive with his left arm in a lightweight plaster cast following a wrist injury suffered in a warm up match in Canada, had started his career at his hometown club, Leicester City, before being snapped up by Everton as a result of his goal-scoring exploits. He had broken into the England side in 1984 and had made his mark the following year with a hat-trick against Turkey in a World Cup qualifier, but hadn't scored for his country since and was perhaps lucky to have kept his place in the side. It was time for him to repay his manager's faith.

Having waited until their third match to score a goal it took just five more minutes for them to score their second. Again it was an end-to-end move, started by Terry Butcher, who played the ball out to Kenny Sansom at left back. His forward ball was cleverly helped on by Beardsley into the path of Steve Hodge, whose early curling cross was inch-perfect for Lineker to score his second from almost the exactly the same spot as his first. Suddenly the World Cup was looking much better for England, but Shilton still had to be on his guard to keep out a Wlodzimierz Smolarek free kick to maintain their two goal lead. At the other end Hodge put the ball into the net from an offside position, but England did make it 3-0 ten minutes before half time, Polish goalie Jozef Mlynarczyk failing to claim a corner and the ball falling perfectly for Lineker who took one touch before smashing the ball into the net to complete his hat-trick.

There were no further goals in the game but England had done enough, and the mood in the squad was transformed, as it was back home. Qualifying as runners-up to Morocco, who were the first African side to reach the second round, they faced Paraguay in the last sixteen. Lineker was in the goals again, scoring two as England recorded their second 3-0 win in a row, the other strike coming from Beardsley. That set them up for a quarter final against Argentina, a match now famous for two Diego Maradonna goals, the first scored using his hand which was later dubbed "the hand of God" and the second a sublime solo goal. England did battle back, Lineker scoring his sixth goal of the World Cup, but they failed to snatch an equaliser and were out 2-1.

Two more Maradonna goals against Belgium saw Argentina through to the final, where they beat West Germany 3-2, but with no further goals for Maradonna that left Lineker as the tournaments top scorer, earning him the Golden Boot.

With the English public feeling that their team had been cheated, Robson remained in charge of the side, but he again offered to resign after a disastrous European Championships in 1988 which saw England lose all three of their group matches. It was again rejected however, despite a media campaign for him to be sacked, and England turned their fortunes around again in 1990, reaching the

World Cup semi final before losing on penalties to West Germany. Lineker was again England's top scorer with four goals, and he went on to score a total of 48 goals for his country, putting him at the time second on the all time list, one goal behind Bobby Charlton. He retired from football in 1994 having scored 330 goals in his career and famously having never been shown a yellow or red card.

14th June 1970
England let West Germany off the hook

It was four years since the greatest moment in English footballing history, when England had beaten West Germany 4-2 in the World Cup final. With the scores level at 2-2 after normal time England had taken the lead courtesy of a controversial Geoff Hurst goal that may or may not have crossed the line. Now, in the quarter final of the 1970 World Cup, the Germans had a chance for revenge, but many in England believed their team was even better than it had been four years before.

England had come through their group despite losing 1-0 to Brazil in a classic, thanks to 1-0 victories of their own over Romania and Czechoslovakia with goals from Hurst and Allan Clarke. West Germany had topped their group with three wins out of three against Morocco, Bulgaria and Peru, scoring an impressive ten goals in the process. Seven of them had been scored by centre forward Gerd Muller, who had achieved the rare feat of scoring hat-tricks in successive matches.

England had lined up against Brazil with six World Cup winners in their side, but they were without goalkeeper Gordon Banks for the quarter final against West Germany, as he had been struck down with a stomach bug and was unable to play. This was a big blow, as Banks was on fine form and had made an incredible save against Brazil seven days earlier. In his place came Chelsea keeper Peter Bonetti. Winning one of only seven England caps it was a fantastic opportunity for the man who had been in the 1966 squad but hadn't made it into the side, but it turned out to be a match to forget.

England started brightly, and Bobby Charlton was soon testing German keeper Sepp Maier as he found the space on the edge of the box to send in one of his famous long range shots. They were ahead with just over half an hour played. Alan Mullery played a beautiful cross field ball into the path of Keith Newton on the right and his carefully timed through ball picked out Mullery, who had continued his run into the box. He got to the ball just before the desperate lunge of a defender to finish the move he started and make it 1-0. England continued to attack, and moments later Franny Lee was bundled over in the German box after a great run from midfield, but nothing was given, and the score remained 1-0 at half time.

It got even better for England just after half time though. With just four minutes of the second period played, Alan Ball played the ball up to Hurst, who held it up and waited for the run of Newton on the overlap. His first time cross picked out Martin Peters at the back post to side foot home for a 2-0 lead. It looked a long way back for the Germans in the searing Mexican heat, but twenty minutes later they pulled one back, Franz Beckenbauer finding half a yard of space around Mullery to shoot from just outside the box and his shot dipping under Bonetti.

England coach Alf Ramsey's response was a surprise one, taking off Charlton to save him for the semi final and replacing him with Colin Bell. Bell however almost made an immediate impact, with a shot saved sharply by Maier then a teasing cross headed inches wide by Hurst. With less than ten minutes to go Ramsey also took off goal scorer Peters for defender Norman Hunter. With time running out West Germany threw men forward, and Muller got the better of Newton only for Bonetti to make a fine save to deny him. The Germans kept the pressure on though, and Karl-Heinz Schnellinger tried a speculative ball back into the England penalty area to find the head of his captain Uwe Seeler. Seeler, with his back to goal, managed to head the ball behind him, over the head of Bonetti and into the goal. England had been just eight minutes from the semi final, but now they had to hang on. Beckenbauer shot just wide, and Hannes Lohr shot just over, but, just as it had in 1966, normal time ended 2-2 and the match went into extra time.

Hurst went close with a header from a Bell cross early in extra time, then Bonetti did well to tip over a Beckenbauer pile-driver before a Hurst strike was harshly disallowed for offside. It was still 2-2 after the first period of extra time, but three minutes into the second period Muller struck to put the Germans ahead for the first time. Dangerous substitute Jurgen Grabowski fired in a cross from the German right to the far post, and Lohr headed it back across goal, stranding Bonetti and setting up Muller to volley into the empty net. England battled to find an equaliser, and had another penalty shout turned down as Bell was brought down in the box. Maier pushed away long range efforts from Mullery and Lee, and that was enough to see the Germans through and the defending champions go out.

England's defeat was a blow to their supporters, and also, it seems, to Prime Minister Harold Wilson, whose Labour Party lost the General Election just four days after England were knocked out having held a comfortable lead in the polls at the start of the World Cup. Many have speculated since that the mood of despondency across the country may have contributed to his defeat.

The Germans again came from behind with a late goal to take eventual runners-up Italy to extra time in their semi final, but despite two more goals from Muller lost 4-3. Muller's ten goals earned him the Golden Boot as the tournaments top scorer, and he scored four more in the 1974 World Cup, helping his country win the title on home soil. His fourteen goals made him the all-time World Cup top scorer until Ronaldo overtook his tally in 2006.

England's World Cup fortunes meanwhile took a turn for the worse, as they failed to qualify for the 1974 and 1978 World Cups. The defeat to the Germans also started something of a curse. They went out at Germany's expense in the 1982 World Cup, lost to them on penalties in the semi-final in 1990, and were knocked out by Germany again in 2010. They fared just as badly in the European Championships, losing to them in the quarter final in 1972 and on penalties again in the 1996 semi final, before finally managing to beat them 1-0 in the group stages in 2000, the first time they had beaten them in a major tournament since 1966.

15th June 2008
Kevin Pietersen's switch hit

Having grown up in South Africa, Kevin Pietersen moved to England as a teenager in 2000 believing that his chances of playing cricket at the highest level were being hampered by the racial quota system that had been introduced as an attempt to address the Apartheid that had prevented black players from representing the country. He had risen through the county cricket ranks at Nottinghamshire and then Hampshire, making his One Day International debut for England in 2004. He scored England's quickest ever one day century against his native South Africa, off just 69 balls, and equalled Sir Viv Richards' record of reaching 1,000 one day runs in 21 innings.

His breakthrough into the Test side in 2005 coincided with England's reclamation of The Ashes for the first time in seventeen years, and he ended the series as the highest scorer. It wasn't all plain sailing though, as fallings-out and controversies began to hit the headlines almost as often as his performances with the bat. His creative, attacking style meant that he remained one of the most exciting players in world cricket though, and spectators made sure they were in their seats whenever he marched out to bat.

In the summer of 2008 New Zealand toured England. The hosts had already won the three match test series 2-0, with Pietersen contributing 115 in the third test. They followed that victory with a comfortable win in a one-off 20-20 match, before the two teams began a five match one-day series. In the opener at Durham's Riverside Ground, New Zealand captain Daniel Vettori won the toss and put England in to bat. England made a steady start, Ian Bell and Luke Wright putting on 49 for the first wicket in eleven overs. A buzz of anticipation went around the ground as Pietersen came in at number three, even though he had not scored a ODI century since the 2007 World Cup. Both he and Bell at the other end made slow progress at first though, and they had only advanced the score to 84 when Bell was run-out in the twentieth over. New Zealand were in a good position, and the balance tipped even more in their favour when Ravi Bopara was caught-and-bowled by Scott Styris a few overs later.

Captain Paul Collingwood was next in to bat. He was on a poor run of form, but on his home ground he was determined to post a decent score, and he dug in to make sure he wasn't out cheaply. At the halfway point England were 101 for 3, and in serious need of acceleration. The pair took 13 off the next over, and it looked like the start of the counter-attack, but the next eleven overs produced just two more boundaries, and with just thirteen overs left England were struggling on 167 for 3. Pietersen had had enough, and began to attack with a couple of boundaries. The best was yet to come though, as he hit a huge six off the next over as Styris came back into the attack. As the bowler approached the crease the right-handed Pietsersen switched to a left-handed stance and grip and blasted the ball over the deep cover boundary. It was a shot no-one had witnessed before. Reverse sweeps had been around for a while, with Pietersen himself famously playing one for six against Sri Lankan spinner Muttiah Muralitharan in a test match in 2006, but this was a genuine, premeditated, ambidextrous shot, and the crowd loved it.

Collingwood followed suit with a six of his own in the next over, as finally the runs started to come more easily for the home side. Pietersen went after Styris again in his next over, pulling off a second stunning switch hit for six, this time over long off.

Collingwood was almost caught off Vettori on the boundary in the forty-fourth over, but Michael Mason couldn't quite hold on and the ball went over the rope for six. Vettori had his revenge with the very next ball though, Collingwood playing on to his off stump for sixty four crucial runs off as many balls. Owais Shah came out to join Pietersen and was there to see his team-mate bring up his century with a pull to fine leg before chipping in with a four and a six of his own in successive balls. England plundered 62 runs off the last four overs, despite Shah falling for a quick-fire 49 off 25 balls, finishing on a highly creditable 307 for 5. They had scored 206 off the second 25 overs, and 109 in the last 10. Pietersen finished on 110 not out off 112 balls, with eight fours and three sixes, surprisingly his first one day century for England on home soil, but it was two of those sixes that were set to change the face of cricket forever.

It was a daunting target for the Black Caps, but with the powerful Brendan McCullum opening the batting they would always be in with a chance. Six boundaries from him in the first eight overs suggested that he could make it a contest, but when Stuart Broad dismissed him with his first ball for 36 it was the beginning of the end for the tourists. The runs dried up as they scored just six runs in the next five overs. The next boundary wasn't until the eighteenth over and the wickets started to fall steadily, with Collingwood wrapping up the tail to finish with figures of four for 15 to give England a commanding 114 run victory.

New Zealand recovered well from that defeat though, winning three of the remaining ODIs to win the series 3-1, but it was away from the pitch that the real debate started. The cricket world was split, with some celebrating Pietersen's skill and innovation but others claiming that the change of stance was unfair on the bowler, who would have set his field for a right-hander, only to find himself suddenly bowling to a left-hander. The MCC (Marylebone Cricket Club) decided that it would not make the shot illegal, but the matter didn't end there. As the shot slowly gained popularity the ICC (International Cricket Council) had to rule on its legitimacy, and it decided in 2012 that the shot was here to stay.

Pietersen continued to court controversy throughout the rest of his career. An unsuccessful stint as England captain ended in 2009, and disagreements with coaches, fellow players and the press were the down sides, but he also scored 23 test and nine ODI centuries, scoring more than 8,000 test runs. He was man of the tournament as England became World 20-20 champions, and was a member of four England Ashes winning sides, before turning his talents to 20-20 cricket with success in the Indian Premier League and Australian Big Bash.

18th June 1963
Henry Cooper floors Cassius Clay

In the summer of 1963 Cassius Clay, who later changed his name to Muhammad Ali when he converted to Islam, wasn't quite "the greatest" as he was later nicknamed. However, he was an Olympic gold medallist and, having turned professional a few months after winning his Olympic light heavyweight crown in 1960 had produced a record of eighteen wins from eighteen fights. He was being touted as a contender for Sonny Liston's World heavyweight title.

Henry Cooper was affectionately known in the UK as "Our 'Enery", and was one of the most popular British fighters of all time. He had British, European and Commonwealth titles to his name, with a record of twenty eight wins, eight defeats and one draw going into the fight in front of 35,000 fans at Wembley Stadium. Although there was no title at stake, the fight was still eagerly anticipated, in the UK and around the world.

Clay had not endeared himself to the British fans with some of his comments in the build up to the bout, describing their hero Cooper as "a bum" at one point, and declaring "It ain't no jive, Henry Cooper will go in five." At the weigh-in he had declared "You got a queen – you need a king. I am king!" and he drew boos from the crowd as he entered the ring sporting a crown and a gown with "The Greatest" emblazoned on the back. To the delight of the home crowd it was Cooper who had the best of the opening round, despite Clay, with a two stone advantage over his opponent, starting the fight as the clear favourite. Cooper went for him right from the start, unleashing a barrage of punches on the American and keeping him on the ropes for much of the round. At the bell Clay had a nosebleed and complained to the referee that Cooper had been roughing him up illegally.

Cooper tried to carry on in the second as he had left off in the first, but Clay was ready for him this time and was able to combat the onslaught and get some shots of his own in, managing to give Cooper a small cut under his right eye in the process. In the third Clay started to demonstrate the supreme movement around the ring that became a feature of so many of his fights throughout his career, forcing Cooper to pursue him and catching him with counter punches. Cooper suffered another cut, this time above his left eye. Clay started to drop his guard and goad Cooper into attacking him, seemingly in complete control of the contest.

Clay seemed to be biding his time in the fourth round, waiting until the fifth to make his prophecy of a fifth round stoppage come true. With seconds to go at the end of the round Cooper fought back though, landing his trademark "'Enery's 'ammer" left hook cleanly on Clay's jaw. Clay toppled backwards and down onto the ropes, fortunately for him catching his arms over bottom rope on his way down to save him from banging his head on the canvas. He was given a count of four before the bell went for the end of the round. It was the epitome of being saved by the bell, and led to one of the most talked about tales of boxing folklore.

As the crowd went wild, thinking that their man was on the verge of causing a massive upset, Clay's trainer, Angelo Dundee, helped his shaky fighter back to his corner, in contravention of the rules. He went on to break another rule, giving him smelling salts to try to clear his head. In addition he called the referee over to point out a small tear on Clay's right glove. Some have accused Dundee of deliberately causing the tear, but footage shows that there was a small split, although Dundee did allegedly admit later that he had made it worse. The story then developed after the fight that, with no spare pair of gloves at ringside a pair had to be fetched from the changing room, causing a delay of five minutes that gave Clay time to recover, but in fact the delay was only six seconds, albeit precious ones, and Clay was soon back in the ring for the fifth round.

And it was a different Clay who came out for the fifth, as he set about Cooper with a vicious series of blows that soon put paid to any hopes that Cooper and the British fans had of a shock. The cut above Cooper's eye took the brunt of the punishment, and soon started bleeding profusely, and the referee had no option but to stop the fight and declare Clay the winner, in the fifth round as he had predicted.

Cooper's moment had been fleeting, but his punch, and the subsequent myths and fables that grew from the fight lived on for much longer. Clay was much more gracious towards his opponent after the fight than he had been before it, telling reporters that Cooper's blow had been "felt by my ancestors in Africa". He admitted his respect for Cooper, and the two men considered each other friends in later life.

Clay went on to beat Liston to claim the world title in his next fight, a title that he would hold, lose and regain a number of times over the next seventeen years, including some of the most famous fights in history. He also fought Cooper again in 1966, at Arsenal's Highbury Stadium. With Ali, as he was now called, now world champion this was Cooper's one and only shot at a world title, but it wasn't to be. Cuts proved to be his undoing again and the fight was stopped midway through the sixth round with blood covering his face.

Despite never becoming world champion, Cooper remained hugely popular with the British public, and became the first person to win the BBC Sports Personality of the Year award twice. He was also knighted in 2000.

18th June 1995
Jonah Lomu destroys England

The 1995 World Cup, held in South Africa just four years after their rehabilitation into international sport following the end of Apartheid, is remembered for the hosts' emotional victory in the final, but the individual star of the tournament was undoubtedly an inexperienced young winger from New Zealand.

The All Blacks had won all of their group matches in impressive style, scoring five tries against Ireland and three against Wales before scoring a staggering 145 points against Japan, running in an incredible twenty one tries. Two of their tries against Ireland had been scored by Jonah Lomu, a twenty year old winger who was about to set the competition alight, combining speed with power to create a formidable presence. He had first been recognised as an exciting young talent with his performances at the 1994 Hong Kong Sevens, but with only two New Zealand caps before the tournament he only made the squad as a late replacement for the injured Eric Rush. He almost missed out due to fitness issues of his own, probably due to yet undiagnosed kidney condition, but managed to put these behind him in time for the tournament.

Five Nations champions England had also topped their group with three wins out of three, but far less convincingly, beating Argentina by six points and Italy by seven before a more comfortable 44-22 victory over Western Samoa. They had found some form however to see off Australia in a nail-biting quarter final, a forty five yard drop-goal by fly-half Rob Andrew winning the game 25-22 in extra time to gain revenge for their defeat at the hands of the Aussies in the 1991 final. New Zealand meanwhile were rampant again in their quarter final, scoring six tries as they beat Scotland 48-30 to set up a semi final encounter with England, Lomu crossing for his third try of the tournament in the process.

The two teams took to the field with all eyes on Lomu, and he was into the action straight away as outside half Andrew Mehrtens aimed his kick off towards his winger rather than, as more usual, his forwards, which England fumbled. Four minutes later New Zealand had taken the lead, a loose Graeme Bachop pass bouncing its way to Lomu who muscled his way past opposite number Tony Underwood and England captain Will Carling before famously flattening full back Mike Catt on his way to the try line. England were visibly rattled, and two minutes later things went from bad to worse, as a flowing All Black move starting with a break from Walter Little in his own twenty two put Josh Kronfeld over for their second try of the match. With six minutes played New Zealand were 12-0 ahead, and England already had a mountain to climb.

Desperate to put some points on the board England turned to the boot of the normally reliable Rob Andrew, but his two penalty attempts both went wide to add further misery to England's day. In contrast, Mehrtens was successful with a long range penalty and even All Black number eight forward Zinzan Brooke joined in the fun, putting the ball between the posts for an unexpected drop goal.

Lomu soon crossed for his second try of the match, a clean break through the heart of the England midfield, and New Zealand were amazingly 25-0 up after as many minutes. Andrew was finally successful with a penalty before the break, but it did nothing to hide the fact that it was a deeply miserable half for England and they were heading out of the tournament.

The onslaught continued at the start of the second half, Lomu completing a hat-trick after Little had raced on to a Mehrtens chip, feeding Kronfield who passed to the winger with Carling powerless to stop him. Bachop was the next to score, completing the move he had started on the half way line after Jeff Wilson and Glen Osbourne had combined to put him clear, but with the score 35-3 and the match already won the New Zealanders then took their foot off the gas and England seized their chance to make the score a little more respectable. Carling and Rory Underwood both scored tries, the first of them a little lucky as Underwood's foot was clearly in touch, before Lomu became the first man to score four tries in a match against England since 1969, handing off Tony Underwood and sidestepping Catt on his way to the line. England kept trying though, and were rewarded with two more consolation tries, again courtesy of Carling and Rory Underwood. Despite outscoring the All Blacks 26-20 in the second half though, the devastating first half display had blown England away and they were grateful for the final whistle, well beaten 45-29.

New Zealand went on to lose in extra time to hosts South Africa in the final, not helped by a dose of food poisoning shortly before the match, whilst England lost 19-9 to France in the third/fourth play-off. Lomu scored eight more tries in the 1999 World Cup to add to his tally of seven in 1995 to claim the record for the most World Cup tries scored. He continued playing for the All Blacks until 2002, winning sixty three caps and scoring thirty seven tries, but his kidney problems continued to dog his career and brought it to a premature end. He received a kidney transplant in 2011, but his body rejected the organ and he sadly died in 2015, a few weeks after watching the All Blacks win the World Cup for the third time, at the age of forty.

18th June 2000
Tiger Woods wins the US Open by 15 shots

By the age of twenty four Tiger Woods was already a global superstar. With two Majors and fifteen PGA Tour wins under his belt at the start of the year, he was also earning millions of dollars from some of the biggest contracts seen in the world of golf, and was also being touted as someone who could seriously challenge Jack Nicklaus' record of eighteen Majors.

His first opportunity of the year to increase his Major tally came at the US Open at Pebble Beach, an event being played under the shadow of the tragic death of the previous year's winner Payne Stewart, who had died in a plane crash four months after his victory. Players with an early start time were definitely the lucky ones on the first morning, with fog making playing conditions difficult later in the day. Woods was one of those players who was out early, and he made the most of his chance, birdying the eighteenth despite having found a bunker to shoot a six under par sixty-five to claim the first round lead, one shot clear of Spain's Miguel Angel Jimenez.

The start of the second round was delayed as many of the players still needed to finish their first rounds, as the fog had forced an early end to the first day, and the weather was still making things difficult on the second morning. Only Woods seemed unaffected, making full use of his distance off the tee to pull clear of the field. On the par five sixth he fired in a sublime approach shot, over the cliffs and the trees to within fifteen feet of the flag. He followed his birdie there with another on the seventh, and was putting daylight between himself and the rest of the field. The real daylight was running out though after the delayed start to the round, and Woods just had time to add another birdie to his round on the twelfth with a stunning thirty foot putt before play ended for the day.

He returned the next morning to finish his second round, dropping a shot to reach the midway point eight under par, a commanding six shots ahead of Jimenez and Denmark's Thomas Bjorn. Fewer players made the cut than usual, due to the fact that the leader was so far ahead of the rest – with players having to be in the top sixty or within ten shots of the leader.

Not even Tiger could shoot below par in the third round, with strong winds making it very tough for everyone. At no time was this more apparent than when the runaway leader triple bogeyed the third after finding a bunker in front of the green, giving his rivals a glimmer of hope, but he managed to made up the deficit over the course of his round, finishing in par for the day with a seventy one, remaining eight under for the tournament. Jimenez had shot a five over par seventy six to slip back to three over, and Bjorn had fallen back even further. Round of the day was by South African Ernie Els, whose three under put him into second place, ten shots behind Woods.

Tiger's lead going into the final round was the biggest in US Open history, but he wasn't in the mood to just play it safe to coast to the title. He did par all of the outbound nine holes, but birdied the tenth, twelfth, thirteenth and fourteenth to get to twelve under, crushing any faint hopes any of his fellow competitors might have had that he would suffer some sort of collapse. Pars at the remaining four holes meant that he finished four under for the round, twelve under for the tournament, a stunning fifteen shots clear of Els and Jimenez in second, an even bigger margin than his twelve shot Masters victory in 1997. It was the biggest winning margin in a Major ever, and he was the only man who finished the week below par. His total of 272 shots equalled the lowest ever US Open score, and it was also the first ever US Open score in double-figures below par. He was only the fifth player to have led the competition from start to finish, and he had played the first twenty two and the last twenty six holes without a bogey, and despite the terrible playing conditions he made just six bogeys in total over his four rounds.

He soon followed his third Major with a fourth, winning The Open at St Andrews by three shots. The US PGA title followed later that year after he beat his compatriot Bob May in a play-off, and when he was victorious in the Masters the following spring he became only the fifth player in history to win all four Majors, and the first player since Bobby Jones in 1930 to hold all four at the same time (although the four tournaments considered to be Majors was different in Jones' day).

When he won the US Open for the third time in 2008 it was his fourteenth Major title, and, still only thirty-two, he looked to have Nicklaus' record of eighteen in his sights. His life was to take an unexpected turn however, as stories about his personal life broke and he started hitting the headlines for all the wrong reasons. He split from his wife, and as more and more stories of his infidelity became known many of his sponsors cancelled their agreements with him. His form suffered, and he took a break from golf to try to get his life back on track. When he tried to rebuild his career he started to suffer a series of injuries, and a number of comebacks failed to see him compete at the highest level. His tally remains fourteen for now, but few people would put it beyond him to add to it at some point.

21st June 1970
Brazil win the World Cup with "perfect goal"

After Brazil had edged out defending champions England 1-0 in a group stage encounter, many people believed that the two would meet again in the 1970 World Cup final two weeks later, but it was Italy and not England who faced Brazil at the Azteca Stadium in front of 107,000 fans.

England had followed Brazil into the quarter final as runners up in their group, but had been undone in extra time by West Germany despite having led 2-0 with little more than twenty minutes to go. Brazil had beaten Peru 4-2 in their quarter final, continuing their free-flowing attacking football and adding to the eight goals they had scored in the group stages. They went on to score three more in their semi final against Uruguay, whilst West Germany lost to Italy in a thriller in the other semi. Italy had taken an early lead through Roberto Boninsegna, with the Germans only equalising in injury time through Karl-Heinz Schnellinger. Eventual Golden Boot winner Gerd Mulller gave West Germany the lead four minutes into extra time, only for Tarcisio Burgnich to level four minutes later. Luigi Riva put the Azzurri back in front just before the break, but West Germany refused to give up and Muller scored again to make it 3-3 with ten minutes to go. A minute later Gianni Rivera scored a fourth for Italy, and that proved to be the decisive strike to see the Italians through to their third World Cup final.

It didn't take Brazil long to take the lead in the final. With eighteen minutes on the clock Tostau took a throw in on the left hand side. He threw it to Rivelino, who hooked the ball into the box where Pele rose high above the Italian defence to power a downward header into the bottom corner of the net. Not only did it put Brazil 1-0 up, it was also Brazil's one hundredth World Cup goal, and Pele's third World Cup final goal having scored two in their victory in 1958.

They held onto their lead for twenty minutes, until a mix up in defence gifted Italy an equaliser. Playing the ball amongst themselves in their own half, Piazza played a pass across to Clodoaldo. With the ball slightly behind him he tried to flick it behind his back with his heel, but he was dispossessed by Boninsegna, who got to the resulting loose ball ahead of the despairing lunge of Brito and goalie Felix to score into the empty net.

Brazil were determined to regain their advantage after half time, and they came close firstly when Jairzinho fed Carlos Alberto on the overlap on the right and his teasing cross just evaded Pele, then when Rivelino's powerful strike following a

Gerson free kick crashed onto the crossbar. With twenty one minutes of the second half gone they did retake the lead though. Jairzinho ran at the Italian defence before laying the ball off for Gerson, and his powerful left-footed strike across goal beat Enrico Albertosi in the Italian goal to make it 2-1. Five minutes later the result was all but decided as Brazil made it three against an Italy side clearly suffering from their exertions in the semi final. Gerson was involved again, playing a long ball forward into the Italian box that picked out Pele in space. He showed great vision to find Jairzinho with a downward header and the winger took one touch to control the ball before getting the faintest of touches as he struggled to keep his balance that was just enough to edge the ball past Albertosi for a 3-1 lead. His strike also meant that he became the first man ever to score in every round.

Brazilian confidence was sky high as the clock ticked down, and they began to enjoy themselves and entertain the crowd with their skills. With four minutes of normal time to go they started a move that would result in what is considered by many to be the greatest World Cup goal ever scored. Tostao won the ball as Italy tried in vain to get back into the game. He played a simple ball to Brito on the edge of the Brazilian box, who in turn passed it to Clodoaldo just in front of him. He played a short ball to Pele, who found Gerson, then it was back to Clodoaldo. Not put off by his error in the first half that had led to Italy's goal he dribbled around four Italians, producing a huge roar from the crowd. He fed Rivelino on the left touchline, just on halfway, who played it up the wing to Jairzinho. He cut inside Italian captain Giacinto Facchetti before feeding it to Pele in the centre just outside the D, who took his time and rolled it into the path of Carlos Alberto arriving into the penalty area at speed, and his first time strike rifled into the net to make it four. It was a goal of true class and beauty, involving eight Brazilian players, and a lesson for everyone in football around the world as to how the game could be played.

With the crowd still celebrating the wondrous goal the final whistle sounded and Brazil had become the first country ever to win the World Cup three times. They were allowed to keep the Jules Rimet trophy to commemorate their achievement. Amazingly it would be another twenty four years before they won it for a fourth time, in the USA in 1994, when they again beat Italy in the final, this time on penalties however after a far less memorable final that had finished goalless. Carlos Alberto died of a heart attack at the age of 72 in 2016.

22nd June 1986
The "Hand of God" and the "Goal of the Century"

England were to face Argentina in the quarter final of the 1986 World Cup in Mexico. Not only was this a match up between two former champions, it was also a match steeped in sporting and political rivalry. England had beaten Argentina on their way to winning the 1966 World Cup in a bad-tempered match that saw Argentine captain Antonio Rattin sent off and the England manager call the Argentines "animals", and the bad feeling from that game had still not gone away. More significant however was the fact that the two nations had been at war just four years earlier, in a dispute over the ownership of the Falkland Islands.

The two teams had made it through the group stages in very different manners. Argentina had been relatively untroubled, topping their group with wins against South Korea and Bulgaria, plus a draw with Italy. England fans however had been made to sweat, with their side having to beat Poland to progress in their final group match having lost to Portugal and drawn with Morocco. A hat-trick from Gary Lineker saw them through however, and they kept that momentum going with a comfortable 3-0 win over Paraguay in the round of 16. Argentina beat Uruguay in their first knock-out match 1-0, setting up their quarter final clash.

In front of 114,000 in Mexico City's huge Azteca stadium, the first half was relatively uneventful. Peter Beardsley had a good chance for England after quarter of an hour but Argentina dominated possession and territory without seriously threatening the England goal.

It was the second half that would live in memory of football fans around the world however. Just minutes after the restart, an attempted pass by Argentina's talisman Diego Maradona was cut out by England midfielder Steve Hodge, but his attempted clearance was sliced up into the air and towards the England penalty area. England goalie Peter Shilton came out to punch the ball clear, and Maradona ran forward to challenge him. Had he used his head, Maradona would have had no chance, but he put up his arm and punched the ball before Shilton could get to it. The ball flew forward and into the England goal. As he ran off to celebrate with his bemused team-mates the England players surrounded Tunisian referee Ali Bin Nasser, but he had not seen the handball and the goal stood.

England were furious and rattled, and just four minutes later things got even worse for them, again at the hands of Maradona. The diminutive playmaker took possession in the Argentine half, turned away from challenges from Beardsley and

Peter Reid and set off towards the England goal with the ball glued to his feet. He swerved around Terry Butcher and Terry Fenwick, pursued in vain by Reid. As Shilton came out to challenge him he calmly ghosted around him and stroked the ball into the open net. It was a breathtaking piece of skill that was voted the Goal of the Century in a FIFA poll in 2002, and prompted BBC commentator Barry Davies to declare "You have to say that was magnificent. There is no debate about that goal. That was just pure football genius."

Now 2-0 down and facing World Cup exit, England boss Bobby Robson made a double substitution, bringing on John Barnes and Chris Waddle to boost England's attacking threat, and the change worked as England suddenly began to look dangerous. They had to wait until the 81st minute for the breakthrough though, as Barnes beat two defenders and his cross was headed home by Lineker to pull one back. Argentina almost restored their two goal advantage straight away but were denied by the post, and it was too little too late for England and the game finished 2-1 to Argentina.

All the attention in the press conference afterwards was understandably on Maradona. When asked about his first goal he agreed that it as "a little with the head of Maradona and a little with the hand of God", and his goal immediately became known as the "hand of God goal". His comments angered English fans even more, and the rivalry between the teams continued with a vengeance at the 1998 World Cup Finals, when David Beckham was sent off before Argentina won on penalties, and 2002 when Beckham gained personal revenge as his penalty on the stroke of half time gave England a 1-0 win. Many Argentines however saw the 1986 incident and result as revenge for the 1966 match and the Falklands War.

With England on the plane home, Argentina went on to beat Belgium in the semi-final and West Germany in the final to claim their second World Cup, making English fans feel even more cheated out of their chance of glory. Lineker's goal had been his sixth of the tournament, winning him the Golden Boot as the competition's top scorer, but yet again, England were left wondering about what might have been.

24th June 1995
Nelson Mandela's Springboks win Rugby World Cup

Rarely, if ever, has a sporting event had such a social and political significance as the final of the 1995 Rugby Union World Cup.

Significant in itself, the tournament was held in South Africa, who had only just been rehabilitated into world sport after six years of a boycott imposed for its racially segregating apartheid policies. Following the release of Nelson Mandela and the fall of apartheid however, South Africa had been welcomed back into the fold, and recently elected President Mandela had urged the whole country to support the Springboks, with the slogan "one team, one country" being coined.

Symbolic in rugby's role in healing some of the nation's wounds was the presence in the side of Chester Williams, only the third non-white ever to play for the Springboks. His image was widely used to show how the country was moving on, although he later stated that he was far from comfortable being used in this way, and that racism wasn't completely banished from the dressing room in 1995.

South Africa made a dream start on their World Cup debut, beating reigning champions Australia 27-18 in Cape Town, the Wallabies' first defeat in over a year. Comfortable but not completely convincing wins over Romania and Canada saw them top their group and took them through to a quarter final against Western Samoa. Here they turned in a more promising performance, scoring six tries to beat the Pacific Islanders 42-14, with four of their tries scored by Williams.

In the semi final they faced France. Thunder storms had saturated the Durban pitch, and the match was in jeopardy. If it couldn't be played France would advance to the final due to their better disciplinary record. Not surprisingly, every effort was made to get the pitch playable, and the nation heaved a sigh of relief as game kicked off, an hour late. With the players slipping and sliding, the Springboks pushed Ruben Kruger over for a first half try and the lead. Joel Stransky for South Africa and Thierry Lacroix for France exchanged penalties as the match progressed, and the Springboks led 19-15 with four minutes remaining. Full back Andre Joubert dropped a high ball though, and French forward Abdel Benazzi gathered the ball and surged to the try line. The ball seemed to be on the line, but the referee disagreed, and the try that would have won the match was disallowed. Seconds later he blew for full time. It looked as though South Africa might be destined for World Cup glory.

One man who stood in their way though was six foot six, nineteen stone Jonah Lomu, New Zealand's talismanic young winger who had set the competition alight with his seven tries, including four in a performance that had blown England away in the other semi final. Despite his size and power he could also run 100 metres in 10.3 seconds, and alongside world class team-mates such as Ian Jones, Sean Fitzpatrick and Zinzan Brooke the All Blacks were formidable opposition and the favourites for the title.

South Africa were only too aware of the threat that Lomu presented, and they hunted in packs to bring the big man down the second he was given the ball. It was a defensive strategy, but it seemed to be working. In attack as well the Springboks were giving nothing away, keeping it tight with their fearsome forwards rather than risking their backs, but it almost paid dividends when they drove Kruger over the line, but the All Blacks held him up to prevent the try. All of the first half points came from the boot, with Stransky and opposite number Andrew Mehrtens both successful twice to make the score 6-6. Then, with eight minutes to go before half time, Stransky dropped a goal to give the hosts a precious 9-6 advantage at the break.

It took the All Blacks quarter of an hour of the second half to get back on level terms, Mehrtens sending over a drop goal of his own after a missed long range penalty attempt and another unsuccessful drop goal effort. Joubert also missed with a drop kick from inside his own half, and remarkably Mehrten's effort was the only score of the second half. He had almost won it late on with another drop goal attempt from a perfect position, but the ball flew wide and the World Cup would be settled in extra time for the first time in its history.

In extra time Mehrtens put New Zealand ahead with his third penalty of the match, but Stransky soon replied to level at 12-12, and it stayed that way, with the tension building by the minute, until there were just seven minutes left to go. The ball came back to Stransky from a scrum. He quickly set himself, and struck a drop goal from thirty metres out, which split the posts and gave the Springboks a precious 15-12 lead.

Moments later Stransky had a chance to give his side some breathing space, but he pushed his penalty wide. It didn't matter though, the All Blacks were unable to respond, and the final whistle blew to seal an emotional victory. Mandela, sporting the green and gold Springboks jersey and cap, couldn't hide his delight as he presented the Webb Ellis trophy to captain Francois Pienaar, reportedly with the words "Thank you for what you have done for our country." Pienaar replied "No, Mr President, thank you for what you have done."

Things did sour slightly afterwards, as the All Blacks were angered by a post-match speech by the president of South African rugby, Louis Luyt , which claimed that South Africa were the first real world champions as they had not competed in the first two competitions. There were also allegations that the All Blacks, many whose players had been struck down by food poisoning two days before the final, had been deliberately poisoned to damage their chances. The South Africans cared little however, as the new Rainbow Nation celebrated their triumph.

24th June 2010
John Isner defeats Nicolas Mahut at Wimbledon... after three days

When American John Isner and Frenchman Nicolas Mahut stepped out onto Wimbledon Court 18 for their first round match, just after 6pm on day two of The Championships, nobody could have imagined that the two would still be battling it out two days later, but it was the start of a truly epic match that smashed numerous records and saw both men go down in Wimbledon history.

The match started ordinarily enough, with Isner taking advantage of two double faults from Mahut to break and take the first set 6-4. Mahut hit back in the second, breaking Isner to love early in the set and holding his own serve to take it 6-3. That was to be the last break of serve for a very long time, as both the third and fourth sets went to tie-breaks, Mahut taking the third set tie-break 9-7 and Isner the fourth 7-3. With the clock ticking past 9 o'clock and darkness starting to set in play was suspended for the day, the players at that point having been playing for 2 hours 54 minutes.

Just after 2 o'clock the next day the players resumed their contest, and they continued where they had left off, with service win after service win. The score had progressed to 10-9 to Isner when he had the first sniff of a break, but Mahut saved the first of a number of match points. When the score reached 32-32 in the fifth set the match officially became the longest of all time. The pressure was immediately on the Frenchman again though as he served 32-33 down, when he was forced the save two more match points. At 47-47 the scoreboard couldn't cope any longer, and the score froze at that score for a while.

Mahut had no match points of his own as he was serving second and hadn't managed a break, but he did push Isner to break points with the score at 50-50, before going on to save a fourth match point himself at 58-59. The light had faded again though, and with the score level at 59-59, to the disappointment of the crowd that had packed the outside court, play was suspended and the match unbelievably would have to run to a third day.

All eyes were on the heroic pair as they locked horns for the third day in a row at 3.40pm on 24th June. The players had been on court for nine hours and fifty eight minutes by that point, and fatigue was becoming a major issue for them both, but they both continued to hold serve. Isner looked to be in trouble at 68-68 when he went 30-love down, but hit his way out of trouble to go 69-68 up.

On the opening point of Mahut's next service game Isner narrowly missed a chance to pass down the line to give the Frenchman a 15-0 lead, but Mahut overhit a forehand on the next point for 15-15. Mahut then put an attempted drop-shot into the net to go 15-30 down. A solid serve and volley made it 30-30, but the next point saw Isner pass Mahut, despite Mahut's approach shot having landed right on the bascline, to bring him his first match point of the day, his fifth in all. Mahut served to Isner's backhand, and the American returned it double-handed. Mahut's forehand volley landed mid-court, and a backhand down the line finally brought Isner the first break since the second set two days earlier, and a final score of 6-4, 3-6, 6-7, 7-6, 70-68. He tumbled onto his back as if he had just won the title, before giving his gallant opponent a hug at the net.

The match had lasted for an astonishing eleven hours and five minutes, and had broken a whole range of records as well as being the longest ever, such as most aces by a player in a match (Isner – 112), most aces in total in a match (215), most consecutive service holds (168), most games in a set (138), longest set (8 hours 11 minutes) and most points won in a match (Mahut – 502). The All England Club honoured the men's achievements, and that of the umpire Mohamed Lahyani, by awarding them with a crystal bowl and champagne flutes, presented by former British players Tim Henman and Anne Haydon-Jones. They later also erected a plaque commemorating the match on Court 18.

Though through to the second round, the encounter had taken too much out of Isner, and he was swept aside by Thiemo de Bakker the next day 6-0, 6-3, 6-3 in less than an hour and a quarter, without serving a single ace.

Unbelievably the pair, who after their efforts became close friends, were drawn against each other again in the first round the following year, but that match, to the relief of the organisers, was a much more straightforward affair, with Isner winning again, 7-6, 6-2, 7-6 in just over two hours. The 34 games played by the two men that day was just half the number won by Mahut in the final set of their match the year before.

24th June 2014
Luis Suarez banned for biting

To say that Uruguayan footballer Luis Suarez had had a chequered career would be a huge understatement.

His first big controversy came in the quarter final of the 2010 World Cup in South Africa. With Uruguay drawing 1-1 with Ghana and extra time running out, Suarez stopped a header from Dominic Adiyiah on the goal-line with his hand. It would have surely been the winning goal, sending Ghana through to become the first ever African World Cup semi finalists, and Suarez was sent off for his offence, but when Asamoah Gyan missed the resulting penalty many thought he had and Uruguay had got away with their foul play. Public opinion wasn't helped by the sight of Suarez celebrating the miss. His side went on to win the penalty shoot-out 4-2 and knock Ghana out, and Suarez showed no regret in interviews, claiming that he had made the best save of the tournament and that "the Hand of God now belongs to me", referencing Diego Maradonna's infamous handball against England in Mexico '86.

Uruguay went on to lose to The Netherlands in the semi final, but Suarez's reputation was well on the way to being made, and later that year he was in the news for the wrong reasons again. Playing for his club Ajax he was involved in a melee following the sending off of PSV Eindhoven's Rasmus Lindgren, in which he bit PSV striker Otman Bakkal. Although the incident wasn't spotted by the referee it was clear to see on TV replays, and Ajax had no choice but to ban the man dubbed "The Cannibal of Ajax" by the shocked Dutch press for two games. The Dutch League went further and banned him for seven matches.

Ajax sold him to Liverpool early in 2011 for a club record £22.8 million, but the change of scenery that he was reportedly seeking failed to keep him out of the headlines for long. After playing for his new club against their arch rivals Manchester United, United's French international Patrice Evra claimed that Suarez had racially abused him. The Football Association investigated, and later found him guilty of using racially insulting language. He received another ban, this time for eight matches, plus a £40,000 fine. Liverpool continued to support him, and some players and former players, notably fellow Uruguayan Gus Poyet, claimed that his actions had just been down to cultural differences, but the ban stood, and others welcomed the firm stance the FA had taken on racism. Again Suarez refused to apologise, and when the two sides next met, having served his ban, he snubbed Evra's attempt to shake his hand before the match.

Then, in April 2013, he bit an opponent again, this time Chelsea's Branislav Ivanovic. Again it was missed at the time, but this time he did apologise, although it didn't prevent the FA giving him a ten match ban. The ban meant he missed the start of the 2014-15 season, but when he did return he finally started to make the headlines for the right reasons, scoring 31 goals to help Liverpool finish second in the Premier League and winning a number of Player of the Year awards. It was good preparation for the 2014 World Cup in Brazil, although a knee injury and surgery in May meant that he was a doubt for the competition starting in June.

He made a speedy recovery though, and was an unused substitute for Uruguay's 3-1 defeat to Costa Rica in their opening match. He started their next match against England, scoring both of their goals in a 2-1 victory. His side went into their final group game needing to beat Italy to progress. With ten minutes to go Uruguay won a corner. When the ball was played into the box Suarez was seen to tangle with Italian defender Giorgio Chiellini, and the two players fell to the ground, with Suarez holding his face as if he had been struck. It was only afterwards that Chiellini was seen to be clutching his shoulder, and he approached the referee to show him the bite marks that Suarez had left. Once more the ref had seen nothing though, and no action was taken. Minutes later Diego Godin scored, sending Uruguay through and Italy out.

Social media went crazy, and the world's press demanded action. The Uruguayan camp claimed it was part of a witch-hunt against Suarez, and that Chiellini had somehow made the marks look worse than they were. Suarez himself claimed to have just bumped into the Italian, but FIFA disagreed and came down hard on him for his third biting offence, giving him a global ban from all football related activities for four months, plus a ban from nine international matches and a £66,000 fine. He was therefore out of the World Cup, and Uruguay complained bitterly, their captain angering many by describing his punishment as a "breach of human rights". Suarez said that he "deeply regretted" his actions and promised never to bite an opponent again.

The reaction to the incident in England meant it would have been difficult for him to return to Liverpool, and he was sold to Barcelona that summer for £75 million, reportedly with a "no biting" clause in his contract. Despite not being able to play until October, his first season in Spain was a success, and he ended the season with twenty five goals, including one in the Champions League final, and he finished the season with La Liga, Copa del Rey and Champions League winners medals.

To date Suarez has missed a total of forty five matches due to his various bans, but none of his misdemeanours have made such a global impact as his bite of Chiellini's shoulder.

25th June 1988
Van Basten volley wins European Championships

If ever the phrase "always the bridesmaid, never the bride" applied to a national football team it would have to be the Netherlands. Twice they had lost in World Cup finals, in 1974 to West Germany despite having taken the lead in the second minute, and four years later to Argentina after extra time in a controversial match where the Dutch felt their opponents had used underhand tactics to try to unsettle them.

Despite their double failure at the final hurdle, the 1970s was a golden era for Dutch football, with superstars such as Johan Cruyff and Johan Neeskens producing a new style of play dubbed "total football". The '80s had not been so successful for them though, and an early exit from the 1980 European Championships was followed by failure to qualify for three major tournaments in a row. By 1988 there was new hope however. New stars had emerged such as Ruud Gullit, Frank Rijkaard and Ronald Koeman, and under returning coach Rinus Michels, who had led them to the 1974 World Cup final, they had qualified for the tournament in Germany in style, undefeated as they topped their group.

Spearheading their attack was Milan centre forward Marco van Basten. He had been prolific at Ajax, where he had scored 128 goals in 133 appearances, and had signed for the Italian giants in 1987, along with Gullitt and Rijkaard. He had also broken into the Netherlands side, netting six goals for them before the tournament, but an ankle injury had meant that he was a doubt for inclusion in the squad right up to the last minute.

Although they were fancied to do well the Dutch got off to a poor start, losing their opening group game to the Soviet Union 1-0. They soon put that disappointment behind them though, bouncing back with a 3-1 victory over England thanks to a van Basten hat-trick. Needing to beat the Republic of Ireland in their final game to leapfrog their opponents, who had beaten England and drawn with the Soviet Union, it looked as though they were going to be frustrated and suffer an early exit, until Wim Kieft scored a late winner in the 82nd minute to break Irish hearts but keep Dutch hopes alive.

They faced their old nemesis West Germany in the semi final, the team that had denied them World Cup glory in 1974. The Germans had been hosts that day as well, but the Dutch were determined not to let them repeat the result. A highly dubious Lothar Matthaus penalty ten minutes into the second half put West

Germany in front and suggested that it might be the same outcome, but the Dutch were awarded an debatable penalty of their own twenty minutes later and Ronald Koeman made no mistake to level the scores. With just two minutes of normal time remaining, van Basten slid in to guide a Jan Wouters through ball past the despairing dive of Eike Immel to give his side some revenge for their 1974 defeat, and their first victory over the Germans since 1956.

In the final they would again face the Soviet Union, the side they had lost their opening group game to, who had beaten Italy 2-0 in their semi final, and it was the Soviets who looked like repeating the result in the opening twenty minutes as they made the more confident start. They were unable to take advantage of their domination though, Hans van Breukelen making two crucial saves to keep the score 0-0. The Dutch slowly played their way back into the match, and Gullit forced Rinat Dasayev to save well, pushing his well hit free kick over the bar.

With just over half an hour gone Dasayev was unable to deny Gullit however. Erwin Koeman sent in a deep cross after the Soviets had failed to properly clear a corner. The Soviet defence tried to play the offside trap, but Van Basten had stayed onside and headed the ball back across goal, where Gullit leapt high to power a header into the Soviet goal.

Ihor Belanov had a chance to equalise almost immediately, the ball falling conveniently to him deep inside the Dutch box, but his shot flew harmlessly over the bar with only Van Breukelen to beat, and the half ended with the Netherlands 1-0 up.

The Soviets pushed forward in the second half, searching for an equaliser, but failed to cause Van Breukelen too much trouble. Instead it was the Netherlands who found the back of the net, and in fine style. Adri van Tiggelen won the ball for the Dutch and brought it forward before feeding Arnold Muhren on the left wing. His first time cross looped towards the back post, where Van Basten was waiting. It looked like an impossible angle, but he hit a dipping volley over Dasayev and under the crossbar for one of the most spectacular strikes ever seen in a major final.

With a 2-0 lead all they had to do was hold on for half an hour, but with their track record in finals they could take nothing for granted. Belanov had another chance with twenty minutes to go, but his shot in a crowded penalty area hit the post. With time running out the Soviets were given a golden opportunity to set up a nerve jangling finish, when Van Breukelen raced out of his goal and brought down Serguei Gotsmanov to concede a penalty. However, the goalie redeemed himself by saving Belanov's spot kick low to his right. That was the Soviet's last chance, and the Dutch were soon celebrating as the final whistle confirmed that they had finally won a major trophy.

Following their European success, many thought that the Dutch could go one step further than their predecessors to win the 1990 World Cup in Italy, but it was not to be. Infighting dogged the squad's preparations, and they disappointed as they scraped through their group only to be beaten, once again, in the second round by eventual champions West Germany in a match remembered more for the spitting incident between Rijkaard and Germany's Rudi Voller than the football itself. The defence of their European Championship title two years later made it as far as the semi finals, but van Basten, in stark contrast to the elation of his winning goal against the Soviet Union, suffered the heartache of missing his penalty kick in the shoot-out against eventual winners Denmark. Further underachievement followed, including a period during which van Basten was the side's coach, with fallings-out and infighting a regular occurrence, until they reached their third World Cup final in 2010. Unfortunately for them they lost yet again, 1-0 to Spain after extra time.

26th June 1996
England lose on penalties to Germany, again

"It's coming home… football's coming home" sang the Lightning Seeds and Baddiel and Skinner, and that's exactly how it felt to England fans as England hosted its first major football tournament since 1966. Hopes were high that home advantage could again help the hosts, but, as the song also pointed out, England had come nowhere near winning anything since then, and they had failed to qualify at all for the last major competition, the 1994 World Cup in the USA.

There had been controversy in the build up to the competition, when members of the England squad were photographed drinking in a Hong Kong nightclub whilst on tour shortly before the competition started. The press had a field day with the story, criticising the players for their lack of professionalism and commitment. Particular attention was given to troubled footballing genius Paul Gascoigne, whose image having alcohol poured into his mouth whilst sitting in a dentist chair featured in all the papers.

The media was also far from impressed by England's start to the tournament, as they struggled to an unconvincing 1-1 draw with Switzerland, managed by future England boss Roy Hodgson, in their opening match. Alan Shearer had opened the scoring, but a Kubilay Turkyilmaz penalty seven minutes from time had denied them the win. There was a huge potential banana-skin facing them next as well, with old rivals Scotland looking to dent the host's chances, but it was England who came out on top, kick-starting their campaign with a 2-0 victory featuring a fantastic solo goal from Gazza, which he celebrated by re-enacting the dentist chair incident. Shearer had got the other goal, his second of the tournament, and the result might have been tighter had Scotland's Gary McAllister not missed a penalty.

The result of the next match was even better, with an impressive England taking apart a fancied Netherlands side 4-1 to top the group. The goals dried up in the quarter final against Spain though, with normal time and extra time finishing goalless and England having to face their first penalty shoot-out since their ill-fated encounter with West Germany in the World Cup semi-final six years before. For once though, England had the better of the shoot-out, even Stuart Pearce exorcising the demons of his miss against Germany to thump the ball home and punch the air in triumph, and they were through to another semi against the Germans.

England got off to a dream start when Alan Shearer found space in the box to head in a Tony Adams flick-on to give them the lead in just the third minute. The advantage was short-lived though, with Stefan Kuntz equalising on sixteen minutes, sliding in to guide the ball home from a Thomas Helmer cross. The rest of normal time passed without too much incident, despite both teams playing some good football.

It was extra time that gave the game perhaps its most memorable image. Both sides had tried to win the match without the need for penalties, and the golden goal rule being used that year would have meant that a single goal would have won a place in the final, making every attack a nail-biting affair for the huge Wembley crowd. Shearer shot just over, and Teddy Sheringham saw his shot blocked, but it was Germany who thought they'd won it, only to see Stefan Kuntz's effort ruled out for a shove in the build-up. Then came the moment that would haunt England fans for years to come. Minutes from the end England broke, and Shearer played a tantalising ball into the six-yard box. With the German defenders out of position Gascoigne hurled himself at the ball feet first, only needing the slightest of touches to guide the ball into the net, but his studs fell agonisingly short and the ball rolled harmlessly across goal. It was to be the last chance of the match, and, once again, an England Germany semi-final would be decided by penalties.

Shearer took the responsibility of going first, and duly drove the ball into the net. Thomas Hassler replied for Germany. David Platt also scored, only to be matched by Thomas Strunz. Pearce was successful again, as was Stefan Reuter, despite David Seaman getting his hands to the ball. Then Gascoigne, Ziege, Sheringham and Kuntz all beat the keeper. With both sides having scored five out of five penalties it went to sudden-death. Up stepped Gareth Southgate for England, but his penalty was weak and along the ground, allowing Andreas Kopke to make the save and leaving Andy Moller the chance to win it for the Germans. He duly dispatched his shot past David Seaman, leaving England and their fans in despair again.

Germany went on to beat the Czech Republic 2-1 in the final with a golden goal. There was some small consolation for England coming in the form of Alan Shearer finishing as the top scorer with 5 goals, but if Gazza had been two inches closer to the German goal at the end of extra time, things might have ended very differently.

Southgate became England manager himself in 2016.

28th June 1997

Mike Tyson bites Evander Holyfield's ear off

It was an eagerly awaited rematch that made the headlines for an entirely unexpected reason.

In November 1996 Evander Holyfield had shocked the world of boxing by taking the heavyweight world title from "Iron" Mike Tyson. Going into that fight Tyson had had a record of 45 wins and 1 defeat, that loss coming against James "Buster" Douglas in another surprise result in 1990. He had reclaimed his title against Frank Bruno in early 1996, defending it once before losing it again to Holyfield. Holyfield's record was 32 wins and 3 defeats, and he had last held the world title in 1994 when he had been defeated by Michael Moorer.

The two had been due to fight back in 1991, but a rib injury to Tyson followed by three years in prison had stopped it from happening then. Tyson, the overwhelming favourite, came out all guns blazing in the opening round, catching Holyfield early on with a heavy blow, but Holyfield defended well from then on and regularly caught Tyson with counter attacks. As the fight progressed Holyfield showed that he was outthinking his opponent, keeping Tyson's attacks largely at bay other than in the fifth round when a combination of punches from Iron Mike did hit their mark. In the following round an accidental head butt by Holyfield caused a cut above Tyson's left eye, then Holyfield caught him with a left hook that knocked him to the canvas. Holyfield stayed on the front foot in the seventh, until another accidental clash of heads hurt Tyson. Tyson became slowly more frantic, allowing Holyfield to pick him off with more and more telling blows, and in the eleventh round the referee had seen enough and stopped the fight with Holyfield raining down blows on Tyson on the ropes.

Seven months later they faced each other again, this time with Holyfield the champion and with a total purse of $65 million. The referee from the first fight, Mitch Halpern, had been due to officiate the rematch too, but stepped down at the last minute, citing the amount of attention that he was attracting following Tyson's camp's attempt to have him removed, probably because of their belief that he had failed to take action over the head butts in the first fight.

Holyfield had the better of the early stages, rocking Tyson in the opening round with a heavy uppercut to the head. Tyson did get some body blows in towards the end of the round, but Holyfield had done enough to win the round.

Early in round two there was a clash of heads, just as there had been twice in their first fight. Tyson was left with a gash above his right eye and looked to the referee to do something about it. Replacement referee Mills Lane noted that it was a head butt, but took no further action, angering Tyson and his corner who were hoping for a stronger response this time from the replacement ref. Holyfield continued to edge the fight and ended the round the stronger of the two.

Tyson came out for the start of the third round without his gumshield, and was ordered to replace it by the referee after Holyfield pointed it out. He was clearly angered by what he perceived to be a deliberate head butt that Holyfield had been allowed to get away with, and began the round with obvious intent, laying into his opponent in a frenzied attack. Holyfield weathered the storm though, and fought back with some hits of his own.

With forty seconds to go before the bell the pair were in a clinch following an exchange, with Holyfield's head against Tyson's. Suddenly, Holyfield pulled away and he jumped in the air clutching the side of his head. Lane called time out, and as Holyfield walked away Tyson came up behind him and shoved him in the back, with Lane having to prevent Holyfield from retaliating. With blood flowing from Holyfield's right ear, Tyson prowled around the other side of the ring, his enraged eyes following his opponent. Replays showed that Tyson had spat out his gumshield, moved his head around and taken a bite out of Holyfield's ear, then spat the piece of ear out onto the canvas.

As Lane consulted with the judges, Holyfield's ear was examined by a doctor, as the disbelieving fans made their opinions clear. Lane called Tyson to him to give him a stern talking to and to give him a two point deduction before allowing the fight to restart. Holyfield got a good punch in on Tyson before they got into another clinch. Incredibly, Tyson bit Holyfield's ear for a second time. This time Holyfield fought on until the end of the round, when the ring quickly filled with officials and representatives of both fighters. Just as the board was being paraded for the start of the fourth round Lane, having seen the further damage to Holyfield's ear, decided that Tyson would be disqualified, and it was bedlam. Tyson flew into a rage and tried to get across the crowded ring to Holyfield, taking a swing at a policeman in the process. Security guards surrounded the Holyfield corner as others led Tyson back to his corner as chaos spread from the ring into the stands, before Holyfield left the ring.

Tyson left the ring shortly afterwards, accompanied by jeers and boos from the disgruntled crowd. Some of the rowdier fans were being led away from the stands but empty and half-empty drinks cups were still being aimed in Tyson's direction. When a bottle of water was hurled at him he started to climb into the stands to confront the thrower before he was held back. Holyfield meanwhile was on his way to hospital for emergency plastic surgery on his ear, the detached part having been recovered by an official.

Tyson later claimed that his actions in the "Bite Fight" as it had now become known had been a reaction to Holyfield's continued head butting, but it didn't stop his purse being withheld. He was also fined $3 million and had his boxing licence removed, although it was restored a year later. He returned to the ring in 1999 but lost his only other world title fight, against Lennox Lewis in 2002. Holyfield defended his belt three more times before losing it to Lewis in 1999.

30th June 1998
Beckham sent off as England lose to Argentina

It's hard to believe when you consider the esteem that David Beckham is now held in around the world, but for a couple of years after the 1998 World Cup he was public enemy number one in England.

In their previous World Cup appearance they had made it to the semi final, narrowly losing out to Germany on penalties in 1990, but a dismal qualifying campaign had seen them fail to qualify in 1994. Another semi final appearance in Euro 96, although ending again in a penalty defeat to Germany, meant that hopes were high for another good run this time round in France.

England had got off to a solid start to their campaign, beating Tunisia thanks to goals from Alan Shearer and Paul Scholes. It was down to earth with a bump in their second game though, as they lost to Romania despite Michael Owen's goal having equalised with nine minutes to go, English based Dan Petrescu scoring a ninetieth minute winner for the Romanians. Needing to beat Colombia to guarantee progression, England came good with a comfortable 2-0 victory, Darren Anderton opening the scoring before Beckham scored his first ever England goal, a rocket of a free kick into the top corner from twenty five yards.

In the round of sixteen England faced their old rivals Argentina, who had won their group with three wins. It was the fourth time the sides had met at a World Cup finals, with England having won the first two encounters, in 1962 and then more famously in 1966 on route to winning the tournament, when Argentina had their captain Antonio Rattin sent off and felt they had been robbed by harsh refereeing decisions. That match had been dubbed "el robo del siglo", the robbery of the century, in Argentina, and it had provided the inspiration for Argentina's defeat of England in their next competitive match, in Mexico '86, the infamous "hand of God" encounter.

This was the first time the two sides had faced each other competitively since, and it looked as though another Argentina victory was on the cards when Gabriel Batistuta scored from the spot after just six minutes. Goalkeeper David Seaman came to gather a through ball, didn't quite make it and was adjudged to have brought down Diego Simeone although replays showed that had been little if any contact. He almost made amends by getting his hands to the penalty, but he could only parry it into the side of the net.

Four minutes later England were level though, also scoring courtesy of a debateable penalty. Paul Scholes headed on to Owen, who sprinted into the box, then went down under the challenge of Roberto Ayala. Referee Kim Morton Nielsen pointed to the spot for the second time in ten minutes of play, despite Argentine protests that there was again little contact. Carlos Roa guessed correctly but couldn't keep out Shearer's penalty, and the score was 1-1.

With sixteen minutes on the clock England scored again. Beckham showed great vision to find Owen just inside the Argentine half, Owen took the ball on the outside of his foot, then used his speed and strength to hold off Jose Chamot and Ayala before lifting the ball over the advancing Roa for a stunning strike that announced him on the international scene. Scholes had a chance to make it 3-1 soon after that, but shot just wide with just the goalie to beat, and he was soon made to rue his miss when Javier Zanetti turned sharply and shot to find the net following a well-worked Juan Veron free kick, meaning that the first half was to end all square.

It had been an encouraging first half for England, but their hopes took a hit right at the start of the second half. Simeone brought down Beckham with a challenge from behind, and in frustration, as he lay prone on the pitch, he lashed out at the Argentine, aiming a kick at Simeone's legs. Simeone went down as if he had been shot. Unfortunately Neilsen was right on the spot, and he reached into his pocket to show Beckham the red card. England would have to battle for a place in the quarter final for forty-three minutes with ten men.

And battle they did, as for the rest of the second half and for extra time they put their bodies on the line for their country. Argentina struggled to make their extra man count, and it was England who thought they had won it near the end of normal time. Sol Campbell found space to power a header into the Argentine goal, only to have his celebrations caught short as he realised that Shearer had been harshly penalised for impeding Roa.

With neither team able to find a third goal it was time for the dreaded penalties yet again. Sergio Berti and Shearer both made no mistake with their penalties, before Seaman dived to his left to save Hernan Crespo's effort. England had the early advantage, but it didn't last long, as Roa saved from Ince in a carbon copy of Seaman's save. Veron and Paul Merson both found the net, and Seaman got a hand to Marcelo Gallardo's strike but couldn't keep it out. Owen scored his penalty, making it 3-3 with one more penalty to go each. Ayala kept his cool to put Argentina, meaning that England's final penalty taker had to score to keep them in it. With regular penalty taker Beckham off the pitch, the duty fell to combative midfielder David Batty, but his shot was far too straight, and although Roa was going to his right he was able to beat the ball gleefully away.

The distraught England players had lost on penalties in a major tournament for the third time in eight years, but it was Beckham who was blamed for the defeat. The papers laid the blame firmly at his door, and some fans burned effigies of him in the streets. However, he concentrated on doing his best for club and country, and the following season helped Manchester United to a famous treble. He was superb in a crucial qualifying victory against Greece in 2001, and gained revenge against Argentina in the 2002 World Cup, scoring the winning penalty. He's now viewed as one of the greats of the English game, as well as being a global ambassador and one of the biggest personal sporting brands the world has ever seen, a far cry from his public image back in 1998.

July

1st July 1977
Virginia Wade wins Wimbledon in Jubilee year

In 1977 Queen Elizabeth II was celebrating her Silver Jubilee. It was also the Wimbledon Championships' centenary year, and a wave of patriotism and national pride swept the country. The Queen was set to watch the Wimbledon final, her first visit to the All England Club since becoming Queen. Everyone was hoping that she would be presenting the famous Venus Rosewater Dish to a British champion.

Despite having had no men's finalist at Wimbledon or any of the other three Grand Slams since Fred Perry in 1936, Great Britain had enjoyed success in women's singles. Angela Mortimer had won three titles in the 1950s and '60s, and Shirley Brasher and Christine Truman had both won the French Open. Ann Haydon-Jones had won two French Opens and Wimbledon in the '60s, and Sue Barker had won the French Open in 1976. Barker was seeded four for Wimbledon, one behind compatriot Virginia Wade, who herself had won the US Open in 1968 and the Australian Open in 1972. That gave the British public good reason to be optimistic of seeing a British winner of Wimbledon in Jubilee year.

Wade opened her campaign against young fellow Brit Jo Durie, coming through in straight sets, as she did in the next three rounds. Barker meanwhile had a bye in the first round, then followed Wade's lead in winning her next three matches without dropping a set.

In the quarter finals Wade beat American Rosie Casals 7-5 6-2, and Barker joined her in the semi final with a 6-3 6-4 victory over Australia's Kerry Melville. With two British players in the semi final it was looking good for a Brit making the final, and an all British final was also a possibility. Wade would have to beat top seed Chris Evert to reach the final, a daunting task against the world number one and defending champion. Wade made a fine start to the match, winning the opening set 6-2, but the American fought back to take the second 6-4. Evert wasn't able to keep the momentum going though, and Wade controlled the decider, taking it 6-1 to claim her place in the final.

Attempting to join her, Barker faced Betty Stove of the Netherlands, who had knocked out second seed Martina Navratilova in the quarter final. Stove took the first set by a single break, 6-4, but Barker levelled at one set all by winning the second set 6-2. A tight third set went the way of Stove though, 6-4, to deny the British public an all British final by the tightest of margins.

On paper Wade was the favourite, ranked higher than Stove and with Grand Slam singles titles already under her belt, although Stove had won Grand Slam doubles titles. Wade was however sometimes prone to nerves, and with the weight of public expectation weighing down on her, and the Queen in attendance, the hard hitting but sometimes unpredictable Stove was more than capable of causing an upset as she had in the previous two rounds. It looked like that might be exactly what would happen too as Stove claimed the first set by a single break, 6-4, despite a thrilling twelve shot rally at set point as Wade struggled to get her game going.

The crowd was delighted though as Wade came storming back in the second set, breaking Stove in the second game and holding her own serve twice to take a 3-0 lead. She had a point for a second break in Stove's next service game and a 4-0 lead, but the Dutchwoman saved it with some excellent serve-volleying and held to get her first game of the set on the board. On the opening point of the next game Wade thought she had gone 15-0 up when a Stove lob was called out, but the umpire overruled and called for the point to be replayed, much to Wade's annoyance. Stove won the point second time round for 0-15, and the incident seemed to affect Wade's concentration as although she had a point to make the score 4-1 she lost her serve as Stove broke back. Wade was still complaining to the umpire at the changeover, before Stove held again to level at 3-3.

Just as it looked like the momentum was back with Stove, Wade regained her composure to hold to love and move back ahead 4-3, and from there she never looked back. Some fine returns and attacking play saw her break Stove for a 5-3 lead, and she moved into a 40-15 lead as she served for the set, giving her two set points. Stove saved the first, but her lob wasn't good enough in the next point and Wade hit an unreturnable smash to bring Centre Court to its feet as she levelled at one set all.

Her confidence growing all the time, Wade continued in the third set where she left off in the second, and had soon built a 4-0 lead, a run of seven games in a row. Unlike in the previous set however there was no way back from Stove, and although the Dutchwoman did win a game to make it 4-1 Wade was in no mood to let her lead slip, and she soon had two championship points. Stove saved the first with some brave volleying as Wade slipped, but Wade's return on the second was too good, and the fairytale had come true. She had become Wimbledon champion at the sixteenth attempt, a few days shy of her 32nd birthday. The crowd sang "for she's a jolly good fellow" as the Queen presented her with the trophy, and the nation celebrated having a Wimbledon champion in Jubilee year.

It was a disappointing end to a fine couple of weeks for Stove though, as she lost not only in the final of the singles but also in the ladies and mixed doubles finals, the first player ever to lose three finals in the same Grand Slam. 1977 was almost made even more memorable for British tennis, as John Lloyd became the first British man to reach a Grand Slam final since Fred Perry, making it to the final of the Australian Open final in December, only to lose out in five sets to American Vitas Gerulaitus.

No British woman has made a Grand Slam final since Virginia Wade that year, although Britain finally had more success in the men's competitions, with Andy Murray winning the US Open in 2012 and Wimbledon in 2013 and 2016.

4th July 1990
Gazza in tears as England lose in World Cup semi final

It had taken England 24 years to reach the World Cup semi final again since their previous, and only other, appearance in one. Time and again since 1966, when England had gone on to win the World Cup, the side had faltered in major championships and failed to progress to the later stages. They had failed to qualify at all for two World Cups and three European Championships. Now though, in Italy, they had made it to the last four, but, almost inevitably, they facing the side they had beaten in the final in 1966 – West Germany.

It had been anything but an easy route to the semi final. A tight group stage saw England, seeded sixth for the tournament, draw their opening game with the Republic Ireland 1-1, Kevin Sheedy's goal cancelling out Gary Lineker's opener. It was goalless in their second against the Netherlands, and with the other two games in the group also ending in draws it took a goal from defender Mark Wright to see off Egypt 1-0 and see England top the group.

In the second round England faced Belgium, who had finished third four years earlier. Normal time ended goalless, and the game looked to be heading for penalties when, with just a minute to go, David Platt hooked in Paul Gascoigne's free kick to produce a wonder goal that put England through in dramatic style.

In the quarter final they faced the challenge of tournament sensations Cameroon, who had stunned defending champions Argentina in their opening game, then had beaten Colombia in the second round to become the first African team to reach the World Cup quarter final. Platt had found the net again to give England a first half lead, but two goals in four second half minutes, from Emmanuel Kunde and Eugene Ekeke had turned the game on its head, and England were on the verge of going out before Lineker stepped up to convert a late penalty to make it 2-2. The Golden Boot winner from the previous World Cup scored from the spot again in extra time and Bobby Robson's men were through to face the Germans for a place in the final.

England made a great start to the game, on a sticky night in Turin, forcing a save from German keeper Bodo Illgner in the first minute. They continued to create openings, but it was West Germany who finished the half stronger and England were grateful for the half-time whistle as the first period ended goalless.

The West Germans started the second half as they finished the first though, and laid siege to the English goal, but they were fortunate to go ahead just before the hour mark, with Andreas Brehme's shot following a free-kick deflecting off Paul Parker, over Peter Shilton and looping agonisingly into the open goal. English heads didn't go down though, and they almost made an instant response, Stuart Pearce's back-header sliding inches wide. When they were denied a penalty minutes later it looked as though their luck might have run out, but with just nine minutes of normal time remaining, Lineker latched onto a Parker cross and rifled the ball home to make it 1-1 and force extra time.

Germany had the better of the chances as extra time began, forcing a fine save out of Shilton, then, five minutes before the break, Paul Gascoigne lost possession and lunged at Thomas Berthold to try to win it back. He brought the German down, and received his second yellow card of the competition. If England made the final, Gazza would be suspended. Tears started to flow as he realised his World Cup final dream was over, and Lineker warned the England bench to keep an eye on him, but he and England played on, and they almost took the lead when Chris Waddle hit the post. In the second period hearts were in mouths all around the ground, as first Platt had a goal ruled out for offside, then Germany hit the post, but there were no more goals, and the game went to penalties.

England went first, and top scorer Lineker found the net, only to be matched by the night's other scorer Brehme. Next was Peter Beardsley, who also scored, as did German captain Lothar Matthias. Platt scored his spot kick despite Illgner getting his fingertips to it, and Karl-Heinz Riedler did too to make it 3-3. Stuart Pearce went next for England, but his shot was too close to Illgner and was saved. Olaf Thon kept his cool to beat Shilton to put West Germany 4-3 ahead, which left Waddle the unenviable task of having to score to keep England in it and make the Germans take their last penalty. Waddle, the nerves etched on his face, placed the ball on the spot and stepped back, but as he approached the ball he never looked confident and his strike flew high and wide. Distraught, Waddle fell to his knees before being helped up by the gallant Matthaus. England fans at home and abroad were left in tears, but proud of their team's performance.

Whilst West Germany went on to beat Argentina in a terrible final, England lost 2-1 to Italy in a lack-lustre third/fourth playoff, but it was their best showing in a World Cup since their famous victory at Wembley, and the players received a hero's welcome and an open-top bus parade when they arrived home, testament to the way their progress had gripped the nation that summer. Unfortunately they weren't able to maintain their form, and they crashed out of the 1992 European Championships without winning a match before failing to qualify for the next tournament in 1994. They did recover for the 1996 Euros, which they hosted, only to lose for a second time in the semi final to Germany on penalties.

5th July 1980
Borg beats McEnroe in Wimbledon final classic

By 1980, Bjorn Borg was the undisputed king of Wimbledon. He had not lost a match there since 1975, winning twenty eight matches in a row and claiming four men's singles titles in the process. Despite being famous for his ice-man demeanour, his great success and polite manner had made him a favourite with the Wimbledon crowds, most of whom expected him to pick up a fifth title that year.

The main contender for his crown couldn't have been more different. Second seed John McEnroe was left handed to Borg's right, had a shock of frizzy dark hair compared with Borg's long blonde hair, and was a serve-volleyer rather than a baseliner. The biggest difference though was in his temperament. The twenty-one year old American already had a terrible reputation for losing his temper on court. He had shot to fame by reaching the semi final at Wimbledon in 1977 and went two steps further at the US Open two years later to claim his first Grand Slam. The pair were scheduled to meet in an eagerly anticipated final.

Borg had reached the final without much fuss, dropping just two sets along the way, but McEnroe had had a bit of a scare in the second round, needing five sets to progress. He was then embroiled in a bad tempered semi final with fellow American and 1974 champion Jimmy Connors. McEnroe won 6-3, 3-6, 6-3, 6-4, but the match was marred by a number of heated exchanges with the officials that earned him an official warning and added to his reputation as "Superbrat".

As a result of McEnroe's outbursts Centre Court witnessed the unique spectacle of one of the finalists being roundly booed as the players walked out for the final. He didn't let it affect him though, as a blistering start to the match saw him take the first set 6-1, the Swede almost helpless against McEnroe's swinging left-handed serve. The second set was a much tighter affair, with Borg using all of his experience to conjure a break of serve with some well-placed passing shots to take it 7-5.

Borg edged ahead for the first time in the match as he took the third set 6-3. It was the fourth set that was to ensure that the match would be remembered forever though. With the set going with serve Borg managed to break McEnroe late in the set and served for the championship at 5-4. It looked like there was no way back for the American now, and Borg moved effortlessly to 40-15 to bring up two match points. McEnroe wasn't ready to concede defeat through, and passed Borg as he approached net to save the first. Then at 40-30 he cut off a Borg volley with both men attacking the net to save the second. A low sliced approach forced an error from Borg at deuce for a break back point, and backhand return winner secured the break. McEnroe was right back in the match with a great cry of "come on!"

The set moved into a tie-break that was to become possibly the most famous of all time. McEnroe held serve at 5-6 to save another match point, but at 6-6 a blistering Borg winner gave the Swede a fourth. McEnroe fired a backhand down the line, and although Borg hurled himself at it he couldn't get it back and the score was level once more. McEnroe had a set point at 8-7, but it was Borg's turn to find a return which left his opponent on the grass. A solid serve and volley from McEnroe put him back in from 9-8, but set point number two was on Borg's serve, and a serve volley of his own made it 9-9. Borg's heavy serve was too good for McEnroe, but McEnroe followed suit to save a fifth match point. Heavy hitting brought up a sixth match point for Borg, but McEnroe's luck was in, the ball hitting the net cord to leave Borg stranded. Borg didn't let it upset him through, manoeuvring McEnroe around the court and forcing an error to give himself a seventh match point, but a superbly controlled backhand volley saved McEnroe again. McEnroe slipped as he hit a volley at 12-12, but still put the ball back behind Borg to lead 13-12. Borg hit his volley on the next point right onto the baseline, which was good enough to save another set point.

At 13-13 Borg netted a volley to give McEnroe his fourth set point. His serve pushed Borg wide but he just missed his volley with the open court beckoning. A fine serve and a perfect stop volley to bring up McEnroe's fifth set point at 15-14. A good serve by Borg though made it 15-15. Borg served out wide, but McEnroe found a great return down the line, forcing him to improvise, but he sent McEnroe cross-court, only for the American to pass Borg down the line at full stretch. Borg saved a sixth set point when McEnroe couldn't control a heavy return though. The Swede just missed the side line with his return with McEnroe beaten, gifting him a seventh set point. Borg put a volley into the net and McEnroe had finally won the tie-break, 18-16, and levelled the score at two sets all.

Many expected the momentum to be with McEnroe in the final set, and Borg dropped the first two points on his opening service game, but after that he didn't lose another point on serve until the tenth game, a run of nineteen consecutive points. McEnroe was holding on to his serve as well though, but, serving second, found himself serving to stay in the match at 4-5 and 5-6, and again at 6-7. At 15-30 McEnroe's serve pushed Borg wide on his backhand, but a strong double-handed return had McEnroe picking the ball off his toes again. He could only pop the ball up, and Borg hammered another backhand at him which he couldn't deal with, giving the champion two more match points. McEnroe again approached after his serve, but his volley wasn't deep enough and Borg passed him cross-court to finally end their titanic battle. Borg sank to his knees in triumph and relief, whilst McEnroe retreated to his seat and held head in hands, contemplating just how close he had come to wresting the Wimbledon title from the hands of the great champion.

The Centre Court crowd's boos turned into cheers as McEnroe received his runners up prize, testament to his bravery and skill that day. He managed to get the better of Borg later that year in the US Open final, and gained his revenge in the Wimbledon final the following year. Borg played little in 1982 and announced his retirement from the game in 1983 at the age of just twenty six. McEnroe went on to win Wimbledon a further twice more and ended his career with seven Grand Slam titles.

5th July 1982
Keegan misses header and England crash out of World Cup

Kevin Keegan was one the best strikers in world football in the 1970s and '80s. Part of the Liverpool side that had dominated throughout the '70s his goals had helped them to three League titles, an FA Cup, the European Cup and the UEFA Cup twice. In 1977 he had then moved to German side Hamburg, adding a Bundesliga title to his collection and being named European Footballer of the Year twice.

For all his domestic honours however he had never graced football's biggest stage – the World Cup. He made his international debut in 1972 under World Cup winning manager Sir Alf Ramsey, but England had failed to qualify for the 1974 finals, famously being thwarted by Polish goalkeeper Jan Tomascewski in the group decider, or the 1978 tournament. With Keegan now in his thirties the 1982 World Cup in Spain was realistically his last chance to make it, but England were again teetering on the edge of failure to qualify. A defeat and a draw in their two games against Romania had set them back, and an unthinkable 2-1 defeat against lowly ranked Norway in a match made famous by commentator Bjorge Lillelien's "Your boys took one hell of a beating" speech left them needing other results to go their way to stand any chance of getting through. For once luck was on their side though, and Romania's failure to win any of their final three matches meant that England needed a point from their last match at home against Hungary. This time there were no slip-ups and they won the match 1-0 thanks to an early Paul Mariner goal to qualify as runners-up to Hungary, one point ahead of Romania.

Although England had qualified, there was still a chance that Keegan, now England captain, would miss out however, as he aggravated a back injury in training shortly before their first game and was ruled out for a couple of weeks. Despite Keegan's injury, hopes were high that the mix of youth and experience in Ron Greenwood's side could recapture the glories of the 1966 team, and they made a dream start to their campaign, Bryan Robson scoring after only twenty-seven seconds in their opener against France. They went on to win that match 3-1, with another goal from Robson and one from Mariner. A Trevor Francis strike and an own goal gave them a 2-0 victory against Czechoslovakia, then Francis scored again to see off Kuwait to make it three wins out of three. England were through to the second round, and, even without Keegan, were looking like genuine contenders.

They were drawn with West Germany and the hosts Spain in the second round group, and opened with a 0-0 draw against the side they had beaten to win the Cup in 1966 but who had knocked them out in 1970. With West Germany beating Spain 2-1 in their second match, England were left needing to beat Spain by two goals in order to progress. Keegan was still not fully back to match fitness, but was able to take a place on the bench.

England were given an early scare when Miguel Alonso battled his way into the penalty area only to blaze his shot over the bar, but after that it was they who created the better chances. Tony Woodcock played a neat one-two with Graham Rix but his shot was wide, then Kenny Sansom saw his effort fly just wide having received the ball from a free kick. Later in the half Sansom was again involved, heading the ball on to Bryan Robson in the Spanish penalty area, but he headed the ball past the post. Woodcock then had another shot on goal, this time drawing a good save from Luis Arconada after intricate build-up play around the box. It wasn't all one way traffic however, and the best chance of the half fell to Spain's Jesus Satrustegui when the ball broke for him midway into the England half. He ran on and pushed the ball past England goalie Peter Shilton, only to see the ball drifting wide of the goal. Santillana almost got to it to turn it into the open goal but couldn't quite direct the ball goalwards, allowing England supporters to breathe a sigh of relief, and the half ended 0-0.

Even though they couldn't qualify, Spain wanted to give their home support something to cheer about, and they almost broke the deadlock at the start of the second half, a superb run by Sastrustegui leading to a chance for Alonso, but he shot wide when it would have been easier to score. England responded, and Greenwood sent on Keegan and Trevor Brooking, who like Keegan has been out with injury. Brooking almost made an instant impact, forcing Arconada into a good save.

With twenty minutes to go and time running out for England, Keegan was given a golden opportunity to score. Mariner's clever reverse pass found Robson on the left hand side of the Spanish box. Robson looked up, saw Keegan in space and played an inch-perfect chip to him on the edge of the six yard area. This could have been Keegan's moment, having waited so long for his World Cup chance. With Arconada out of position Keegan just needed to head the ball straight to give England a priceless lead, but he tried to direct it away from the keeper and ended up glancing it wide of the goal. Perhaps he was still rusty having not played for weeks, but he knew it was a chance he should have taken, and he fell to his knees and slapped his thighs in frustration.

It proved to be the last serious chance of the game, and with the final score 0-0 England were out, even though they hadn't lost a single game. West Germany went through at their expense, beating France on penalties in the semi final in a match famous for German goalkeeper Harald Schumacher's challenge on Patrick Battiston that left him in hospital, before losing in the final to Italy.

Greenwood resigned after the World Cup, and new England manager Bobby Robson left Keegan out of his first squad. Keegan was unhappy that he had learned the news via the press rather than being told by Robson, and he never played for England again. He did however become England manager himself in 1999. His side qualified for the European Championships in 2000, where they blew a 2-0 lead against Portugal to lose 3-2, then beat Germany 1-0 before losing 3-2 to Romania, again after being in front. Later that year Keegan resigned after England lost their first qualifier for the 2002 World Cup, 1-0 against Germany, in the final game played at the old Wembley Stadium.

5th July 1987
Pat Cash climbs into the crowd

There have been many memorable Wimbledon men's singles finals over the years, but none have featured as memorable a celebration as when Pat Cash beat Ivan Lendl for the title in the 1987 Championships.

Australian Cash was no stranger to the All England Club, having won the junior singles title there in 1982. He also won the 1982 US Open junior title, and was ranked junior number one in the world before turning professional later that year. It wasn't long before he was making his mark on the senior tour, winning tournaments and fans with his classical serve-volley play and distinctive headband. The following year he helped his country beat Sweden to win the Davis Cup, before reaching the semi finals at Wimbledon and the US Open in 1984, losing in the latter to Lendl in a fifth set tie-break. He continued his progress and reached his first Grand Slam final in January 1987, losing in the Australian Open final to Stefan Edberg in five sets.

Despite his performances he was still only seeded eleven at Wimbledon later that year. That didn't stop him cruising through the first week however, as the draw opened up with top seed and defending champion Boris Becker suffering a shock defeat in the second round. Cash dropped just one set on route to the quarter finals, where he faced, on paper, a tougher challenge against number three seed and four-time Grand Slam champion Mats Wilander. However, Cash's grass-court game was too good for the clay-court favouring Swede, and the Aussie won again in straight sets. In the semi final his opponent had eight Grand Slams under his belt, including two at Wimbledon, but Jimmy Connors was also no match for the on form Cash, and he made it comfortably through to his first Wimbledon final 6-4 6-4 6-1.

In the other half of the draw number two seed Ivan Lendl had found things tougher. He had been taken to four sets in the first round, five in the second and four again in the third before more straightforward three sets wins in the fourth round and quarter final. In his semi final he dropped the opening set to Edberg 6-3 but came back to win the next three 6-4 7-6 6-4 to reach his second successive Wimbledon final.

Lendl had won the French and US Opens twice, and had reached the Australian Open final, but had always been thwarted on the grass courts of SW19, although he had reached the semi finals in '83 and '84 before losing to Becker in the final in '86.

The first set went with serve until the tenth game, with Lendl serving at 4-5. A poor volley into the net at deuce gave Cash a set point, but Lendl managed to save it with a winning volley. Two strong first serves got him out of trouble to level at 5-5, and both men held their next service games to take it to a tie-break. Cash raced into a 4-1 lead, and two winning backhand returns of serve gave him a 6-1 lead and five set points. Lendl wasn't beaten yet though, saving the first with a well placed lob and the second after putting pressure on the Cash volley. A backhand volley of his own saved a third set point, and a smash got the score back to 6-5. With just one set point remaining and Lendl looking dangerous Cash hit a well placed serve that was too strong for Lendl though, and he took the first set 7-6 in just under an hour and a quarter.

The loss of the opening set seemed to have got to Lendl, and he struggled to find any kind of form in the second set. Errors beset his game as he gifted points to his opponent, and he hurled his racket to the ground in frustration. Cash won the set comfortably 6-2 without losing a single point on his serve to take a two sets to love lead.

Lendl regrouped at the start of the third set, and earned himself two break points with Cash serving at 1-2. The Australian missed an easy volley on the first and Lendl was back in the match. Both men continued to hold serve to leave the Czech serving for the set at 5-3, but he double faulted at 30-40 to hand the break back to Cash. That was all that Cash needed, and after he held serve for 5-5 he converted the second of two break points to break Lendl again and give himself a chance to serve for the match. Unlike Lendl moments earlier he had no problems serving out, and a cross court forehand volley saw him hold to love to take the set 7-5 and along with it the match and the championship.

Amazingly Cash had only lost 15 points on serve in the entire match, and he punched the air and threw his spare ball into the crowd in celebration. Moments later he was in the crowd himself, as he ran across the court towards the players' box and hopped over the low fence and into the stand. Helped by slightly bemused supporters he made his way up to just below the box, before clambering up onto the commentary box roof and into the players' box to embrace his father, coach and other family members. He re-emerged on the court a while later to receive his trophy. Centre Court had never seen anything like it, although numerous players have repeated his climb in subsequent years.

Cash reached the Australian final again the following year but lost to a Swede in five sets for the second year in a row, this time to Wilander. Injuries then began to dog his career, and he never made it further than the fourth round of a Grand Slam after that. Lendl meanwhile won his third straight US Open title later that year, and added two Australian Opens to his collection in 1989 and '90. He was never able to claim the Wimbledon crown to complete the career slam however, coming close again in '88, '89 and '90 but losing in the semi final on each occasion. He is considered to be one of the greatest players never to win Wimbledon, but he did coach Great Britain's Andy Murray to the title in 2013 and 2016. Murray continued the tradition of climbing up to the players' box, but a gate was installed the following year to stop it happening again.

7th July 2013
Andy Murray ends Britain's wait for a Wimbledon champion

When Fred Perry won the Wimbledon men's singles title in 1936, his third win in as many years, no-one could have thought that Britain would be waiting for the next home grown winner seventy seven years later.

A few men had come close. Tim Henman had given the British public belief, reaching four semi-finals in the nineties and naughties, but he fell just short of the final each time, the weight of expectation surely playing a part in his downfall. Most memorably he had led wild-card Goran Ivanisevic by two sets to one and looked to be in complete control of the match and heading for the final in 2001 before rain interrupted the match and gave the Croat the chance to get back into the match and win in five. British players had won the ladies singles and doubles, men's doubles and mixed doubles since Perry, but the British public wanted to celebrate a British men's singles champion at long last.

And so up stepped Andy Murray. The Scot had made his Wimbledon debut in 2005 at the age of eighteen, reaching the third round and impressing in a tight match against former finalist David Nalbandian, taking the first two sets before losing in five. His performance then had given the nation hope, but we'd been there before, only to see young prospects fail to make a breakthrough. This time though, it looked as if Britain finally had a serious contender, as Murray worked his way up through the rankings into the world top 10. In 2012 he really got everyone believing he could be the one by reaching the final and taking the first set, but lost out to seven time champion Roger Federer in four sets.

He had though gained revenge soon after that by beating Federer 6-2 6-1 6-4 to become Olympic champion on Centre Court, and became the first British man to win a grand slam in seventy six years by winning the US Open, beating Novak Djokovic in a epic final 7-6 7-5 2-6 3-6 6-2. Now there was a definite chance that he could give Britain the Wimbledon victory it craved.

His progress through the early rounds of the 2013 Championships had been comfortable, with straight sets victories seeing him safely into the second week. Things got tougher in the quarter final though, with Murray battling back from two sets to love down to beat Spain's Fernando Verdasco in five. He had to come from behind in the semi final as well, losing the first set on a tie break to Jerzy Janowicz of Poland before winning in four sets.

Murray's opponent in the final, world number one Novak Djokovic, had an even harder time of it in his semi final, taking four hours and forty three minutes to overcome Juan Martin Del Potro_in five gruelling sets. All but the most even-handed British tennis supporters were hoping that Djokovic's fitness would suffer in the final as a result, giving their man a possibly crucial edge. Against the seven time grand slam champion, the man who had twice beaten Murray in major finals in the past, he would need every advantage he could get, although Murray's victory over him in the previous year's US Open final gave some optimism.

A huge cheer greeted the two contenders as they stepped out onto Centre Court, with a nervous nation glued to their televisions at home. Murray himself showed few signs of nerves though, as he earned an early break against the Djokovic serve, but the world number one soon broke back. It was the Serb who was making more errors though, and Murray moved a break ahead again for a 4-3 lead and kept his nose in front to take the first set 6-4.

Djokovic regrouped though, and started to show his class at the start of the second set, breaking the Murray serve twice to move ahead 4-1. Many of his supporters would have been looking ahead to the third set, but Murray hadn't given up on the second yet. Three games in a row saw him level at 4-4, and he broke again in a bad-tempered game at 5-5 for the chance to serve for a two set lead. He made no mistake, and Centre Court erupted as their man put himself just six games away from making history.

The momentum was with the Scot now, and he started the third set with yet another break of the top seed's serve. Djokovic wasn't ready to concede defeat though, and looked like putting the celebrations on hold as rattled off four games in a row to move into a 4-2 lead. Murray supporters started to bite their fingernails now – would he be denied the title again? He didn't see it that way however, and promptly won the next three games for a 5-4 lead and the chance to serve for the title.

All seemed well as he went 40-0 up, but Djokovic saved three match points to level at deuce and raise the tension level even further. Despite Murray's lead Djokovic was refusing to give up, and the crowd feared that a comeback could be on the cards if Murray didn't take his chance now. A forehand into the net gave Djokovic a break point, but a powerful first serve got it back to deuce. A drop shot off the net cord after a long rally gave the Serb a second break point, but Murray held his nerve in another lung-busting exchange to pass Djokovic cross court. Djokovic earned a third break point as he was too quick for Murray's drop shot, only for Murray to put away a simply volley to deny him. Brilliant defending from Murray forced an error from Djokovic at the net for a fourth championship point. A deep first serve forced a defensive return from Djokovic and Murray attacked with a forehand. Djokovic's backhand found the net and Murray had done it. He sank to his knees in triumph, exhaustion and relief, and a nation, finally, celebrated a Wimbledon men's champion.

He went on to win his second Wimbledon crown in 2016, before defending his Olympic title the following month, and he became World Number One for the first time later that year.

8th July 1982
German goalie puts French striker in hospital in World Cup semi final

The 1982 World Cup proved to be one to forget for West Germany, despite finishing as runners-up. They made no friends on route to the final as a result of a highly controversial match against neighbours Austria in the group stage, then a horrific foul committed by their goalkeeper in the semi final against France.

The tournament had started badly for them, beaten 2-1 by Algeria in a result that was considered to be one of the biggest upsets in World Cup history. They recovered quickly though, a Karl-Heinz Rummenigge hat-trick helping them to a 4-1 victory over Chile. With Austria having beaten Chile and Algeria in their opening two matches, and Algeria victorious over Chile, that left Austria top of the group on four points, ahead of Algeria on goal-difference, with West Germany facing a humiliating exit on two points, with one match to go.

That meant that a German win in the El Molinon stadium in Gijon by one or two goals would see both they and Austria qualify for the second round. A bigger win would see Austria go out though, and unfortunately both teams used their advantage of playing after Algeria to dictate their tactics. The Germans took the lead after ten minutes through Horst Hrubesch, leaving both teams in a position to go through, and for the remaining eighty minutes neither side looked remotely interested in scoring. The players spent most of the match passing amongst themselves with no attacking intent, with the only half-hearted efforts on goal going well wide. The only touches the goalkeepers got were back-passes, and plenty of aimless clearances up field were played. The largely Spanish crowd were outraged, and the few Algerian supporters in the stadium threw banknotes at the players. German and Austrian commentators either stopped commentating or urged viewers to switch off, and one Spanish newspaper even moved their match report to their crime section. The rules were changed for future World Cups so that the final two group matches would be played simultaneously to prevent it happening again, but that was scant consolation to Algeria who found themselves out of the World Cup.

France had also made poor start to the tournament, falling behind to England within thirty seconds in their opener, which they lost 3-1, only to win their second match 4-1 against Kuwait with goals from Bernard Genghini, Michel Platini, Didier Six and Maxime Bossis. They conceded a late penalty to draw their final match against Czechoslovakia 1-1, but that was enough to qualify for the second round as runners up to England.

It was West Germany's turn to face England in the second round group, and they fared better than France with a 0-0 draw, then beat Spain 2-1. When England failed to beat Spain the Germans were through to the semi final, where they would face France after a stunning Genghini free kick secured them a 1-0 win over Austria before they dispatched Northern Ireland 4-1.

Neutral supporters were rooting for France, both because of Germany's antics against Austria and for the attractive, attacking football that the talented French side preferred. It was West Germany who took the lead though, Pierre Littbarski seizing on to a loose ball after Klaus Fischer had challenged goalkeeper Jean-Luc Ettori and firing home after seventeen minutes. They were only ahead for ten minutes though, French playmaker Platini equalising from the spot after Bernd Forster had been penalised for holding Dominique Rocheteau, and the half finished 1-1.

The second half featured some fine chances for both teams, especially the French, but was marred by a horrific injury to France's Patrick Battiston. Fifteen minutes into the half Battiston was chasing a long ball played through into the German half. Battiston beat defender Manfred Kaltz to the ball and knocked it past the advancing goalkeeper Harald Schumacher on the edge of the box, but he never got the chance to try to turn the ball in. Schumacher launched himself at Battiston, feet up, and clattered into him hard. The ball rolled harmlessly wide, but Battiston remained on the ground, lying still as he had been knocked unconscious. As concerned team-mates gathered round him and called for the team doctor, referee Charles Corver unbelievably awarded West Germany a goal kick. It took some minutes for Battiston to be taken off the pitch on a stretcher, and he was taken to hospital where it was found that he had broken ribs, cracked vertebra and had lost two teeth. It was generally considered to be one of the worst fouls ever seen on a football field, and the fact that the perpetrator wasn't booked let alone sent off, and a free kick wasn't even given, made it even more shocking.

The French were visibly shocked by the fate of Battiston, but Manuel Amoros still came agonisingly close to scoring a late winner in, but his injury time shot rebounded off the crossbar, and the score remained 1-1 at full time. Two minutes into extra time justice seemed to have been done, as France took the lead through a Marius Tresor volley, and six minutes later France went 3-1 ahead when Alain Giresse's shot glanced off the post and into the net. The Germans didn't give up hope though, and Rummenigge pulled one back for them five minutes after coming on as sub, squeezing the ball in from a tight angle. They were back on level terms just after the break, a brilliant bicycle kick by Fischer making the first ever World Cup penalty shoot-out a definite possibility.

Extra time did indeed finish with the score 3-3. Giresse, Amoros, and Dominique Rocheteau were all successful for France, as were Manfred Kaltz and Paul Breitner for West Germany, but Ettori saved Uli Stielike's strike to give France the advantage. Schumacher, who many thought shouldn't have been on the pitch, responded by saving from Six, and Littbarski scored to level. Platini and Rummenigge were both successful, but then Schumacher saved again, guessing correctly and beating out Bossis' kick. Hrubesch knew that if he scored his side would be through, and he made no mistake. It was harsh on France, who should have been playing against ten men for most of the second half and extra time, and the fact that Schumacher saved two penalties in the shoot-out just rubbed salt into the wound.

West Germany went on to lose 3-1 to Italy in the final, and France lost 3-2 to Poland in the third/fourth playoff, but did go on to become European Champions two years later, and finally managed to become World Champions in 1998.

8th July 2014
Germany thrash Brazil

Many people thought that Brazil were lucky to have reached the 2014 World Cup semi final, but the hosts had made it through somehow, and the five time champions now faced the three time winners Germany for a place in the final.

Comparisons will always be made with the great Brazil teams of the past, but the 2014 squad seemed to lack the flair and talent of many of their predecessors. Added to this the fact that there had been a series of protests and even riots leading up to the competition, by Brazilians unhappy with the amount of money that had been spent on hosting the tournament in a country where poverty was so widespread, and there was significant pressure on the squad. Apart from star striker Neymar, the team looked fairly average, but nevertheless they had battled through, swept along on a tide of public expectation and with more than a bit of luck at times, to be on the verge of their seventh final. For a side unbeaten at home in competitive matches for twelve years, there was certainly hope.

They had got off to a good start in the group stage, beating Croatia 3-1, before a dull 0-0 draw against Mexico. A 4-1 victory over an admittedly disappointing Cameroon side had seen them into the next round, where they faced South American neighbours Chile. With the score 1-1 after normal time, Chile came within a whisker of winning when Mauricio Pinilla hit the crossbar in the last minute of extra time, but Brazil survived the scare to win 3-2 on penalties to reach the quarter final.

Facing Colombia, Brazil took the lead through a scruffy Thiago Silva goal, then doubled their lead thanks to stunning David Luiz free kick, but Colombia pulled a goal back through a James Rodriguez penalty ten minutes from time. They were unable to score a second though, and Brazil had scraped through to the semi final. The down side for Brazil though was that Silva had picked up a yellow card during the game and would miss the semi final through suspension, and Neymar would also be missing, having gone off injured, later diagnosed as having a fractured vertebrate after being kneed in the back by Juan Zuniga.

Germany meanwhile started impressively by thrashing Portugal 4-0 in their opener, before being held to a 2-2 draw by Ghana and beating the USA 1-0. They had surprisingly been pushed to extra time by Algeria before beating them 2-1, and had beaten France 1-0 in a tight quarter final. The Germans were favourites to beat Brazil, but nobody foresaw the manner in which they would do so.

The Brazilians paid tribute to their missing talisman Neymar during the national anthem, but it didn't take long for the passionate start to the match to descend into stunned silence. It took Germany just eleven minutes to take the lead, Thomas Muller finding acres of space in the Brazilian box to score from a corner. Twelve minutes later Miroslav Klose made it 2-0, scoring at the second attempt after Julio Cesar had blocked his initial strike, becoming the top goalscorer in World Cup history in the process with his sixteenth goal. The Brazilian defence, brittle at the best of times but clearly missing Silva, was all at sea, more interested in charging forwards to attack than in defensive discipline, and Toni Kroos was gifted Germany's third and fourth goals, completing a chaotic three minute period during which the Germans tore through the Brazil defence at will. When Sami Khedeira unbelievably made it 5-0 only twenty nine minutes of the match had passed.

The contest was already over in less than half an hour, with the only thing left to be decided whether Germany could continue to humiliate Brazil or the hosts could salvage a little bit of pride. Brazil did manage their first shot on target in the fifty first minute, but it didn't trouble Manuel Neuer in the German goal.

It got even worst for Brazil after the break. Substitute Andre Schurrle scored two more as the Brazilian defence continued to make things easy for their opponents, making it 7-0. By now the shock, disbelief and tears in the stands had given way to anger, and the crowd even started cheering the Germans as they gave their own once-great side a footballing lesson. Brazilian players were also being booed when they touched the ball, particularly Fred, who looked completely out of his depth up front. Brazil did manage to find the net late on through Oscar, but never has a consolation goal given less consolation to a grieving nation.

It had been an incredible match that broke all kinds of records – the first time a team has scored seven goals in a World Cup semi final and the time five goals had been scored in the first half; the shortest ever time to score five goals in World Cup history; Brazil's heaviest ever World Cup defeat. Social media erupted during the match, with the game becoming the most discussed sporting event on Twitter ever. 35.6 million tweets were sent during the match, including 580,000 sent in one minute following the fifth goal, a record in itself. Stand in captain Luiz sobbed through his post-match interview as he attempted to apologise for their performance, but the buck stopped with manager Luis Filipe Scolari, who was sacked shortly after the tournament ended.

Germany went on to beat Argentina in the final, but only by one goal to nil after extra time, whilst Brazil suffered more embarrassment in the third / fourth playoff, losing 3-0 to The Netherlands. Brazilians were glad the tournament was over.

9th July 2006
Zidane ends career with a headbutt

Zinedine Zidane might not even have been playing in the 2006 World Cup final. Having retired from international football following France's disappointing display in the 2004 European Championships, he had changed his mind barely a year later. Along with fellow World Cup winner from 1998 Lilian Thuram, who had also come out of retirement, Zidane turned France's flagging qualifying form around and helped them top their group. At the end of the domestic season though he announced that the World Cup would be his last competitive action on the football pitch. Could one of the greats go out on top of the world?

Nothing in France's early form in Germany suggested that he would. A misfiring performance in their group opener against Switzerland saw the match end goalless, and despite taking the late in their next game against South Korea they could only draw 1-1. With Zidane struggling to fine his own touch he was substituted off before the end, and having picked up a yellow card in each match and set to miss their must-win game against Togo there was a danger that the World Cup had seen the last of him. However, his team-mates laboured to an unconvincing 2-0 victory and this was enough to secure second place in the group, progression to the knock-out stages and another chance for Zidane to shine, should coach Raymond Domenech choose to bring him back into his side.

He did, and their round of sixteen match against the thus far impressive Spanish would prove to be a turning point. With the score 1-1 and time running out, Patrick Vieira headed in Zidane's floated free-kick to put the French in front, and soon afterwards Zidane was on the score-sheet himself, finishing a powerful run with a searing shot that left Spanish keeper Iker Casillas with no chance.

French hopes were rejuvenated for their quarter final against defending champions Brazil. Zidane was back on form, and he bossed the game from start to finish, taunting the Brazilians with keepie-ups and splitting the defence with inch-perfect passes time and again. Again, it was a free-kick that gave France the lead, Zidane's delivery catching the defence out at the back post for Thierry Henry to score. That was enough to win the match and put them through to face Portugal for a place in the final. Again, Zidane was imperious, playing with joy and precision, and he led his side to a 2-1 victory, scoring the winner himself from the penalty spot.

Whatever the result, the World Cup final, against Italy, was to be Zidane's last ever match, played out in front of a packed Olympic Stadium in Berlin. It should have been a fitting end to the career of one of the most talented players to have graced football's ultimate stage, and it looked as if it was heading that way when Zidane opened the scoring after just six minutes. Marco Materazzi was harshly penalised for bringing down Florent Malouda in the box, replays showing there had been minimal contact, and Zidane calmly chipped home a penalty off the crossbar. That goal made him only the fourth player to score in more than one World Cup final, but French joy was short-lived, as Materazzi made amends ten minutes later, jumping highest to power home a header from Andrea Pirlo's corner to equalise. Italy almost scored twice more from Pirlo corners, but another Materazzi header was cleared off the line and Luca Toni's came back off the bar.

Both teams had chances to win it in the second half too, Italy having a Toni effort ruled out for offside and Henry forcing Gianluigi Buffon into a sharp save, but normal time ended 1-1 and the game moved into extra time. France looked the more likely to score, with Malouda and Franck Ribery going close before Buffon tipped Zidane's header over the bar. That was to be Zidane's last real contribution however, as with ten minutes to go he became embroiled in an angry exchange of words with Materazzi. Moments later Materazzi was on the floor. Few people had seen the incident, including the referee, but replays showed that Materazzi had said something to Zidane as he was walking away, and although he had made a meal of it, Zidane had turned back and headbutted the Italian in the chest. The assistant referee had seen it though, and after a short discussion Zidane was shown the red card.

The game petered out after that, leaving Materazzi to have the last laugh, scoring his penalty along with Pirlo, Daniele de Rossi and Alessandro del Piero. Sylvain Wiltord, Eric Abidal and Willy Sagnol scored theirs for France, but David Trezeguet's strike hit the underside of the bar and the ball bounced down but didn't cross the line. Fabio Grosso made no mistake with the decisive penalty and the World Cup was Italy's. It was a sad end to a brilliant career.

Afterwards it emerged that Zidane had reacted to abuse from Materazzi involving his sister. Opinion in France was split, but most fans seemed to forgive the man who had helped to bring so much success to French football for his moment of madness.

12th July 2009
The most thrilling draw ever?

For non-aficionados of cricket, the fact that test matches can last for five days and still not produce a winner can be something of an anathema, but the first test of the 2009 Ashes series produced a finish that was gripping enough to excite the most demanding of sports fans.

England had won the Ashes back for the first time in two decades four years earlier, but had promptly relinquished them back to the Aussies in 2006-07 by a resounding 5-0 scoreline. The teams looked well matched for the first series on English soil since the historic 2005 series, with the series opener being played at Glamorgan's Swalec Stadium, the first ever test match played on Welsh soil.

Having won the toss and chosen to bat first, England showed great resilience in their first innings, recovering from a shaky start that saw them slump to 90 for 3. Alistair Cook, Andrew Strauss and Ravi Bopara had all fallen cheaply, before Kevin Pietersen and Paul Collingwood steadied the ship with a crucial partnership of 138. Just as it looked as though they had seized the initiative with the score on 228 for 3 Australia struck back, with Collingwood and Pietersen falling within five overs of each other, and Peter Siddle taking two late wickets to see the home side end the day on 336 for 7.

The England tail attacked at the start of day two, with Graeme Swann hitting a rapid 47 from 40 balls to help the England total to a reasonable looking 435 all out shortly before lunch. However, Australia set about England's total in fine style, despite the early loss of Phillip Hughes. Simon Katich and Ricky Ponting both had centuries by the end of the day, Ponting scoring his 11,000th run in the process, and the tourists were in a strong position at the close at 249 for 1.

They carried on where they had left off the following day, with Katich and Ponting taking their partnership to 239 before Katich was trapped LBW by Jimmy Anderson for 122. Ponting was out having played on against Monty Panesar for 150, and Hussey was also out in an even morning session, but the afternoon belonged to the Aussies as England failed to take a further wicket in the session. Rain and bad light cut short the final session of the day, but Australia still had time to pass England's total, with five wickets in hand and a chance to build a commanding lead.

Marcus North and Brad Haddin set about doing just that on the fourth day, with both batsmen adding centuries to the Australian innings with some ferocious hitting. Ponting eventually put the England attack out of its misery by declaring on 674 for 6, the fourth highest Ashes total ever and an impressive lead of 239. With more than four sessions of play left England were up against it, and knew that they would have to bat well to avoid defeat, but they started their task badly, with both Alistair Cook and Ravi Bopara losing their wickets before tea. England were helped out by the arrival of rain during the tea break, and there was no further play that day, but with a dry day forecast for day five they would still have to improve their batting if they were to save the match and avoid going 1-0 down in the series.

It wasn't a promising start however, as three further wickets fell in the morning session, and England were staring at defeat at lunch with the score 94 for 5. Collingwood wasn't going anywhere though, and he set his stall out to bat out the day for his side. He was let off the hook when on 35, when Katich, one of many Aussie fielders crowded around the under pressure batsmen, failed to hold on to a sharp bat-pad catch chance. It was all-out defence for him, and at one point he scored just one run in ten overs. The normally all-out-attacking Andrew Flintoff was also playing cautiously, scoring 26 off 71 balls before Australian captain Ricky Ponting took a fine low catch at slip to dismiss him. The tourists needed just four more wickets for victory.

Stuart Broad was next in to join Collingwood, and he managed to hang around for just over an hour after surviving a loud appeal for LBW the first ball he faced. The Aussie bowlers gave next man Swann a good going over, but despite causing him some discomfort it gave England the opportunity to see off some time as physio Steve McCaig was called into action a couple of times. Collingwood and Swann made it through to tea, and England fans were starting to believe that if those two could stay in they might just salvage an unlikely draw.

Swann managed to hang around for another sixteen overs after tea, but Australia were able to take the new ball, and the extra pace contributed to his mistake in trying a pull shot, and England had lost their eighth wicket. With eighteen overs left in the day, England had just two wickets in hand, and apart from Collingwood had only Anderson and Monty Panesar left to bat, neither of whom boasted a good batting record. Collingwood tried to dominate the strike to protect Anderson, but his vigil finally came to an end when he was caught by a grateful Michael Clarke off the bowling of Nathan Hauritz for 74. He had faced 245 balls and batted for 344 minutes, a monumental effort, but it looked like it would be in vain as Anderson and Panesar were unlikely to be able to survive the remaining eleven overs.

England were now six runs away from avoiding an innings defeat, and if they could make Australia bat again that would eat up some precious time. The Aussie bowlers threw everything they had at England's number ten and eleven batsmen, but they refused to budge. Every ball they survived was met with a cheer, and the pair bumped gloves with each other at the end of each over they managed to see off. They were blocking and leaving whenever they could, but at one point Anderson managed two boundaries, putting England in front to the delight of the crowd. They would now have to survive two overs fewer, and word went round that if they cou'd make it through to 6.41pm the match would be over. Physio McCaig and twelfth man Bilal Shafayat were both sent out to the middle for spurious reasons, only to be sent packing by Ponting. At 6.39 Australia had time for one last over, to be bowled by Hauritz. Anderson blocked the first ball, then the second, the cheers getting louder each time. With a bye off the final ball time was up, the final wicket pairing had survived 69 tension-laden balls and England had done it. The noise in the stadium was deafening.

A buoyant England went on to win the next test at Lords, and despite Australia levelling the series with an innings victory at Headlingley, a comfortable victory in the final test at The Oval gave England the series.

18th July 1976
Nadia Comaneci scores the first perfect ten

To achieve something never achieved before at the Olympic Games is something special. To do it again six more times in the space of five days, at the age of fourteen, is incredible.

Nadia Comaneci had been training for her Olympic moment since the age of six, when she was sent to a boarding school for promising young gymnasts in Romania run by Bela and Marta Karolyi. Many years later criticism was levelled at their methods, labelling it brutal, with stories emerging of the girls being hit whenever they made a mistake, but at the time all anyone was aware of was that it had produced a prodigious talent. Comaneci immediately caught the eye when she first competed in adult competition in 1975 at the age of thirteen, and shortly after her debut won four golds and a silver medal at the European Championships.

Her performances had not gone unnoticed in the Soviet Union. Their gymnast Olga Korbut had been the star of the 1972 Munich Games, winning three gold and one silver medal, but with attention turning to Comaneci after her showing at the European Championships, the pressure was on Korbut to keep her young rival at bay. A fierce rivalry grew between the two gymnasts and their coaches, as well as with another Soviet competitor, Ludmilla Tourischeva, who herself had won two golds, a silver and a bronze in Munich, and the pressure gave them all an intense focus to practice even harder for the Games. The Soviet officials expected Korbut to be the one to beat, but her preparations were hampered by injuries and she was not at her best when the competition began.

The team all-around event was the opening event, and therefore the first chance to see the rivals in action. When the Romanian team moved to the asymmetric bars it wasn't long before Comaneci took to the stage. What followed was eighteen seconds of perfection. From the moment she leaped up onto the bars every release, every catch and every handstand were flawless, her rhythm superb right up until her clever dismount. The crowd knew they had witnessed something special.

There was confusion though when her score was displayed. The Montreal Olympic committee had assured scoreboard suppliers Omega that gymnastics scores could never be as high as 10.0, even though it was theoretically possible. As a result the scoreboard only went up to 9.99, so the decision was made to show her score as 1.0. The confused crowd was soon told that she had actually scored 10.0, the first perfect score in Olympic history, and they gave her a standing ovation.

Comaneci returned to the stage to wave the crowd before stepping back down, but as the applause continued she had to return to acknowledge them once more.

One of the judges that day, Jackie Fie, later said that awarding ten was "an enormous leap" as one had never been given before, but said that she felt she had no choice. "You wanted to give her 10.2 out of 10. That would have reflected the difference between her and the rest" she said. Her performance may have been head and shoulders above everyone else's, but it only earned her a silver medal as Romania finished behind Korbut and Tourischeva's Soviet team.

Gold medals were just around the corner though. Not content with achieving the impossible once, she continued her amazing form throughout the rest of the competition, scoring three more perfect tens on the asymmetric bars and three on the beam on her way to winning gold in the individual all-around and on the bars and beam. She also picked up a bronze on the floor for good measure.

Inspired by the performances of Comaneci, the Soviet response came not from Korbut and Tourischeva but from eighteen year old Nellie Kim, who produced three perfect ten performances of her own, in the individual all-around, vault and on the floor, earning her two gold and one silver medal to add to the gold she had won at the team event. Tourischeva meanwhile added two silvers and a bronze to her gold in the team event, and Korbut, unable to repeat her exploits from four year before, added just one silver.

Comaneci competed again at the 1980 Moscow Games, winning two more golds and two silver medals, and being awarded two more perfect tens in the process. Her feats will never be repeated however, as in 1981 the minimum age for competitors in Olympic gymnastics competitions was raised to fifteen, then in 1997 to sixteen. The scoring system has also been changed so that the score given varies depending on the difficulty of the routine, so there is no longer such thing as a "perfect ten".

Following her retirement from competitive gymnastics Comaneci became a coach, helping the Romanian team at the 1984 Olympics in Los Angeles. In 1989, shortly before the Romanian revolution, she fled the country, making her way eventually to the USA where she now lives.

21st July 1981
Botham's Ashes – The Headingley Test

One nil down to Australia after the first two tests, England were on the ropes. It had been a dismal few months for England. Under the captaincy of Somerset all-rounder Ian Botham they had lost four and drawn eight, and their captain's own form had plummeted. England lost the first Ashes test at Trent Bridge and drew the second at Lords, but Botham had resigned as captain having suffered a pair, replaced by former captain Mike Brearley.

The Aussies continued their domination as the third test began at Headingley. Captain Kim Hughes won the toss and chose to bat, and his side steadily put together a decent first innings total. It was slow going on the first day, not helped by rain breaks, but Australia had reached 203 for 3 at the close, and they continued their innings on the second day in the same steady manner. John Dyson, having been dropped whilst in the 50s, scored 102, before Botham finally found his rhythm and took 5 for 35 after tea. Hughes eventually declared at 401 for 9, leaving England openers Geoff Boycott and Graeme Gooch a tricky couple of overs to survive at the end of the day.

They survived, but didn't last long on day 3: Gooch going for 2 and Boycott for 12. Botham's half century was the only resistance, and England were all out for 174. Hughes enforced the follow-on, and Gooch fell again before bad light gave them a much-needed reprieve. Still 221 runs behind with 9 second innings wickets in tact, no-one gave England any chance of preventing Australia going 2 tests up with 2 to play. The bookies were offering 500-1 on an England win, and the odds were so attractive that Aussies Dennis Lillee and Rodney Marsh both put a bet on their rivals, just for fun.

The England players even checked out of their hotel the next morning, believing that the match would be over by the end of the day. It looked like they would be proved right as English wickets continued to tumble, and when Graham Dilley came out to join Botham mid way through the afternoon session with the score 135 for 7, England were still 92 behind and staring down the barrel of a dismal innings defeat. But then things started to change. Dilley started the throw the bat around, and Botham soon followed suit. Riding their luck at times, the pair put the Aussie bowlers to the sword, hitting boundary after boundary and putting a smile on the England supporters' faces for the first time in a long while. It seemed like it would be a futile gesture, but it would be fun while it lasted. They put on 117 in just 80 minutes, taking England's score to 252 for 8, edging the home side into the lead and at least ensuring that Australia would have to bat again, and Botham, with a century under his belt, kept up the onslaught with Chris Old when Dilley finally fell. That ninth wicket produced a further 67 runs before Old was bowled by Geoff Lawson with the score on 319. Bob Willis came out to join Botham, facing just 5 balls before the end of play whilst his partner added another 31 to end the day 351 for 9.

With England now ahead by 124, and having to check back into their hotel, the bookies who had offered 500-1 were starting to worry, but they would surely need a profitable last wicket stand to set a target that could be defended. In Botham's own words "Fifty or sixty more and it could be interesting", but it wasn't to be, and only 5 more runs were added to the total before Willis was out, leaving Botham 149 not out off 148 balls. The tourists would need just 130 to win, and England's brave fightback seemed to have been in vain.

An early wicket for Botham gave the home supporters hope, but Greg Chappell and Dyson saw their side to 56 for 1, just 74 short of their target. Then, Willis swapped ends and the match turned again. He dismissed Chappell, Hughes and Graham Yallop in quick succession to leave the Aussies 58 for 4 at lunch. Old dismissed Allan Border shortly after the break, then three more wickets for Willis left Australia reeling at 75 for 8. Lillee and Ray Bright tried to copy England and hit their way out of trouble, adding 35 for the ninth wicket, but a sharp catch by Mike Gatting gave Willis his seventh wicket of the innings and left England needing one more wicket and Australia 20 more runs. England stumbled on the brink of victory, dropping two sharp chances in the slips, but Willis was not to be denied, smashing out Bright's middle stump to finish with figures of 8 for 43 and his side an incredible victory by 18 runs as the jubilant crowd poured onto the pitch.

It was only the second time a test match had been won by a side following-on, and the rejuvenated England went on the win the next two tests as well to clinch the series and The Ashes 3-1. The series became known as Botham's Ashes, and it would have been scant consolation to Marsh and Lillee that they were able to visit the bookies to claim their winnings.

22nd July 2012
"Allez Wiggo!" - Bradley Wiggins becomes first British Tour de France winner

It was the 99th Tour de France, but in the race's 109 year history there had never been a British winner. No British rider had even been in the top three until 2009, when Bradley Wiggins had finished the race in fourth position but had then been promoted to third following the disqualification of Lance Armstrong for doping.

With that result and his glittering track cycling record – Olympic gold in 2004, two more golds in 2008 plus six World Championship gold medals – Wiggins was tipped for further success on the road with his new team Team Sky, but he disappointed in the 2010 race, finishing back in 24th before being upgraded to 23rd. Disaster struck in the 2011 when he crashed out in stage seven and left the race with a broken collarbone.

His form going into the 2012 Tour was superb however. He had won the Paris Nice race, the Tour de Romandie and the Criterion de Dauphine, and he started the tour as a firm favourite, alongside defending champion Cadel Evans and Italy's Vincenzo Nibali.

Wiggins got off to a good start, finishing second in the prologue time trial, seven seconds behind Fabian Cancellara. The Swiss rider was to keep the yellow jersey and his slender lead for the first six stages. Stage seven was the first real mountain test of the race, and a group of five riders broke clear around a kilometre from the summit at La Planche des Belles Filles, including Evans, Nibali, Wiggins and his team-mate and fellow Brit Chris Froome. Evans attacked, but Froome stuck with him and went clear to win the stage, but more significantly, Cancellara finished almost two minutes further back and Wiggins claimed the race lead and the yellow jersey, ten seconds clear of Evans. He was only the fifth British rider to wear the coveted leader's jersey, but unlike the others he wasn't going to relinquish it.

After Wiggins had seen off attacks from Evans and Nibali in stage eight there was another individual time trial, and Wiggins put in a blistering performance, winning by thirty five seconds from Froome, and gaining two minutes on Evans and Nibali. As the race hit the mountains no-one was capable of gaining time on Wiggins, who was helped tirelessly by his Team Sky domestiques. By now the French crowds lining the mountain passes had taken to the Englishman, and cries of "Allez Wiggo!" were to be heard as his battled his way up the steep climbs. Only once did Wiggo look like he might crack, on stage eleven, when Froome, having been helping his team leader up the final climb to La Toussuire, broke clear, only to be told by his team to wait. The incident led some to suggest that Froome should have been allowed to attack, and to take over the team leadership if he was able to put himself in yellow, but the moment was gone and Froome would have to wait for his chance the following year.

Drama hit the fourteenth stage, when thirty riders suffered punctures in the Pyrenees after saboteurs threw tacks onto the road 200 metres from the summit of the Mur de Peguere. One of the riders affected was Evans, and, realising that something had happened, Wiggins ensured that the peloton slowed down to allow them to catch up. Evans went on to lose time two stages later anyway, putting him out of contention. With four stages to go Wiggins led by over two minutes, with Froome in second and Nibali, seemingly the only man who could deny him victory, a further twenty seconds back, but in the final Pyrenean stage he fell a further eighteen seconds behind the yellow jersey. With another time trial to go, Wiggins' speciality, it was hard to see anything other than a crash denying him.

Wiggins again delivered, winning the time trial from Froome by a commanding minute and fourteen seconds, giving him a lead of over three minutes with just the largely processional final stage to Paris to go. Britain's Mark Cavendish won on the Champs Elysees, his fourth victory on the Paris streets in as many years, to cap a memorable Tour for British riders. It was a dominant victory for Wiggins, who had been in yellow for thirteen of the twenty stages, finishing 3 minutes 21 seconds ahead of Froome and 6 minutes 19 ahead of Nibali.

Britain's first ever winner of La Tour went on to play a starring role in the London 2012 opening ceremony, then capped a golden year with Olympic gold in the time trial.

Wiggins' victory opened the floodgates for more British Tour de France success. After waiting 109 years for the first British winner, Froome went on to claim the yellow jersey in 2013 to make it two in two years, and won it again in 2015 and 2016. In 2016 there were also stage wins for Brits Steve Cummings and Mark Cavendish, who claimed his 30th victory n 2016 to become the second most prolific stage winner in the history of la Tour.

24th July 1908
Dorando Pietri collapses at end of Olympic marathon

70,000 people were packed into London's White City stadium waiting expectantly for news of the men's marathon. It was an eagerly anticipated event, but one which had been riddled with chaos and controversy at previous games. In 1904 in St Louis the first to finish was Fred Lorz, but he was later disqualified when it was found that he had been given a lift in a truck for some of the race. Thomas Hicks had finished second, but he had consumed strychnine, eggs and brandy in the later stages of the race to try to give himself a boost, yet had still had to be helped by two officials as he neared the finish. Despite it being against the rules to receive any sort of help the result stood and Hicks was given the gold medal.

The British officials would have been hoping for the race to run more smoothly this time, but it wasn't to be. The games had already had its issues, with the USA unhappy right from the start when their flag was initially omitted from those in the stadium for the opening ceremony. One was found for them for the athletes' parade, but their flag bearer refused to dip it as he passed King Edward VII, and the antagonism continued as the games progressed, reaching a head when a British official declared the men's 400 metres void and disqualified the American athlete who had finished first. His two compatriots refused to take part in the re-run, leaving one British athlete to run on his own and take the gold medal. The American sense of injustice would prove to be significant for one Italian athlete.

Dorando Pietri had only taken up running four years previously. Whilst working in a pastry shop he had run fifty kilometres to deliver a letter for his boss, then raced against Italy's leading distance runner when he visited his town, only losing by a small margin. He ran his first competitive marathon in 1906, winning on the streets of Rome. Now representing his country in his first Olympics, he was faced with an unusual start to the race, as the start line at Windsor Castle was moved so that it was outside the window of the room where Princess Mary's daughter was having a birthday party. That meant that the race would be an extra 385 yards long, seemingly insignificant to the athletes, but the additional distance made a huge difference in the end. Marathon's are now always twenty six miles and 385 yards as a result of the 1908 race.

The early leaders set off too quickly, and were soon suffering in the muggy conditions. South African Charles Heffernon made the first significant move of the race, taking the lead and pulling away from the field, giving himself an advantage of four minutes over his nearest rival Pietri by the twenty mile mark. The Italian began closing the gap however, and when Heffernon foolishly accepted a glass of champagne from one of the estimated million spectators lining the route, and soon suffered stomach cramps and dizziness, Pietri sensed an opportunity. He made the mistake of trying to catch Heffernon too quickly however, and was soon suffering himself.

Nevertheless, Pietri took the lead half a mile from the stadium. A man with a megaphone announced to the crowd when the leader was ten minutes from home, a gun blast sounded when he passed the last station on the course, and the excitement was growing. A cheer went up as the little Italian entered the stadium in his white vest and red shorts, but by now he was dazed and confused with exhaustion. He started to run to his left instead of right as he was supposed to, and he argued with the officials who tried to get him to turn around, thinking they were trying to trick him. Finally he gave in, and started the one lap of the track that stood between him and gold, effectively the extra 385 yards of the race.

He had nothing left to give though, and he collapsed at the first bend. Officials helped him up, but with 300 yards to go he was unable to make it on his own. He collapsed three more times as he made his tortuous way around the track on legs that were barely able to bear his weight, let alone convey him onwards. Meanwhile, almost unnoticed by the crowd who were cheering on the Italian's brave efforts, American athlete Johnny Hayes had also entered the stadium. Shortly after Pietri finally made it over the line he also finished the race, and the Americans soon protested that Pietri should be disqualified for having been assisted and their man given the gold. Their protest was upheld, despite Hicks having got away with it four years before, and Hayes was given the gold.

Touched by Pietri's bravery, and perhaps feeling a little guilty for her daughter having extended the race, Queen Alexandra awarded him with a silver cup at the closing ceremony. Despite his disqualification, Pietri had become a global hero. He went on a tour of London music halls, and Daily Mail readers raised £300 for him. A crowd cheered him off when he finally departed London, and another greeted him when he arrived home. A few months later he was on his way to New York for a rematch with Hayes. The two ran 262 laps of Madison Square Gardens in front of 20,000 spectators, with a reported 100,000 unable to get in. Pietri won by half a lap, and won again when they faced each other once more the following year. Irving Berlin was even inspired to write a song about him. Pietri may not have won the gold medal, but he certainly became more famous as a result than he would have done if he had.

24th July 2005
Lance Armstrong "wins" seventh Tour de France

It seemed to be one of the greatest stories of triumph over adversity that the world of sport had ever seen. A victory over cancer followed by a new record for the most Tour de France wins, but all was not as it seemed, and the legend of Lance Armstrong was destined to come crashing down.

Armstrong had competed as a youngster first as a swimmer and then as a triathlete, but it was the cycling element that he excelled at, and he signed his first professional contract with the Motorola cycling team at the age of twenty one. He won his first Tour de France stage the following year, before going to on to win the World Road Race Championships. Over the next few years he won further stage races, including another stage of La Tour, but he dropped out of the race after just five stages in 1996 due to ill health, and he was to receive devastating news soon afterwards when he was diagnosed with stage three testicular cancer that had already spread to other parts of his body, including his lungs and brain.

The diagnosis wasn't good, and he was given just a 20-50% chance of survival. He began a course of chemotherapy specially formulated to avoid damage to his lungs should he survive, and underwent several operations. Amazingly though he survived, and was declared free from cancer in 1997. He established the Lance Armstrong trust to help fellow cancer patients, and began the long journey to restart his career. He was signed up by the US Postal team, and a remarkable comeback seemed to be complete with victory in the Vuelta a Espana in 1998.

It was to get even better for Armstrong though in the 1999 Tour de France. He got off to a great start, claiming the yellow jersey by winning the prologue time trial, although he lost it the next day to Estonian rider Jaan Kirsipuu. Kirsipuu wore yellow for the next week, despite Italian Mariano Cipollini winning a record four stages in a row, until Armstrong reclaimed it after another time trial victory. The American then kept the maillot jaune for the remainder of the race, winning a stage in the Alps and a third time trial along the way to finish seven and a half minutes ahead of Swiss rider Alex Zulle to claim his first Tour de France. His victory was celebrated as an incredible achievement for someone who had been facing possible death less than three years before, and he was an inspiration for others battling the disease.

However, some claimed that the absence of the winners of the previous two Tours, Marco Pantani and Jan Ullrich, meant that Armstrong was yet to really prove himself. He quickly began to address the criticism, beating both Pantani and Ullrich the following year, and adding further victories in 2001, 2002 and 2003 to make it an incredible five wins in a row. He joined Jacques Anquetil, Eddy Merckx, Bernard Hinault and Miguel Indurain as a five time winner, although he was the only one to have won five in successive years.

However, rumours were emerging that all was not what it seemed, and that Armstrong's success was built on the use of performance-enhancing drugs. A book entitled *LA Confidential* was published in 2004 that claimed that members of his Motorola team had been using drugs since 1995, and when the allegations were printed by the Sunday Times Armstrong sued them for libel. The matter was settled out of court, but some of the mud had stuck and from thereon his achievements were treated with suspicion, especially in France.

It didn't stop him winning Tour titles though, and he won five stages on the way to his sixth victory in 2004, including three consecutive mountain stages. He reportedly considered retirement before the 2005 race, but decided to compete. His countryman David Zabriskie won the time trial on the opening day, but Armstrong was just two seconds behind him, and he took the yellow jersey on stage four when his new Discovery Channel team won the team time trial, with Zabriskie falling during the stage and losing time. The six time champion held on to the lead despite numerous attacks from his rivals, until Germany's Jens Voight briefly took it from him on stage nine after being part of a small group that escaped from the peloton and managed to stay clear. Armstrong, ably assisting by his team, took the lead back the following day however, and remained in yellow until the penultimate day.

The last but one stage was another time trial, Armstrong's last realistic chance to claim a stage win, and he took it in style, beating his old rival Ullrich by twenty seconds. He made his triumphant entrance onto the Champs Elysees four minutes forty clear of Italian Ivan Basso in second, claiming an unprecedented seventh straight Tour victory, and promptly announced his retirement from cycling.

The story was in no way over however. Firstly, he made a comeback in 2008, and rode La Tour again in 2009, finishing third behind Alberto Contador, then for a final time in 2010, finishing in twenty third. However, more significant were the developments away from the races. In 2005 L'Equipe newspaper alleged that six of Armstrong's urine samples taken during his first Tour win in 1999 had subsequently failed drug tests using new testing methods, but the International Cycling Union (UCI) cleared him due to unscientific testing of the samples. The following year another French newspaper, Le Monde, ran a story that one of Armstrong's former team-mates, Frankie Andreu, had heard him admitting to taking performance-enhancing drugs, and in 2006 a Los Angeles Times article claimed that he had taken blood-doping hormone EPO in 1999.

The evidence against him was building, and by 2010 former riders were admitting their own drug use and accusing Armstrong of doing the same, most notably American rider Floyd Landis. A criminal investigation was started, although this was later dropped. In 2012 the United States Anti-Doping Agency (USADA) charged him with taking banned substances and of pressurising team-mates into doing likewise, and he announced that he would not be fighting the charges. His sponsors all immediately dropped him, costing him millions of dollars. USADA and the UCI stripped him of all seven Tour titles and banned him for life. Finally, during an interview with Oprah Winfrey in 2013, Armstrong admitted cheating. It was a sad but by then not unexpected end to what had appeared to be the most incredible of cycling careers.

30th July 1966
"They think it's all over... It is now"

England didn't enter a team into any of the first three World Cups, following a disagreement with FIFA, and in the four tournaments they had taken part in since they hadn't got further than the quarter finals.

England fans hoped that home advantage would make a difference in 1966 however, as England was hosting the competition. They also had a new manager in Alf Ramsey, but jury was still out on him as he had used almost fifty players since taking over, and still seemed undecided on selection and formation as the tournament grew closer.

Results in World Cup year were encouraging however, with seven straight wins, including a 1-0 defeat of West Germany. Making his debut in that match was West Ham striker Geoff Hurst, whose prolific goal scoring for his club had caught the eye of the England boss. He scored in his second game, but struggled in the final couple of warm up games, and Spurs centre forward Jimmy Greaves got the nod for the starting line-up.

England kicked off against Uruguay, an unconvincing 0-0 that did nothing to convince anyone that their side could become World Champions. Goals from Bobby Charlton and Roger Hunt gave them a 2-0 win over Mexico in their next match, and they secured a quarter final place with another 2-0 victory, this time over France, with Hunt on the score sheet twice more.

They still hadn't found top gear though, and they weren't about to either, as they overcame an Argentina side intent on kicking, diving and even spitting at their opponents. Their captain, Antonio Rattin, picked up his second yellow card after thirty five minutes after a foul on Hurst, who had come back into the side as Greaves had been injured against France. Rattin refused to leave the pitch though, and the match was delayed as he and his team-mates remonstrated with the referee. Eventually he was escorted from the pitch by policemen, but the ten men of Argentina kept the scores level until twelve minutes from time, when a glancing Hurst header saw England into the semi final.

Ramsey refused to let his players swap shirts with their opponents, and famously referred to them as "animals" in a post-match interview. His comments greatly angered the Argentines, who already felt that refereeing decisions had cost them the match.

If England were to reach the final they would have to find a way to deal with the star of the tournament, Portugal's Eusabio. He had scored seven goals already, including four in an incredible quarter final that had seen Portugal come from 3-0 down against outsiders North Korea to win 5-3. Nobby Stiles did a fine job of keeping Eusabio quiet though, and two goals from Charlton gave England a 2-0 lead. Eusabio did score a penalty with eight minutes to go, but England held on to reach their first ever World Cup final.

Their opponents would be West Germany, who, like England, had topped their group. A comfortable 4-0 win over Uruguay in the quarter final had also been marred by arguments over a goal-preventing handball and two sendings-off. Their semi final followed a similar pattern to England's too, with West Germany going 2-0 up before a late goal by their opponents, the Soviet Union, gave them a nervy end to the match.

An expectant nation gathered around television sets to watch its team try to become World Champions, with almost 97,000 excited fans packed into Wembley. Hurst kept his place in the side with Greaves not quite recovered, and he was immediately involved. It was West Germany who took the lead though. A speculative volley into the box from Karl-Heinz Schnellinger was headed away by Ray Wilson, but only to Helmut Haller, and his well-placed shot beat Gordon Banks to make it 1-0 after twelve minutes.

England weren't behind for long though. Six minutes later the Germans failed to deal with a Bobby Moore free kick and Hurst headed home to make it 1-1. Banks made a sharp double save first from Wolfgang Overath then Lothar Emmerich to keep the scores level, and Hans Tilkowski was on good form at the other end too, beating away a Roger Hunt shot and saving a Hurst attempt, and the efforts of the two keepers kept the score 1-1 at the break.

The two defences were on top at the start of the second half, with the Germans in particular having to cope with a series of English attacks. The deadlock was finally broken twelve minutes from time, when Horst-Dieter Hottges sliced a clearance into the path of Peters, who couldn't fail to score from six yards out. England were 2-1 up and on the verge of glory. The Germans weren't giving up though, and in the final seconds English fans' hearts were broken when an Emmerich free kick bounced around in the English box, the England players claimed off the arm of Schnellinger, and Wolfgang Weber pounced to score a dramatic equaliser.

England had to keep their heads up for extra time, and Ramsey told his players "You've beaten them once, now you've got to go and beat them again." It seemed to do the trick, and England pushed Tilkowski into action time after time, although West Germany had their chances too. Ten minutes into extra time came one of the most talked about World Cup final goals ever. Alan Ball crossed from the right and found Hurst, who turned and shot. His strike beat Tilkowski and hit the underside of the crossbar, bouncing down on or over the line. The English players claimed a goal, the Germans disputed it. Swiss referee Gottfried Dienst consulted his Soviet linesman Tofik Bharamov, then signalled a goal. The German players were furious, but the goal stood.

Could England hold onto their lead this time? With time running out and the Germans pushing desperately for another late equaliser, Hurst found acres of space inside the German half. Just at that moment commentator Kenneth Wolstenholme spotted some over-excited supporters making their way onto the far side of the pitch. "And here comes Hurst. He's got... Some people are on the pitch. They think it's all over." Hurst carried the ball forward, into the German penalty area, then thumped a powerful shot that flew into the top corner of the net. "It is now" added Wolstenholme, completing one of the most famous pieces of commentary of all time.

Seconds later it was all over, and England were the World Champions, thanks to the first ever World Cup final hat-trick. The Queen presented the Jules Rimet trophy to Bobby Moore, and a jubilant nation celebrated.

England's defence of their title in 1970 ended at the hands of the West Germany at the quarter final stage, the Germans coming from two goals down to win 3-2 in extra time. Apart from a semi final appearance in 1990, when they again lost to West Germany, they haven't looked like winning it again. Remarkably, of the nine World Cups they have qualified for since the 1966 victory, they have gone out at the hands of the Germans four times.

August

1st August 1980
Coe v Ovett

Despite being one of the fiercest rivalries of the 1980s, British middle distance runners Sebastian Coe and Steve Ovett surprisingly only raced each other six times in their entire careers. Four of those races were Olympic finals, with their greatest battles coming in the 800 and 1,500 metres at the 1980 Moscow Olympics.

Despite both being prodigious talents, the pair could hardly have been more different. One from the north, one from the south, one came from a working class background, the other more privileged. After racing each other in a junior race in 1972 they would then not compete for another six years, the 800 metres final at the 1978 European Championships being their next encounter as they avoided each other either by chance or deliberately until the Olympics (Ovett finished second and Coe third).

The two were still driven to outdo each other however, each desperate to be the best in Britain and the world, and they both laid a good claim to that title. In 1979 Coe broke the 800 metres, 1,500 metres and mile world records, adding the 1,000 metres best in 1980 to hold four world records. Less than an hour later Ovett broke his mile record though, and a few weeks later broke Coe's 1,500 metre time as well.

Their first event in Moscow was the 800 metres, with World Record holder Coe favourite for gold. Both had won their heat and semi final, with just one tenth of a second separating their semi final times. Coe seemed to be struggling with the tag of favourite however, and was reportedly agitated during the build-up to the final, finding it difficult to sleep the night before and not himself on the morning of the race. In contrast, Ovett seemed to relishing the occasion. Both were off the pace during the first lap, with another British athlete, Dave Warren, in a better position at the front of the pack. Ovett was happy to sit at the back, although he was slightly boxed in, and Coe slowly moved his way around the outside.

At the bell Ovett spotted half a gap on the inside and muscled his way up to fourth, whilst Coe was still struggling to make up ground. Nikolay Kirov of the Soviet Union took the lead down the back straight, with Ovett tracking him. Ovett was right on his shoulder round the final bend, and made his move in the home straight, with Coe finishing fast in fourth. Ovett sprinted clear, with Coe straining to catch him and Kirov. Coe finished fastest, but he had left it too late. He overhauled Kirov for silver, but the gold was Ovett's. He said afterwards that he was waiting for Coe to challenge him as the line approached, but the challenge never came. Coe described the race as the worst of his career. He was determined to learn from his mistakes and put things right in the 1,500 metres.

Again both men came through their heats and semi final comfortably, setting the stage for their second showdown. This time the roles were reversed though, with Ovett, unbeaten in three years, the favourite, but seemingly struggling with nerves.

Coe's determination not to leave it too late this time was obvious from the start, as he put himself on the shoulder of the leader, East German Jurgen Straub. It was a cautious, slow race, which suited 800 metre favouring Coe, and Ovett was happy to stay back in sixth place, running wide though to ensure that he wasn't boxed in and was able to follow any move. On the second lap Ovett decided to get closer to Coe, and fell in behind him, with fellow Brit Steve Cram also at the front of the pack. Straub made his move with a lap and a half to go, putting his foot down on the back straight. Coe followed him, with Ovett just behind, and at the bell it looked like the medals would be decided between the three. Straub still held a metre lead coming around the final bend, but Coe was ready to strike and accelerated past the German with 100 metres to go. Straub tried to respond but Coe slowly edged clear. Ovett was trying to make his move, but was too far back to catch Coe, and Straub held his form to hold on to second. Coe crossed the line a couple of metres ahead of Straub to take the gold, with Ovett having to settle for bronze, his first defeat at the distance for three years.

Both men returned home with a gold medal, but surprisingly at the distance the other was expected to triumph at. They continued to break records but avoid each other for the next couple of years, exchanging the mile world record a number of times, before they faced each other again in the Los Angeles Games in 1984. Ovett's preparations were hampered by bronchitis however, and the LA smog brought on a relapse. He was taken to hospital after his 800 metre semi final, and although he lined up for the final he was unable to challenge and finished eighth before being taken back to hospital. Coe again took silver, with gold going to Brazil's Joaquim Cruz. Ovett bravely competed in the 1,500 metres, making it to the final but having to drop out on the final lap, but Coe went on to sprint clear to retain his title.

After the two men had retired their relationship, always depicted in the press as testy, became closer, although in reality they probably had just never got to know each other when they were competing. Coe went on to become a Member of Parliament, then led the organisation of the London 2012 Olympics, before becoming president of the IAAF (International Association of Athletics Federations). Ovett emigrated to Australia and switched from competing to commentating.

1st August 1992
Linford Christie wins 100m Olympic gold

Only two British men had ever won the Olympic 100 metre title, the showpiece event of the Olympic athletics – Harold Abrahams in 1924, as immortalised in the film *Chariots of Fire*, and Allan Wells in the boycott hit Moscow games of 1980.

In 1992 Britain had another genuine contender though. Linford Christie, born in Jamaica but raised in London, was the reigning European and Commonwealth champion and was regularly running times that put him as one of the favourites for gold in Barcelona. He had finished third in the event in the previous Olympics in Seoul in 1988, only to be later awarded the silver medal following the disqualification of race winner Ben Johnson for anabolic steroid use. In a Games tarnished with drug scandals, Christie had himself failed a test, with traces of a banned stimulant being detected after his 200 metre heat, but a disciplinary panel had given him the benefit of doubt that he had unwittingly consumed the substance whilst drinking some ginseng tea and he was allowed to keep his medal.

Christie eased through his first round heat in a comfortable time of 10.48 seconds, but was pushed close by Leroy Burrell in the second round, beating the American by one hundredth of a second in 10.07. Burrell went one better in the semi final, beating Christie into second with a time of 9.97, with the Brit finishing in 10 seconds dead. Almost a second behind them both was Johnson, who had served his ban after 1988 and was trying to rebuild his career and his reputation. He had stumbled out of the blocks and finished last, but even if he hadn't stumbled his times were down on what was needed to make the final. The other semi final was won by Namibia's Frankie Fredericks, but it was a slower race, and his time would only have been good enough for fourth place in Christie's semi final.

As always the pundits speculated about who might have been holding something back for the final, but Christie and Burrell went into the race with the fastest times in qualifying and were expected to fight it out for the medals, along with Fredericks and Burrell's fellow American Denis Mitchell. With Johnson out and 1984 and '88 champion Carl Lewis having failed to make the USA team for the event and also missing, it looked like being a four way battle for gold. With Burrell and Mitchell, along with Lewis, having kept Christie out of the medals at the World Championships the previous year, the British athlete was hungry for revenge.

Lining up alongside the four favourites were two Nigerians, Davidson Azinwa and Olapade Adeniken, Bruny Surin of Canada and Jamaica's Ray Stewart. As the athletes were introduced to the capacity crowd in the Montjuic Stadium a large British contingent gave Christie the biggest cheer, but not a flicker of acknowledgement was visible on his face as his famous concentration never wavered and he stared, unmoving, towards the finish line.

He was also unfazed as Burrell, in the lane next to him, false-started. Then Mitchell, in the lane the other side of him, raised his hand from his position on the blocks, perhaps unsettled by something in the stadium or maybe trying to break his opponents' concentration, and the competitors had to stand and try again. As the gun sounded Surin made the fastest start, with Fredericks hot on his heels. The slower starting Christie began to get into his stride though, his strides lengthening and his speed increasing as he made up ground on the field. At fifty metres he was right in contention, and as one of the strongest in the second half of the race he was in a great position to pull clear. With every stride he started to pull clear, arms and legs pumping as he maintained his tunnel vision, leaving the struggling Burrell in his wake. Only Fredericks looked briefly capable of catching him, but Christie wasn't going to be beaten, and he flew across the line in a time of 9.96, the fastest time of the competition, with Fredericks second in 10.02 and Mitchell just overcoming Surin to take the bronze medal in 10.04.

The new Olympic champion held his arms aloft in triumph, then made his way to the crowd to pick up a Union Flag for his lap of honour, stopping to thank the British supporters dotted around the stadium. Later that evening he choked back the tears as he watched the Union Jack raised and listened to the national anthem, determined not to produce any photos that might embarrass him in the future, but there was nothing embarrassing about his achievements that day, as the oldest man ever to become Olympic 100 metre champion.

The following year Christie added the World Championship title to his collection, and became the first man to hold to Olympic, World, European and Commonwealth 100 metre titles at the same time. He attempted to defend his title in Atlanta in 1996 at the age of 36, but was disqualified from the final after two false starts. He retired from international competition the following year, but continued competing occasionally, just for fun. His career came to an end in 1999 under a cloud however, when he received a two year ban after a drug test suggested that he had been taking anabolic steroids. He claimed that the traces had come from legal supplements, and has continued to insist his innocence. UK Athletics initially agreed with him that there was reasonable doubt, but the IAAF upheld its ban. There is nothing to suggest that his Olympic gold medal was won anything than fairly though.

3rd August 1992
Derek Redmond's dad helps him finish 400m semi final

Olympic crowds and fans around the world have taken many athletes to their hearts over the years, celebrating with them and commiserating with them as their fortunes fluctuate. However, never has the pain of an athlete been felt by so many watching all around the world, and never have as many tears been shed at the sight of a truly poignant moment as when Derek Redmond competed in the 400 metre semi final in Barcelona in 1992.

Redmond had been an exciting prospect when he came to prominence by breaking the British 400 metre record as a nineteen year old in 1985, but injuries soon began to thwart his early promise. A hamstring injury meant that he missed out on a place in the individual event at the 1986 Commonwealth Games, although he was a part of the relay team that won gold, as he was the same year in the European Championships. World Championship silver followed the following year, again in the relay, but disaster struck as he sought for an individual medal at the 1988 Olympics in Seoul. Suffering from an Achilles tendon injury he had been given two painkilling injections in an attempt to make it to the start line, but ten minutes before his first race he was forced to admit defeat and pulled out.

He had considered giving up athletics as injuries continued to dog him the following year, but he refused to let them beat him despite undergoing surgery five times. It looked like he'd made the right decision in 1991, when he was part of the Great Britain four that shocked the favourites the USA to claim World Championship relay gold. It proved to be the highlight of his career.

The following year brought another Olympic Games, and another chance to show the world what he could do and to put the disappointment of Seoul behind him. He had had eight operations by then, but his form was good and he was hopeful that he could win an individual medal at a major championship for the first time. The signs were good when he qualified with the fastest time of the first round, his own fastest time for four years, and he followed it up with another impressive performance in the second round, crossing the line first again.

He looked to be in fine form and a definite medal contender going into the semi final. Together with his coach and his father Jim he had decided to go for another quick time in the race, which would secure him a preferential lane for the final. He got out of the blocks well, and was well in contention round the first bend and into the back straight, but twenty seconds into the race his luck gave out on him yet again. He clutched his hamstring and fell to his knees. He said later that he had felt a pop as his hamstring snapped, and as he clutched his leg in agony his rivals sprinted away from him, and along with them his dreams.

He wasn't about to let his Olympics finish mid way around the track though, and he picked himself up, his face creased with pain, and began limping his way towards the finish. Afterwards he explained that in his anguished state he actually believed he might be able to limp fast enough to catch the other athletes up. With more than 250 metres to go it was going to be a tortuous journey, but determination and the support of the crowd as they realised what he was doing helped him forward. An official tried to tell him to wait for a stretcher, but he was having none of it. As he reached the final bend his father ran from the crowd to help, waving away another official who tried to hold him back. After initially telling him to stop in case he made the injury worse, he quickly realised what his son needed to achieve, and he put his arm around his boy as the two of them carried on down the final straight, slowing to a walking pace. Redmond asked his father to help him back into his lane, lane five, to finish the race, and the two of them crossed the line together to the biggest cheer of the day and possibly of the whole Games.

Officially, as he had received help, the result was recorded as "Did not finish", but he had finished, and in doing so he created a moment of Olympic history that no-one who witnessed it would forget, with barely a dry eye in the house.

The race spelled the end of Redmond's athletics career, as he finally admitted defeat following yet another operation. He wasn't finished with the world of sport though, going on to play basketball for the Birmingham Bullets, before launching a career as a motivational speaker. No-one could wish for a better example of pure determination than that semi final.

4th August 2012
Super Saturday

Despite the smart money being on Paris to host the 2012 Olympics, the Games had come to London. The tone had been set by a breath-taking opening ceremony; now it was down to the athletes to do their bit. Set a challenging target of 48 medals, one more than they had achieved four years before in Beijing, Team GB had got off to a good start, topping the podium eight times already in rowing, cycling, shooting and canoeing.

It was the middle Saturday of the Games that would live in the memories of British sports fans forever though. The first action of the day was in the rowing at Eton Dorney, where British athletes had already delivered gold medals in the women's pairs and women's double sculls. The men's four of Andy Triggs Hodge, Pete Reed, Andy Gregory and Tom James made a powerful start to the final, gaining a psychological advantage over their main rivals Australia by leading them at 500m. The Aussies had beaten them in the last World Cup, and they refused to let the Brits get away from them, staying less than a length behind going into the final 500m. The crowd gave the British four a life though, and they put in one final effort, slowly pulling away to put clear water between the crews to win by a length.

Less than half an hour later there was more British gold on the water. Women's lightweight double sculls pair of Sophie Hosking and Katherine Copeland faced stiff competition from World Champions Greece and an in-form Chinese pair, and it was the Greeks who made the quickest start to lead at 500m, with China in second and Britain third. Hosking and Copeland made progress through the next 500m though, and were up to second at half way. It was in the second half of the race that they made their move, and they upped their strokes to pull clear of the field, a move that was to prove decisive. The Greeks couldn't respond, and although China did their best to close them down it was too late. The British pair, who had only started rowing together earlier in the season, had claimed a remarkable victory.

Next it was off to the velodrome for Laura Trott, Dani King and Jo Rowsell's team pursuit final. Hot favourites for the title after breaking the world record in the first round, the British team faced the USA in the final. Led out by Rowsell the team got off to a powerful start and the result never really looked in any doubt. Their lead grew and grew, much to the delight of the crowd, and they pulled away from the Americans over the 12 laps to win by five seconds, taking another half a second off their own world record time in the process.

The evening's action was on the track, with Jessica Ennis leading the way in the heptathlon. Ennis had come into the final day with a comfortable lead of 184 points, having set personal bests in the 100m hurdles and high jump, 309 points ahead of then World Champion Tatyana Chernova (although she was later stripped of her title for doping, with the gold being given to Ennis). Chernova's strongest events were to come though, and Ennis would have to be on her game to hold off her rival, and she was up to the challenge, starting the day with a fine long jump of 6m 48 to respond to Chernova's 6m 54. Next came the javelin, an event that had caused her problems in the past, but she reeled off another personal best to take a lead of 258 points into the final event, the 800m, with Chernova's challenge fading. All she needed to do for the gold was to stay close to her rivals, but that was never going to be enough for the Games' poster girl, and she stormed through to finish first and secure gold to a rapturous ovation.

Moments later the crowd was on its feet again. Greg Rutherford was by no means the clear favourite for the long jump, and it was his compatriot Chris Tomlinson who led after the first round. Rutherford put in a leap of 8m 21 in the second round to take the lead though, and improved further in the fourth with a distance of 8m 31. With two rounds to go jumper after jumper tried in vain to match Rutherford's jump, but try as they might no-one managed to, leaving him and the crowd to celebrate a second British gold of the night.

There was yet more for the 80,000 crowd to cheer, with Mo Farah going in the 10,000m final, and he didn't disappoint. Farah was content to sit in the pack for most of the first 5,000m, well-placed to cover any potential attacks, and when they began, first from Zersenay Tadese then from Moses Masai he made sure they didn't get away. Running side-by-side with Kenenisa Bekele of Etheopia, who had won gold at the previous two Olympics, Farah bided his time as the pack thinned out and he slowly moved up to third. The crowd roared as Farah took his turn to push the pace, and at the bell he kicked hard, quickly putting distance between himself and the rest of the field. He was a metre clear coming into the final straight, and still had another gear to move up into as he accelerated clear to cross the line with his arms aloft to deafening cheers, before treating the crowd to his trademark "Mobot" celebration.

It was an amazing end to an incredible day – six gold medals making it Great Britain's most successful Olympic day for 104 years. Mark Hunter and Zac Purchase had also won a silver medal earlier in the day in the men's lightweight double sculls, adding to a medal haul that saw Team GB finish third in the medal table behind USA and China, with 29 gold, 17 silver and 19 bronze medals. Their performance was in stark contrast to the 1996 Atlanta Games, where the team had won just one gold medal and only 15 in total. A month later they also finished third in the Paralympic medal table, behind China and Russia, to cap a stunning summer of British sport.

7th August 2005
England beat Australia by 2 runs

Having suffered a disappointing heavy defeat to Australia in the first test at Lords, England were desperate to level the series as the two teams headed to Edgbaston for the second test.

England were bidding to win back the Ashes for the first time since 1985, a period of 20 years when they had been regularly humiliated by the dominance of a Aussie side featuring greats such as Allan Border, Merv Hughes, Mark and Steve Waugh, Glenn McGrath and Shane Warne. Now though England were going into the series on the back of six consecutive series wins, and there was a belief amongst English cricket fans that their team could actually do it this time. Their hopes had taken a knock at Lords though, and England badly needed to get back on level terms if they were to succeed. Perhaps the fact that the Aussies would be without McGrath, who stood on a ball whilst warming up before the match and injured his ankle, would give England the edge.

England had posted a decent total in their first innings after surprisingly being put in by Ricky Ponting - all out for 407 with Marcus Trescothick top-scoring with 90 having put on 112 for the first wicket with Andrew Strauss. Andrew Flintoff and Ashley Giles then took 3 Australian wickets each as the tourists replied with 308 to give England a useful first innings lead of 99. England were looking to build a match-winning lead in their second innings, but their top order batting faltered, and Warne took 6 for 46 to skittle them out for 182, Flintoff making the score respectable with 73. That set Australia a challenging but gettable 282 to win and take a commanding 2-0 series lead.

The run chase started badly for the tourists, with wickets falling steadily, including Ponting for a duck. Flintoff took three wickets and Australia finished the day on 175 for 8. Surely England were heading for victory.

As the two sides took the field on the fourth day no-one could have predicted the drama that lay ahead. With Australia still needing 107 more for victory with just 2 wickets remaining, and England's pace attack quartet of Flintoff, Steve Harmison, Matthew Hoggard and Simon Jones in fine form, it looked as though they should have the game comfortably wrapped up by lunchtime, but the Aussies had other ideas. England's nemesis Warne was never one to give up without a fight, and he started to play some shots to chip away at the total before he was dismissed by Flintoff for 42. He had put on 45 in just 9 owners for the 9th wicket with Brett Lee, who was joined at the crease by last man Michael Kasprowicz still needing 62 to win.

Lee and Kasprowicz played cautiously but were picking up runs, slowly hauling themselves closer and closer to the target despite suffering body blows during an aggressive spell by Flintoff. As they closed in on an unlikely victory their confidence started to grow, and they started adding boundaries to the ones and twos, spinner Ashley Giles in particular coming in for some stick.

Both batsmen had played and missed a couple of times, and a few edges had flown clear of the fielders' despairing fingertips, and it started to look as if it could be Australia's day. With Australia just 15 runs short of their target England produced a chance though, as Kasprovicz skied a ball from Flintoff, but Jones was unable to take a difficult catch at third man. Would that be England's last chance gone?

The tension in the ground was almost unbearable as Australia moved to within a boundary of victory. Then, in ran the ever-willing Harmison, who bowled a short ball to Kasprovicz. The tail-ender sensed a chance to win the game and tried to pull the ball, but was hit on the glove and the ball flew through to wicket-keeper Geraint Jones who took the catch. The players and the crowd screamed to umpire Billy Bowden, whose finger went up after what seemed like an eternity. England had won by 2 runs, the narrowest margin in Ashes history.

It was a brave effort by Lee, who finished 43 not out, and Kasprovicz, who made 20. The two had put on 59 for the last wicket, but as man of the match Flintoff consoled the distraught Lee in an admirable sporting gesture and Edgbaston let out a huge sigh of relief and celebrated, television replays showed that the wicket should not actually have been given, as the batsman's hand had not been on the bat when the ball struck it.

It was a decision that may have changed the outcome of the whole series, as England went on to win again at Trent Bridge and draw at Old Trafford and The Oval to win the Ashes 2-1, with a jubilant nation rewarding the team with MBEs and an OBE for captain Michael Vaughan for their efforts.

England's joy was short-lived however, as Australia reclaimed the Ashes urn with a comprehensive 5-0 victory in the next series in Australia the following year. England bounced back with three series wins in a row, before suffering another whitewash in Australia in 2013-14, only to regain them on home turf in 2015.

9th August 1936
Jesse Owens wins four Olympic golds

The 1936 Olympics in Berlin were, in the opinion of German leader Adolf Hitler, an opportunity to promote Nazi ideals, to show the world how the Aryan race was superior and just how inferior races such as Africans really were. As offensive as this was to many, the Games had been awarded to Berlin in 1931, two years before the Nazis had come to power, and although it was debated whether the Games should be moved elsewhere when Hitler declared that Jews should not be allowed to compete at all, when he backtracked they went ahead as planned.

Part of the US team was Jesse Owens, a young black American who had set the world of athletics alight the previous year when he had set three world records and equalled a fourth within the space of forty five minutes. Despite being the antithesis of Nazi ideology, he received a hero's welcome from many when he arrived in Germany, with crowds of fans shouting his name and trying to touch him as he tried to get off the train. He was also visited by the founder of German sportswear company Adidas in the athletes' village, signing a sponsorship deal, possibly the first ever for an African-American.

Owens was entered into three individual events, the 100 metres, 200 metres and long jump, and was also due to be part of the 4x100 metre relay team. His first chance of gold in front of the 110,000 strong crowd came in the 100 metres, and he made an immediate impact in his heat as he won in an Olympic record time of 10. 3 seconds. He bettered his time by 0.1 seconds in the second round, and cruised through his semi final into the final, where he again ran 10.3 to claim the gold ahead of compatriot Ralph Metcalfe, also an African-American.

It was reported at the time that Hitler, in his fury that a black athlete had won, refused to congratulate Owens in the way that he had for all successful white athletes. Reports since have painted a slightly different picture however. It seems that he had been shaking hands with German athletes who had won but nobody else, until Olympic officials demanded that he shake everyone's hand or nobody at all and he chose the latter. His failure the shake Owens' hand was therefore not a personal snub, and accounts emerged years later that suggested that the two had exchanged a wave whilst Owens was on his way to an interview, and that he had shaken his hand in private. Owens himself also made the point that he was at least allowed to stay in the same hotel as white athletes whilst in Germany, something he was still unable to do in many parts of the USA at that time.

There was another Olympic record as Owens won his first round heat of the 200 metres before the qualifying round for the long jump, where he was set to do battle with German favourite Luz Long. An error led to a no-jump in the first round, as he ran through into the pit whilst still checking his run-up, allowed in US competitions but not in Europe. He overstepped marginally in the second round, putting pressure on his final jump. The story since is that Owens was helped with his run-up by Long before his attempt, but this is probably an embellishment. With or without assistance, he played it safe and took off a foot before the board but still qualified comfortably.

He went from the long jump pit to the second round of the 200 metres, where he matched his first round time of 21.1 seconds, before returning for the long jump final.

Owens led Long by 20cm after the first round. Long equalled Owens' mark in the second round, only to see the American increase his distance by 13cm. Long closed the gap in the third round to just 3cm, but was unable to take advantage of an Owens foul in the fourth. Both improved with their fifth round jumps, giving Owens a lead of 7cm with one jump each to go. Long fouled as he strained to find the winning jump, leaving Owens to break the Olympic record with his final leap of 8m 6cm as he claimed his second gold medal. Long congratulated his rival and the pair left the stadium together, meeting up later to swap stories as they forged an unlikely friendship.

Fellow American Mack Robinson had matched Owens' 21.1 seconds in the 200 metres semi final, slightly quicker than Owens' semi final time, but normal service was resumed in the final as Owens finished in a World Record time of 20.7 seconds, with Robinson taking silver 0.4 seconds behind him.

With three golds under his belt that just left the 4x100 metre relay, and controversy again raised its head with the US selectors changing their minds about picking Jewish athletes Marty Glickman and Sam Stoller, replacing them with Owens and Metcalfe. It was an understandable decision to pick the individual gold and silver medallists, but with the backdrop of anti-Semitic propaganda in Nazi Germany at the time, questions were asked. Alongside Foy Draper and Frank Wycoff they equalled the World Record of 40 seconds in their heat, then took 0.2 seconds off it as they stormed to victory in the final.

Owens had done it. He had won four Olympic gold medals in the space of a few days, a feat not repeated on the track until 1984 when another American, Carl Lewis, achieved it. He tried to cash in on his fame after the games, but was then deemed to be a professional, and was unable to compete in a major competition again.

9th August 1984
Daley Thompson wins second Olympic decathlon gold

Daley Thompson had won the decathlon at the 1980 Moscow Olympics, but in the absence of world record holder and 1976 silver medallist Guido Kratschmer due to West Germany's boycott of the games there were some who cast doubt on his achievement. He was determined to do it again in Los Angeles in 1984 to prove beyond all doubt that he was the greatest all round athlete in the world.

Thompson had continued to win titles after his 1980 win. By 1984 he was the reigning Olympic, World, European and Commonwealth champion, and was unbeaten in six years, but he had been battling with another West German, Jurgen Hingsen, for the world record. In May 1982 Thompson had broken the record, only for Hingsen to break it in August. Thompson claimed it back whilst winning the European title in Athens one month later, beating Hingsen into second, but the German had improved his best twice in 1983 and early 1984 to go into the Olympics as the world record holder.

It was one of the great rivalries of the 1980s, and the world looked forward to a titanic battle between the two, with Kratschmer back and another good West German, Siggi Wentz, expected the challenge as well. The first event in the baking hot and smoggy LA Coliseum was the 100m, and Thompson set down a marker right from the start, sprinting clear of Hingsen and Kratschmer to win in a personal best time of 10.44 seconds, almost half a second ahead of Hingsen. That gave him a lead of 122 points over his rival to take into the long jump. One of Thompson's best events, he improved over each of his three jumps to post 8.01 metres, another personal best and 21cm further than Hingsen managed. With two personal bests in the opening two events and his lead now up to 164 points it was clear that Thompson was a man on a mission.

However, at six foot seven Hingsen's height gave him an advantage over the six foot Thompson in some of the events still to come, so there was no question that Thompson was going to run away with it. The German disappointed in event three though, the shot put, with his 15.87 metres well down on his personal best. Thompson, in contrast, achieved his third PB of the day, and despite losing some ground to his rival with a throw of 15.72, he was more than happy with the state of play.

Hingsen again used his height advantage to gain more ground on the leader in the high jump, clearing 2.12 metres to Thompson's 2.03, cutting the Englishman's lead by a further 77 points. Thompson ended the day on top though, posting a time of 46.97 seconds in the 400 metres, three-quarters of a second ahead of the German, to end the first day 114 points ahead.

With ground to make up if he was going to catch Thompson, Hingsen started day two with two events that suited him, the 110 metre hurdles and the discus, and he took the opportunity to chip away at the lead. Thompson made the faster start in the hurdles, but Hingsen caught him before the mid point. Thompson refused to let the German get away from him though, and although Hingsen finished ahead of him, the gap between them was only 0.05 seconds. Hingsen had only taken six points out of his lead.

The pressure was on Thompson in the discus though. Hingsen posted a personal best of 49.8 metres in the first round, and Thompson struggled to respond. His first effort was only 37.9 metres, and he was in danger of conceding considerable ground. Hingsen improved to 50.82 with his second throw, and Thompson could only add a couple of centimetres to his distance. Hingsen's third throw was no better than his second, meaning that Thompson had one more throw to limit the damage. As it stood Hingsen was set to move into the lead. It was a crucial point in the battle, but Thompson was up for the challenge. He hurled the discus out from the circle. "It's a better one, it's a better one, it's a better one!" exclaimed commentator Ron Pickering, and he was right. The distance was 46.56, still short of Hingsen but a personal best, and it meant that he still held the lead, although now only by 34 points.

With three events to go time was running out for Hingsen. Next up was the pole vault, but Hingsen was feeling unwell, which hampered his chances of putting the pressure on Thompson. The German could only manage a disappointing 4.50 metres, leaving Thompson to edge his lead bigger and bigger as he cleared 5.00 metres. The Brit's lead was back up to 152 points, and it would be tough for Hingsen to close him down now.

Hingsen needed to make up ground in the javelin to put himself into contention in the final event, but it wasn't to be. Thompson threw 65.24 metres, and Hingsen could only manage 60.44. That gave him an almost unassailable lead, and the 1,500 metres was really just a formality. Knowing the size of his lead, Thompson didn't push himself, and he finished well down on Hingsen in a time of 4.35 minutes, eleven seconds slower than his personal best. If he had pushed himself he would have smashed Hingsen's world record, but instead he finished just one point behind the German's tally, scant consolation for the man who had to settle for the silver medal, 124 points behind. Wentz took the bronze with Kratschmer in fourth, ending any doubts that Thompson was a worthy champion.

There was a controversial end to the event for Thompson, who attracted some criticism as he grinned and whistled along to the national anthem as he was awarded his gold medal. He went on to wear a controversial t-shirt in his press conference and joked about the conversation he had had with Princess Anne as she congratulated him on his success, tarnishing the reports of his achievement in the press.

His time for the 110 metre hurdles was later rounded down, giving him one extra point to match Hingsen's best and a share of the world record. He went on to win further golds in the 1986 Commonwealth and European Championships, beating Hingsen and Wentz into silver and bronze again, but was unable to achieve his ambition of three Olympic gold medals as injury disrupted his preparations for Seoul in 1988 and he could only finish fourth.

10th August 1984
Zola Budd v Mary Decker

Middle distance runner Zola Budd was already a controversial figure before the 1984 Olympics in Los Angeles. Born and raised in South Africa, her world best 5,000 metre time, set in early 1984 at the tender age of seventeen, was not recognised as a world record as South Africa were banned from world athletics due to their policy of apartheid. That meant that the record stayed in the hands of American athlete Mary Decker, and a further, much more memorable contest between the two was yet to come later that year.

Budd's 5,000 metre time meant that she shot to global prominence, and she received countless offers of scholarships from American Universities as well as an offer of Italian citizenship that would enable her to compete against Decker and the world's best. Her father though had British citizenship in mind, due to the fact that his father, Zola's grandfather, was British. He thought that she might be able to compete in the 1988 Olympics, as the process could take up to two years, but The Daily Mail found out about their intentions and set about trying to make it happen much more quickly. They flew the Budd family to Britain, giving them a house and £100,000 cash, then started lobbying Margaret Thatcher's government to fast-track the application. The idea split the Cabinet, as being seen to be breaking the South African boycott was extremely controversial, but ten days after the application was submitted, Budd had her British passport.

A few months later she won the 3,000 metres at the British trials and was selected for the team for Los Angeles. Protesters regularly camped outside her house however, and on one occasion she was jeered as the crossed the finish line of a race. Also on the British team was Wendy Sly, who had finished fifth in the event at the World Championships the previous year but whose place on the team had been completely overshadowed by her new team-mate and who had spoken out against allowing Budd to compete for Britain.

Another contender who was receiving little attention during the lead-up to the Games was Romanian Maricica Puica, despite the fact that she had run the fastest time of the year. Instead the event was being billed as a contest between Budd and Decker, the American having set six world records in 1982 before becoming 1,500 and 3,000 metres World Champion the following year. Budd's coach tried to play her chances down, but still all eyes were on her in her heat. She qualified comfortably, but was beaten by Puica, who broke the Olympic record in the process that Decker had set minutes before in winning her heat.

Decker showed clear intent to win the final from the front, taking the lead from the gun. Budd made a steadier start but had moved through onto Decker's shoulder by the end of the first lap. Sly and Puica settled in just behind them, and the four remained in those positions for the next three laps. At the start of the fourth lap Budd decided to make a move, edging ahead of Decker, the two sharing the inside lanc with Decker on the inside, slightly behind Budd.

Running barefoot, as she always preferred to do, Budd had a slightly ungainly running style, with her elbows wide, and with the two running so closely together some sort of collision was inevitable. Their first coming together happened shortly after the half way point, Decker catching one of Budd's legs, causing both to check their stride. The next contact, just a few strides further on, was more significant though, with Budd's foot catching Decker's thigh, causing Budd to stumble. As she tried to regain her balance her left leg went out to the side, and Decker tripped over it, crashing to the ground to the inside of the track. Puica and Sly saw their chance and pressed on, leaving Decker writhing on the floor in agony, physical, mental or both. Budd had suffered a badly spiked ankle in the clash, but was able to carry on and quickly made up the ground to Puica and Sly.

Shortly afterwards she retook the lead, and was booed by the crowd, angry that their home favourite was out of the race. It looked as though the medals would be decided between the three, but at the bell Budd fell away, leaving Puica to attack down the back straight and power away from Sly, winning the gold by twenty metres. Sly was jubilant with her silver medal, no doubt feeling vindicated as her rival trailed in in seventh place. As Decker was helped away from the track in tears by her husband, British discus thrower Richard Slaney, Puica started her lap of honour, for some reason taking her shoes off along the way. One bare footed athlete was celebrating whilst another was wondering what the future would hold for her.

Budd was temporarily disqualified, before she was reinstated on the grounds that she had done nothing wrong and it was simply an accident. Decker was still convinced that it was Budd's fault, although others, including Puica, blamed Decker for the incident, and the American did soften her stance on the debate years later. Budd later claimed that her final lap slowdown had been intentional, and that she couldn't face standing on the rostrum and facing the boos that would inevitably have greeted her.

She still faced a hostile reception back in Britain, and even received death threats. After a brief spell back in South Africa she returned to compete for Great

Britain, winning World Cross Country titles and breaking the 5,000 metre world record again, this time her time being recognised, but her hopes of competing in Seoul were dashed when she was banned for attending a race in South Africa, even though she had not competed. She did compete in the 1992 Olympics in Barcelona, for South Africa, as their international ban had ended, but she failed to make the final.

11th August 1984
Carl Lewis wins four Olympic gold medals

At the 1938 Berlin Olympics Jesse Owens had completed the incredible feat of winning four gold medals, in the 100 metres, 200 metres, long jump and 4x100 metre relay. In 1984, in Los Angeles, fellow American Carl Lewis was considered to be in with a great chance of emulating Owens.

Lewis had missed the 1980 Moscow Games due to the US boycott, but in the meantime had established himself as one of the stars of world athletics, winning gold in the 100 metres, long jump and relay at the inaugural World Championships in Helsinki in 1983. By the time the Los Angeles Games began he was ranked number one in the world in the 100 metres and long jump, and he was all set to match Owens' achievement and become the hero of the Games.

His first event was the 100 metres, and he qualified for the final comfortably, winning all three rounds with times of 10.32 seconds, 10.04 and 10.14. He saved his best time for the final though, breaking the ten second barrier to win his first gold medal in a time of 9.99 seconds, 0.2 seconds ahead of countryman Sam Graddy, with Canada's Ben Johnson in third. His victory wasn't greeted with quite the warmth he might have expected however. He had already been criticised for his decision not to stay with the other competitors in the athlete's village, and some felt that his celebrations were over the top and choreographed as he took a lap of honour with a giant American flag.

His relationship with the American public soured further during the long jump. The media had built up the competition as a chance for Lewis to break Bob Beamon's long standing world record, and the crowd in the stadium and the audience at home eagerly anticipated a possible moment of history. His opening was jump was long, and he led the competition easily with a distance of 8 metres 54. This was still well short of Beamon's 8 metres 90, and he fouled on his second attempt. With none of his competitors coming close to his mark though, and the semi final and final of the 200 metres plus the relay still to come, Lewis was reluctant to waste energy or risk a possible injury, and he passed his remaining four jumps. He had won his second gold medal by 30 centimetres with just one legal jump, a tremendous achievement, but the crowd, feeling short-changed by his failure to attempt to break the record, started booing. It was a common approach in long jump events, and he had done the same in winning the world title the previous year, but that didn't prevent the anger of the crowd.

Having won his first and second round heats of the 200 metres prior to the long jump final, he was back on the track for the 200 metre semi final. He won that race as well, before leading home an American clean sweep in the final, winning in an Olympic Record time of 19.80 seconds, with Kirk Baptiste and Thomas Jefferson taking silver and bronze behind him.

Having won five out of six individual sprint medals, the US team was the clear favourite for gold in the 4x100 metre relay. Such was their strength in depth that they could afford to include two sprinters who hadn't won individual medals, but it didn't slow them down one bit. Graddy gave them the lead on the first leg, passing on to Ron Brown who extended their lead. He passed the baton to Calvin Smith who put in a blistering bend to hand over to Lewis with a clear lead. Lewis streaked away from the field and crossed the line in a World Record time of 37.83 seconds. Finally he had helped to deliver a World Record for the crowd.

On a personal level Lewis had achieved his goal – to win four gold medals – but he still hadn't become the megastar that you would have expected him to. He failed to attract any of the big endorsement deals that other big American sports stars were landing, probably due in part to the public perception of him following his 100 metres and long jump wins and also to rumours regarding his sexuality that were circulating. Furthermore, Nike and Coca-Cola actually ended their association with him following the Games. An attempt to make it as a pop star failed, and rumours of a failed drugs test in the lead up to the 1988 Olympics kept potential sponsors away from him.

He kept on winning on the track though, with three more World Championship golds in Rome in 1987, two in the Seoul Olympics in '88, including the 100 metres after Ben Johnson was disqualified for failing a drug test, two at the Tokyo World Championships in '91 and two at the Barcelona Olympics in '92. In 1996 the Olympics returned to the USA, to Atlanta, and it proved to be Lewis' swansong, as he found form to win his ninth and final Olympic gold medal in the long jump. This time he received a standing ovation from the American crowd, a fitting end to the career of one of America's greatest ever, but one of its most contentious, athletes.

14th August 1948
Don Bradman misses out on test average of 100

Going into his last ever test match, Australian cricketing legend Don Bradman had the chance to achieve the unthinkable – to end his career with a test average of over 100.

Bradman had tormented bowlers, especially English ones, throughout his career, and had amassed an incredible number of runs in test matches by the time he faced England in the Ashes series of 1948. Folklore tells of how as a boy he spent hours practicing his batting with a stump for a bat and a golf ball, honing his skills and developing unparalleled hand/eye coordination. The effort was worth it, and at the age of twenty he became the youngest man ever to score a test century, against England, in just his second test match.

He continued to enjoy batting against England, scoring nineteen of his twenty nine centuries against them. The exception was England's tour of Australia in 1932-33 – the infamous Bodyline series. Bradman had scored heavily in England in 1930, posting scores of 131, 254, 334 and 232 and averaging 98 as his side unexpectedly won the series 2-1. England devised a tactic known as leg-theory, later bodyline, to try to stop him scoring, where the fast bowlers delivered quick, rising deliveries into the batsman's body. It was dangerous – the Aussie batsmen received many painful blows – but also effective, and it succeeded in blunting the Bradman threat. He still managed to average 56 for the series, disappointing by his high standards though, and scored just one century as England won the series 4-1.

Australia and Bradman bounced back from that defeat to win the next two series however, with their star batsman making four more big centuries in the process, posting 304, 244, 270 and 169. In the process he became the first man to score two test match triple centuries, both of which had been against England.

Another double century followed in the 1938 series, which was drawn, along with three other triple figure scores, then he scored a further two tons after the war in 1946 as Australia won the Ashes yet again.

It was therefore something of a relief when Bradman announced that he would be retiring from international cricket at the end of the 1948 tour, but he hadn't finished tormenting England yet. He scored his eighteenth century against them as his side won the first test by eight wickets, and they followed that with a 409 run victory in the second test. England did manage to draw the third test, but

Bradman's nineteenth Ashes century in the fourth test anchored a record run chase of 404, giving them an unassailable 3-0 series lead.

With the Ashes decided, that just left the final test, at The Oval, which would be Bradman's last ever test match. He needed to score just four runs in the first innings to keep his batting average above the magic 100 mark, a seemingly simple task for a man who had already scored more than 500 runs in the series at an average of 84.

He would have to wait for his chance though, as England captain Norman Yardley won the toss and chose to bat. It was a bad decision, on a wet pitch that helped the Australian bowlers, and England were all out for only 52, with only opener Len Hutton reaching double figures before he was out for 30, Ray Lindwall taking his wicket to claim his sixth of the innings for just 20 runs.

In contrast Australia looked completely untroubled, openers Sid Barnes and Arthur Morris passing England's total and taking the tourists' total to 117 before Barnes was caught behind off the bowling of Eric Hollies for 65. Leg spinner Hollies had been recalled to the side following an impressive performance for his county Warwickshire against the tourists, where he had taken eight first innings wickets, including taking the prize one of Bradman. The two now faced each other again as Bradman was the next man in.

He was given a standing ovation and three cheers by the crowd and the England fielders as he walked out to the crease, and everyone expected to see one final display of sublime batting. He defended his first ball from Hollies, but the next was a googly that snuck between bat and pad and into the stumps. Unbelievably he was out for a duck. A stunned silence descended on the stadium, before another round of applause accompanied him back into the pavilion. Some speculated that emotion of the occasion had brought a tear to the great man's eye, preventing him from seeing the flight of the ball, but Bradman himself denied that, sportingly giving Hollies credit for delivering a great ball.

Despite Bradman's failure to score, Australia were 152 for 2 at the end of the day, and they piled on the runs the next day thanks to Morris, who made 196, finally being dismissed for 389, with Hollies claiming 5 for 131. With a first innings lead of 337, Bradman was in the unusual position now of needing England to post a big second innings score in order to require him to bat again and hopefully take his average back over 100.

England looked like they might well do him a favour, reaching 54 for 1 by the close and 121 for 2 at lunch on the third day, but once the top four had been dismissed the middle and lower orders collapsed, and they were facing an innings defeat on 178 for 7 when the rain came to their rescue and brought the day's play to a halt. Bill Johnston quickly wrapped up the innings the following morning with the rain gone, and Australia had won the match by an innings and 149 runs. More importantly, Bradman would not bat again in a test match, and his average ended on 99.94, incredible, but just shy of three figures. The crowd sang "For he's a jolly good fellow" in his honour as they marked the end of an amazing career.

The Aussies won their remaining county matches to end the tour unbeaten, earning themselves the title "The Invincibles". No-one has come close to matching Bradman's achievements, with the next highest test average thirty runs lower, by South Africa's Graeme Pollock. Even other cricketing legends such as Garry Sobers, Sachin Tendulkar and Brian Lara failed to challenge his record, ending with averages of 57, 53 and 52 respectively, putting into context just how good Bradman actually was.

16th August 2008
Usain Bolt breaks world record whilst slowing down

The men's 100 metres final, for so long the blue riband event of the Olympic Games, was in danger of losing the public's respect. Ben Johnson had infamously brought the event into disrepute with his disqualification for failing a drug test after initially claiming the gold medal in Seoul in 1988, but Carl Lewis, Linford Christie, Maurice Greene and Justin Gatlin, all the winners bar one between 1984 and 2004, had been tainted by drugs in one way or another. Only 1996 gold medallist Donovan Bailey was beyond suspicion. Olympic sprinting badly needed a hero.

There was little in his early career to suggest that Jamaica's Usain Bolt would be that man. A leg injury in his first Olympics in Athens in 2004 hampered his performance and he went out in the first round of the 200 metres, his only event that year. He reached the final of the event in the Helsinki World Championships the following year, but an injury in the final saw him finish last. However, World Championship silvers in 2005 in the 200 metres and 4x100 metre relay gave a glimpse of his potential, and when he broke the 100 metre world record in May 2008 with a time of 9.72 seconds the world woke up to the fact that he was a real contender for the Olympic gold.

With defending champion Gatlin serving a ban for failing a drug test in 2006, the new world record holder was the clear favourite, but he posted only the fifth fastest time of the first round, running well within himself to win his heat in 10.20 seconds. He was more dominant in the second round, finishing in 9.92 seconds, the fastest time of the round. He improved his time slightly in the semi final, finishing in 9.85 seconds, 0.06 faster than fellow Jamaican Asafa Powell, the winner of the other semi.

It looked like the final would be a showdown between Powell, the former world record holder and Commonwealth Games champion, and the current world record holder Bolt. Powell's chance to beat Bolt lay at the start, where the favourite, at six foot five, traditionally struggled. He did indeed make the better start, with the third fastest reaction time compared with Bolt who was the second slowest, but Bolt's pick-up was far better, and by half way his long strides had propelled him into the lead whilst Powell had slipped back to fourth. Over the next twenty metres he powered clear of the pack to streak two metres clear of his rivals. Looking round, he knew the gold medal was his, and he started to celebrate with more than ten metres left. It was a stunning performance, and then he saw his time – 9.69

seconds, a new world record. He introduced the world to his trademark "lightning bolt" pose before hugging some Jamaican fans in the crowd and collecting a flag for his lap of honour.

It was disappointment for Powell, who never got going and finished back in fifth, with Trinidad and Tobago's Richard Thompson claiming the silver and American Walter Dix the bronze. Some criticised him for showboating, but Bolt himself said he was just happy to have won his first senior gold medal.

He wasn't finished there either. Four days later he was back in the Bird's Nest stadium bidding for his second gold medal in the 200 metres, and again he blew the opposition away. This time there was no slowing down, and he won in a time of 19.30 seconds to break Michael Johnson's world record. He was soon on top of the podium for the third time, winning gold in the 4x100 metres along with teammates Nesta Carter, Michael Frater and Asafa Powell. Yet again it was a world record time.

Scientists later estimated that Bolt could have clocked a time of 9.55 seconds if he hadn't slowed down in the 100 metre final in Beijing, and he almost did run that time the following year at the 2009 World Championships in Berlin, winning gold in a time of 9.58. Not content with taking more than a tenth of a second of the 100 metre world record, he again followed up with gold and a world record in the 200 metres, as well as the biggest winning margin ever in the World Championships, and once more the Jamaican team won gold in the relay. It was just the start of a domination that carried on throughout the next Olympics and the next two World Championships, where Bolt incredibly won eleven of the twelve sprint gold medals up for grabs, the only blemish being in the 100 metres in Daegu in 2011, when a false start saw him disqualified in the World Championship final.

With the only stories of his training methods emerging revolving around his considerable consumption of chicken nuggets rather than anabolic steroids, he continued to be seen as the saviour of sprinting, most notably in the 2015 World Championships, again in Beijing. With Gatlin, back from his second suspension for drug use, on a twenty-eight race unbeaten run going into the 100 metre final and Bolt having struggled to find form all season, it looked as though his status as the fastest man on the planet might be under threat. Athletics fans around the world were willing him to pull something out of the bag though, with many outraged that Gatlin was able to compete at all in light of his previous attempts to cheat. Bolt didn't disappoint them, rising to the occasion to beat his American rival by one-hundredth of a second in a thrilling final. Of course, he followed up his victory with further wins in the 200 metres and relay. Bolt had played his role as the saviour of sprinting once again, and he beat Gatlin again in the 2016 Olympics as he became the first man to win three 100 metre gold medals before adding 200 metres and relay golds once again to complete an incredible "triple-triple".

17th August 2008
Michael Phelps wins 8 Olympic golds

It was no surprise that American swimmer Michael Phelps won a glut of gold medals at the 2008 Beijing Olympics. With four golds at the 2003 World Championships, six at the 2004 Olympics, five and seven more at the 2005 and 2007 World Championships respectively, he was almost unbeatable when it came to the big races. He had however set himself an even greater challenge for the 2008 Games – to surpass countryman Mark Spitz's record of seven gold medals at a single Olympic Games, achieved at the 1972 Munich Games.

Phelps had turned to swimming during a difficult childhood. Having found it difficult to concentrate at school he was diagnosed with ADHD, but found the swimming pool a safe haven. His rise to success was a broadcaster's dream, and NBC even managed to pull some strings to ensure that his races at Beijing could be shown at primetime in the USA.

His first success came in the 400 metre individual medley, where he set an Olympic record in the heats before taking almost two seconds off his own world record in the final. The following day he doubled his haul, swimming the first leg of the 4x100 metre freestyle relay, also in a world record time, anchor leg swimmer Jason Lezak making up half a body length to touch eight hundredths of a second ahead of France's Alain Bernard.

The 200 metre freestyle was next, and it was a third gold and a third world record for Phelps, his ninth gold medal in total, making him the joint most successful Olympian of all time alongside Spitz, Carl Lewis, Larisa Latynina and Paavo Nurmi. It took him just one more day to become the sole holder of that record with ten golds, another world record in the 200 metre butterfly providing his fourth victory of the Games, despite his goggles filling up with water half way through the race, and a fifth followed an hour later in the 4x200 metre freestyle relay. Once again the quartet set a new world record in the process.

With heats but no final the next day, Phelps had to wait a couple of days to top the rostrum again, but he duly did for a sixth time, winning the 200 metre individual medley by two seconds, yet again setting a new world record.

One gold medal short of Spitz's record, his seventh gold medal chance, the 100 metre butterfly, was to prove the closest and most controversial. Phelps' main rival for gold was Serbia's Milorad Cavic, who beat Phelps in the heats in a new Olympic record time. They avoided each other in the semi final, both men winning their race but with Cavic's time slightly faster than Phelps', although Phelps may have been disadvantaged by the fact that he had only just made it to the start in time following the medal ceremony from his 200 metre individual medley win. Cavic was quoted as saying that he would like to be the man who denied Phelps the chance to win eight golds, and that it would be good if Phelps lost. If Phelps needed any further motivation, this certainly provided it, but maybe Cavic had got to him as the American made an uncharacteristically slow start to the race and was back in fourth at the turn, with Cavic in the lead.

Phelps did his utmost to catch the Serb, and was dragging himself closer and closer with every stroke in a thrilling finish as they neared the wall, but it looked as though Cavic would hold on. Right at the death, having trailed throughout the race and with his record at stake, Phelps got the touch one hundredth of a second ahead of Cavic to win his seventh gold of the Games. There was no world record this time, just an Olympic record, but that didn't matter to the jubilant but relieved Phelps.

It didn't end there though, as the Serbians, having studied the video replays, mounted a complaint about the result. Whilst FINA (the International Swimming Federation) reviewed the result, the fact that the official images of the finish were not immediately released to the public, plus Phelps being sponsored by official timer Omega, led to some suspicions about the result. His victory was confirmed however, meaning that Phelps now shared the record for the most gold medals in an Olympic Games with Spitz. Cavic, despite his bullishness before the race, was magnanimous in defeat, saying "There's nothing wrong with losing to the greatest swimmer there has ever been."

Phelps needed one more gold medal to be confirmed with that title however, and that meant he and his team-mates winning the 4x100 metre medley relay. Phelps had been rested for the heats but the Americans had booked their place in the final as the fastest qualifiers anyway, and he took his place for the final, swimming the third butterfly leg. Aaron Peirsol gave the USA the lead after the first leg, but Brendan Hansen was overhauled by Japan's Kosuke Kitajima on the second leg, threatening a major shock. When Phelps took off he was 0.21 seconds down, but he again showed his class and he handed over to Jason Lezak 0.26 seconds in front. Lezak wasn't going to be caught, and he saw the team home for Phelps' record-breaking eighth gold medal in yet another world record time. With pandemonium inside the National Aquatics Centre, Phelps found his mother in the crowd and went to her to celebrate his astonishing achievement of eight gold medals and seven world records.

He didn't stop there either. Nine more gold medals followed at the next two World Championships, plus four more at the London 2012 Olympics, taking his total up to an incredible eighteen. He announced his retirement at the end of the 2012 Games, and hit the headlines for the wrong reasons, not for the first time, in 2014 when he was arrested for drink-driving. His subsequent suspension from the US swimming team hampered his intended comeback and meant that he missed the 2015 World Championships, but he did win three golds at the US National Championships instead. In 2016 he competed in his fourth Olympics, in Rio de Janeiro, and promptly took his gold medal tally up to 23 before announcing that he was retiring again, this time for good.

31st August 1968
Garry Sobers hits six sixes in one over

The match had begun as a fairly meaningless end of season affair. The home side, Glamorgan, were second in the County Championship but with no hope of catching runaway leaders Yorkshire, and their opponents Nottinghamshire were lying in fifth. Nevertheless, the match produced one of the most memorable few minutes of cricket ever seen.

West Indies captain Garry Sobers, playing for Notts in the first season that overseas players were allowed, won the toss and chose to bat first on the St Helen's pitch in Swansea. Brian Bolus and Bob White had got them off to a fine start, putting on 126 for the first wicket before falling for 140 and 73 respectively. Glamorgan bowler Malcolm Nash took four wickets and Brian Lewis one, bringing Sobers to the crease. Keen to score quick runs so he could declare and have a bowl at Glamorgan before the end of the day, Sobers started to accelerate. Glamorgan captain Tony Lewis threw to ball to Nash to see if he could put the brakes on. Nash was ostensibly a seamer, but had been experimenting with spin bowling, and Lewis asked him to try out some of his left arm spin. It was a plan that definitely didn't work.

Sobers smashed Nash's first ball over the midwicket boundary and out of the ground for six, the ball eventually being returned by a passer-by. The second ball followed the same way, bouncing off the concrete terracing and hitting a nearby house, BBC Wales commentator Wilf Wooller suggesting that "Glamorgan could do with some fielders on that wall over there, some seven footers."

Nash bowled his third delivery at middle stump, but to no avail as Sobers struck it for a straight six over long on and into the members' enclosure. At that point Lewis suggested that Nash returned to his more familiar seamers, but the bowler chose to persevere with spin. He soon regretted his decision, as the fourth ball was too short and was pulled over backward square leg, crashing into the concrete terraces and flying back onto the pitch. With four sixes off the first four balls one of the Glamorgan slips told Sobers "I bet you can't hit the next one for six."

The crowd also sensed what could be on the cards, and started chanting "six, six, six!" Their entertainment almost came to an end on the fifth ball though. Nash pitched it up, but Sobers hit it straight back over the bowler's head. He hadn't timed it right though, and Roger Davis raced back and leapt into the air to take the catch. However, he was too close to the boundary by that point, and he landed over the rope. The umpires consulted for an age as the rules governing that very situation had been changed earlier that season. Davis thought he had taken a fair catch, and Sobers started heading back to the pavilion, but eventually umpire Eddie Phillipson signalled a six, the fifth six in five balls, to the delight of the crowd. The previous season he would have been out, but now, thanks to the rule change, he had five sixes off five balls.

Nash prepared to bowl his sixth ball, with all the fielders being sent to the boundary in an attempt to prevent the inevitable attempt by Sobers to clear the ropes. He now decided to revert to seam, but Sobers guessed that he would bowl a quicker ball, and he stepped back and heaved the ball high into the air. It flew over the midwicket boundary and out of the ground, Wooller exclaiming "And he's done it! He's done it! And my goodness it's gone all the way down to Swansea."

Sobers modestly raised his bat to acknowledge the crowd, then immediately declared with Nottinghamshire's score on 394 and his own 76 not out, almost half of those runs coming in that one over. To add insult to injury he went on to bowl Nash for 8 in Glamorgan's innings, and the home side was all out for 254. Notts then stumbled to 139 for 6 in their second innings before declaring again, Sobers out for 72, setting Glamorgan 280 to win. Glamorgan fell well short though, all out for 113, the win moving Notts up to fourth and helping Sobers to win a bet and a couple of bottles of champagne.

The story didn't end there though. Mystery still surrounds the whereabouts of the ball that was hit around the ground that afternoon. A local boy picked it up from the street outside the ground after the sixth six, and gave it back. It was then presented to Sobers, who put it in his kit-bag and later gave it to the Nottinghamshire Supporters Association. In 2006 a ball purporting to be the Sobers ball was put up for auction and sold for £26,400, but it was a Duke ball, whereas Glamorgan always used Stuart Surridge balls. The ball was put up for auction again in 2013, but was withdrawn due to doubts about its authenticity. The likeliest explanation is that Sobers accidentally took the wrong ball out of his bag, but the whereabouts of the real ball remains unknown.

No one matched Sobers' achievement for another sixteen years, when India's Ravi Shastri managed it. It has only ever been managed a handful of times since. Sobers was knighted and became Sir Garfield Sobers for services to cricket in 1975.

September

1st September 1991
Kris Akabusi clinches GB 4x400m relay gold

Great Britain's men's 4x400m relay team had built a fine tradition in the event during the 80s and 90s, winning gold medals at the European Championships and silver and bronze medals at the Olympic Games and World Championships, but their achievements were eclipsed by the USA, who had won every Olympic and World Championship title since 1984.

At the 1991 World Athletics Championships in Tokyo both teams had comfortably qualified for the final by winning their heats, even managing to rest some of their big guns before the final, GB bringing in the less favoured Ade Mafe and Mark Richardson and USA fielding Jeff Reynolds and Danny Everett. The two teams had posted almost identical times, GB being fractionally quicker, but with personnel changes to come and neither being pushed to the limit in the heats, the US were still firm favourites.

The GB quartet for the final featured individual 400m silver medallist Roger Black and semi-finalist Derek Redmond, but also included non-400m specialists John Regis, a 200m runner, and 400m hurdles bronze medallist Kriss Akabusi. They were up against a US team consisting of individual 400m champion Antonio Pettigrew and bronze medallist Danny Everett, plus finalist Andrew Valmon and Quincy Watts, who would go on to become Olympic champion the following year. It was a formidable team with an intimidating history, and the British boys knew they would have to produce something special if they were to challenge the Americans.

4x400 relay teams usually put their strongest runner on the last leg, but the British team knew that too often in the past the US had built an insurmountable lead by then that the anchor runner had little chance of overhauling. This time, just ten minutes before the race started, they made a brave decision. Black, on paper their fastest runner, would run the first leg, in the hope that GB would be ahead or only just behind going into the final leg, putting pressure on the Americans. It was a gamble that could easily backfire and see them slip out of the medals altogether if it didn't pay off.

When the gun went Black made a strong start from lane three, and at the changeover he was very slightly ahead of Valmon as he handed the baton to Redmond. When the runners broke from their lanes Redmond led the field, with Watts just behind him but making up ground. Watts edged inches ahead in the back straight though and handed over to give Everett a slender lead, despite Redmond's stunning 44 second leg. With the US now ahead it looked as though Britain's gamble had been in vain, and with the individual gold and bronze medallists to come for the Americans, it was difficult to see GB coming back at them.

Regis tucked in behind him though, and refused to let the lead grow. In the last hundred metres of his leg he tried to make up ground, but Everett's superior 400 metre pedigree saw him finish the stronger and he stretched ahead by a couple of metres. When Akabusi took over he was about three metres down on the world champion. Surely the gold medal was heading to the US yet again. Akabusi was patient though, and waited for the right time to launch an attack. He fought his way onto Pettigrew's shoulder coming around the top bend, and with fifty metres to go he kicked, drawing level and then moving ahead of the American. Pettigrew tried to respond, and for a moment it looked as though he would run Akabusi down, but the Brit wasn't to be denied and found something extra from somewhere, keeping himself inches ahead to cross the line first.

As the breathless British quartet celebrated the American team just stood around looking stunned. Pettigrew shook his head in disbelief at what had just happened. It was Great Britain's first gold medal in the event at either the World Championships or Olympics since 1936, and they had smashed the British, European and Commonwealth records with the second fastest time ever of 2 minutes 57.53.

Normal service was resumed the following year at the Barcelona Olympics, where the USA took gold ahead of Cuba, with Great Britain having to settle for bronze. The Americans also won at the 1993 and 1995 World Championships, with Great Britain failing to claim a medal, and the two teams went head to head again in the 1996 Olympics, Anthuan Maybank holding off the challenge of Black to win gold by just over half a second. There was an even closer finish at the 1997 World Championships, with the USA finishing just two tenths ahead of Great Britain, but eleven years later Pettigrew admitted taking performance enhancing drugs and the US team was stripped of its gold medal. The gold was instead awarded to the GB four of Black, Iwan Thomas, Jamie Baulch and Mark Richardson, keeping the fine tradition in the event going.

1st September 2001
Germany 1-5 England

The greatest moment in English football history had come against West Germany, when England had beaten them 4-2 in the World Cup final at Wembley to become World Champions. They had a bit of luck that day, with their third goal given even though it was highly debateable whether the ball had actually crossed the line or not. They had used up their full ration of good fortune that day though, with fate transpiring to prevent them from beating their rivals in a competitive match for another thirty four years.

Their bad run began in the quarter final of the 1970 World Cup, when the defending champions, already playing without the world's best goalkeeper Gordon Banks, who had succumbed to a stomach bug, saw a goal dubiously chalked off for offside and a good penalty appeal turned down as they surrendered a 2-0 lead to lose 3-2 in extra time. A defeat and a draw against them in qualifying for the 1972 European Championships saw England fail to qualify, and a 0-0 draw in the 1982 World Cup second stage was enough for West Germany to progress at England's expense. In the 1990 World Cup the teams met in the semi final, West Germany reaching the final on penalties, and exactly the same thing happened in the semis of Euro '96. England had beaten the unified German team 1-0 in the 2000 European Championship, but the result was effectively irrelevant as both teams failed to progress from their group.

The two nations were drawn together to seek qualification for the 2002 World Cup, and the Germans had got back to winning ways in the first encounter, winning 1-0 thanks to a Dietmar Hamann goal that signified the end of the old Wembley Stadium, which was redeveloped after the match, and England manager Kevin Keegan, who resigned shortly after the defeat. England turned to a foreign coach to succeed him for the first time in their history, appointing Swedish Sven Goran Eriksson, and after a disappointing 0-0 draw against Finland they had won the return match as well as beating Albania and Greece to get their qualifying campaign back on track.

With five wins and a draw from their first six matches it was Germany who were in pole position by the time they hosted England in the Olympic Stadium in Munich. They were six points ahead of England and England badly needed a win, but it looked like it would be yet another disappointing night for English fans as they fell behind to an early goal. With just six minutes gone Michael Ballack chipped the ball into the England penalty area, Oliver Neuville headed it down and

Carsten Jancker got to the ball before England goalie David Seaman to prod the ball home.

Germany's lead was short lived however, as seven minutes later England were awarded a free kick in an attacking position when Michael Owen was needlessly shoved over on the left of the box. David Beckham curled in the free kick, and although the ball was initially cleared Gary Neville headed it back into the box, Nick Barmby headed it down and Owen volleyed it into the net.

Sebastian Deisler spurned a golden opportunity to regain the lead, shooting well wide with only Seaman to beat, but it was England who went in at half time with their noses in front. On the stroke of half time Beckham was brought down on the right, and his second attempt to get the ball into the box after his free kick had been cleared was headed down by Rio Ferdinand to Steven Gerrard just outside the box, and he slammed the ball past Oliver Kahn to put England 2-1 up.

It got even better for England three minutes into the second half, Beckham picking up a loose ball just outside the German box and firing in a cross on the turn. Emile Heskey showed great vision to pick out Owen with his knock-down and the Liverpool striker kept his shot down to beat Kahn for his second of the match. Germany had a chance to pull a goal back, but Ballack blasted over when Jancker's header found him in space in the England box. His miss proved costly, as with just over twenty minutes to go Owen completed his hat-trick and effectively sealed the win for England. Gerrard had won possession in midfield and played an early through-ball for Owen to run onto. Two touches took him into the penalty area, he looked up, then shot into the roof of the net to become the first Englishman to score a hat-trick against Germany since Geoff Hurst in the 1966 final.

English fans were ecstatic, but German supporters had seen enough and started streaming for the exits. Those who remained in the stadium witnessed further humiliation for their side, as eight minutes later Ferdinand snubbed out a German attack and passed to Paul Scholes, who played a neat one-two with Beckham before hitting a first time ball through to Heskey. He took one touch and fired it into the goal. Unbelievably England were 5-1 up in Germany's own backyard, and that proved to be the final score. Not only was it a vital win for England's chances of qualifying, it was all the sweeter for all the heartache that English fans had suffered at German hands over the years. It was also the first time Germany had conceded five goals in a match since 1958.

England beat Albania in their next match four days later to draw level with Germany on points and ahead of them on goal difference. If they could match or better Germany's result in their final match at home to Greece they would top the group, but it was far from plain sailing. In a disappointing performance they fell behind twice and only equalised through a ninety-third minute free kick from an inspired Beckham. With Germany only managing a 0-0 draw against Finland, England were through, and Germany were forced to win a play-off against Ukraine to make it to the Finals.

The Germans had the better tournament in South Korea and Japan however, going all the way to the final where they lost 2-0 to Brazil whilst England went out in the quarter finals, also to Brazil. The next England v Germany encounter was not until 2010, when the tables were turned in the second round of the World Cup in South Africa, the Germans enjoying a comprehensive 4-1 victory on their way to the semi final. England's 5-1 victory in Munich is still fondly remembered as one of England's finest hours though.

4th September 1972 Mark Spitz wins 7 Olympic golds

American swimmer Mark Spitz had told the world in 1968 that he was going to return from the Mexico City Olympics with six gold medals. He won two, both in relays, plus a silver and a bronze. It was a disappointing haul for a man who had entered the event as the holder of ten world records. What went wrong for him remains unclear. Perhaps it was the pressure he had heaped upon himself at the age of just eighteen, but he changed his coach the following year in search of a fresh start, hoping that things would go better for him in Munich in 1972, where he was aiming for not six but seven gold medals.

The first indication of whether it had worked or not was in the 200 metre butterfly. He was clearly in fine form, having broken the world record twice one month before the Games, but the question was whether he could reproduce that form when it mattered most, as he had failed to in Mexico. He set out to put any doubts to bed from the gun, opening up a lead of almost a second and a half at the first turn. His teammate Gary Hall had closed a little by half way, but he pulled further clear in the second half of the race to win his first gold medal of the Games by more than two seconds in a new world record time, Hall taking the silver behind him.

He didn't have to wait long for his second gold, with the 4x100 metre freestyle relay final scheduled just forty minutes after his first final. With his frantic workload Spitz had been rested for the qualifying race, but even without him the USA had broken the world record. With Spitz back for the final they took a further two seconds off the record time, three seconds clear of the Soviet Union in second. It was a good day's work for Spitz, and he was on track for his seven golds and had already proved that he had put the disappointment of Mexico City behind him.

The following day it was the 200 metre freestyle final. Three world records in three years had made him the favourite again, especially as his main rival, fellow American Steve Genter, had been hospitalised just days before. As he had in the 200 metre butterfly, Spitz tried to break his opponents at the start of the race, leading at the turn, but Genter, having recovered miraculously from his health problems and determined to beat the man who had urged him to withdraw from the race, wasn't going to let him get away and edged ahead of him at the midway point. Genter held off Spitz's challenge to lead at the final turn, but Spitz powered away in the final 50 metres to claim his third gold medal by almost a second. It was also his third world record in as many finals.

It was back to butterfly for his fourth final, two days later, this time over 100 metres. Again, he was the world record holder and favourite, having broken the world best time five times in the preceding years, including twice already in 1972. There was no way anyone was going to deny him his fourth gold medal, and he dominated the race from start to finish, winning by over a second as the world record fell yet again.

He was back in the pool later the same day chasing his fifth title, as part of the USA's 4x200 metre freestyle relay team. With the gold and silver medallists from the individual event, Spitz and Genter, back in their team for the final, the USA was expected to dominate, but it was the Soviets who led at the first change. Normal service had been resumed by halfway however, and with Genter on the third leg and Spitz bringing them home it was a comfortable victory in the end by almost six seconds, and another world record.

With two more events to go he was on track for the seven golds he set out for, and with the US 4x100 metre medley relay team an almost cert to win that, Spitz's final event, his last big hurdle was in the 100 metres freestyle. He was expecting a challenge from team mate Jerry Heidenreich, and he had been beaten in both of the earlier rounds of the event, although as world record holder Spitz was still the favourite and it was suspected that he was conserving his energy. He even considered withdrawing from the race just in case he blemished his perfect record, settling for six golds, but decided to race for fear of being labelled a "chicken". As he had with his other finals he went out hard, touching well ahead of Heidenreich at the turn. From there it was a question of just hanging on, and although Heidenreich pushed hard and closed the gap considerably he was unable to catch Spitz, who took the gold medal by 0.4 seconds. Of course, it was a sixth world record.

That just left the relay, and even though East Germany led after the first leg through their 100 metre and 200 metre backstroke gold medallist Roland Matthes, Tom Bruce put the USA into a slender lead after his breast-stroke leg. Spitz then took over swimming the butterfly leg and extended their lead to two seconds, before Heidenreich put the result beyond doubt on the anchor leg with his freestyle. Spitz had won his seventh gold medal, each of them won with world record times, and his team-mates lifted him into the air to take a lap of honour.

It was the most gold medals anyone had won at a single Olympics, and he became only the third competitor to win nine Olympic golds, joining Soviet gymnast Larisa Latynina and Finnish distance runner Paavo Nurmi. Only Michael

Phelps has won more since, picking up eight golds in the pool in Beijing in 2008 as well as six in Athens in 2004, four in London 2012 and five in Rio 2016.

Unfortunately the world's attention turned from his astonishing achievement to more sombre matters, when the following day Palestinian terrorists took members of the Israeli Olympic team hostage, demanding the release of Palestinian prisoners. The ensuing siege lasted for almost twenty four hours and left eleven members of the team plus a German policeman dead. 80,000 spectators and 3,000 athletes attended a memorial service for the victims, and the tragedy left a cloud over the rest of the Games.

Nevertheless, Spitz is remembered as one of the greatest ever Olympians. He retired from competition after the Munich Games so never added to his tally, and although he did attempt a comeback at the age of 41 in 1989 he was unable to meet the qualifying standard for the Barcelona Games.

10th September 2012
Andy Murray wins US Open

It was seventy six years since a British man had won a grand slam tennis singles title. Fred Perry had been the last, back in 1936. John Lloyd had come close, losing in the Australian Open final in 1977, as had Greg Rusedski, who had made the US Open final in 1997, but British success since the Second World War had been scarce.

Finally though Britain had found a genuine contender, with Scotland's Andy Murray making his way to the world's top ten. Unfortunately for him he was in a golden age for men's tennis, with anyone wanting to claim a grand slam having to overcome multi-grand slam winning greats Roger Federer, Rafael Nadal and Novak Djokovic. Murray reached his first major final in 2008, losing in the US Open final to Federer. In 2010 he was again beaten by the Swiss, this time in the Australian Open final, and the following year he was again the runner-up in Melbourne, this time losing out to Djokovic. In 2012 he suffered his fourth grand slam final defeat, the third at the hands of Federer, at Wimbledon, despite having taken the first set.

It was beginning to look like Murray would be always the bridesmaid and never the bride, having come so near and yet so far on four occasions. However, the breakthrough in his career came less than a month after his Wimbledon defeat, on the same court against the same player, as he gained revenge against Federer in the Olympic men's singles final, having also beaten Djokovic in the semi final. That victory seemed to have given him belief, and he went into the US Open later that year with renewed hope of winning his first grand slam title.

Murray, who had seen an improvement in his performances since engaging the services of eight time grand slam champion Ivan Lendl as his coach in 2011, was seeded three for the tournament. He was no stranger to success at Flushing Meadows, having won the junior title there in 2004, and he came through the first two rounds without any problems, winning both matches in straight sets. His third round match was much tighter, as he beat Spain's Feliciano Lopez in four sets, winning all of his three sets on tie-breaks. He brushed aside big-serving Canadian Milos Raonic in the fourth round, before a tough quarter final battle against Croatia's Marin Cilic. Having lost the opening set he won the second on a tie break before dropping just two games in winning the third and fourth sets. He also dropped the first set against Tomas Berdych of the Czech Republic in the semi final, but came back to win 5-7 6-2 6-1 7-6 to reach his fifth grand slam final.

If he was to finally win a grand slam he would have to overcome Djokovic, who in contrast to Murray's record of four final and six semi final defeats had five grand slams under his belt, including the US Open the previous year. It was first blood to Murray though, as he won a mammoth first set in a difficult swirling wind after 87 minutes, 24 of those taken up by a tie-break that the Scot won 12-10 on his sixth set point. There had been nothing between the two in the opening set. Each had broken the others serve twice, and at one point they had played out a 54 shot rally.

Murray held the advantage after edging the opening set, and quickly moved into a 4-0 lead in the second. Djokovic found his form again however from 5-2 down, winning three games in a row to level at 5-5. Murray refused to be rattled though, as he maybe would have been without Lendl's influence, and he broke the Serb again to pinch the set 7-5.

Djokovic came out fighting in the third set, and broke Murray twice to take it 6-2, with Murray becoming increasingly angry with himself. Djokovic was dominant in the fourth as well, breaking Murray to take an early 2-0 lead and winning it 6-3. It now looked like the momentum was with the defending champion, and that the tired-looking Murray's chance had gone. He was in danger of losing his fifth grand slam final and his second in a row, but he dug deep and broke his opponent in the opening game of the fifth. Djokovic did his upmost to break back, but Murray held him at bay with some brilliant defensive play. Not long later he had a double-break under his belt, and it looked like he was in the home straight, but the Serb wasn't beaten yet, and managed to break back to cut Murray's lead. The Scot kept his head though, and was soon serving for the championship. He showed no signs of nerves, and moved to 40-0 to give himself three championship points. Djokovic saved the first, but his return of serve on the second flew long to give Murray the title.

It had been a nerve-jangling, almost five hour encounter for fans of Murray and of British tennis, but he finally put 76 years of history and 287 disappointing grand slam tournaments behind him and the nation. He had avoided extending the record he shared with his coach Lendl, of four open era grand slam finals without winning, and as he crouched down with his face in his hands he looked almost in disbelief that he had finally fulfilled his dream.

The two faced each other again a few months later in the 2013 Australian Open final, but Djokovic was on top again that day as he won in four sets, but Murray won his second grand slam title and ended Britain's long wait for a Wimbledon champion later that year, beating Djokovic in straight sets. The two men, separated in age by just one week, were good friends off the court despite their intense rivalry on court, and Murray was even best man at Djokovic's wedding in 2014. The Serb had the upper hand in their meetings since the Wimbledon final though, beating Murray in two more Australian Open finals, in 2015 and 2016, the fourth time he had beaten Murray in the final at Melbourne, plus the 2016 French Open.

Murray did win his second Wimbledon title and a second Olympic gold medal in 2016 however, and became World Number One later that year. Whether or not he wins any more major titles in his career though, Murray will always be remembered as the man who broke Great Britain's grand slam hoodoo.

20th September 1969
Nicklaus concedes Jacklin's putt to tie Ryder Cup

Great Britain had only won the Ryder Cup once in thirty four years, losing twelve out of thirteen ties. They had been thrashed the previous time in 1967, losing by 23.5 to 8.5. As a result the British team was determined to make amends at Royal Birkdale, and had set out to take every advantage they could, with captain Eric Brown reported to have told his team not to give the Americans any help finding their balls if they found the rough.

There was a surprise on the first morning, as US captain Sam Snead left seven time major winner Jack Nicklaus out of the morning foursomes. Perhaps, given their dominance in the event, he underestimated the British team, but the Brits got off to a great start, ending the morning 3.5 0.5 up. It was a bad tempered morning, as the tone set by Brown was continued by both teams, the biggest flashpoint occurring when America's Ken Still insisted on standing too close to his opponent Maurice Bembridge as he was about to putt. It hadn't prevented Bembridge and Bernard Gallacher beating them 2&1, but the dispute was a taste of things to come.

Snead immediately introduced Nicklaus, who was making his debut as PGA rules had prevented his participation in previous years, for the afternoon foursomes. He was rewarded as The Golden Bear and his partner Dan Sikes beat Peter Butler and Bernard Hunt by one hole to help the USA cut the deficit to just one point, ending the first day 4.5-3.5 behind.

Friday morning was Great Britain's though, as they won two of the four four-balls, with the USA winning one and the other halved. That made their lead 7-5, and Snead responded by dropping Nicklaus and Sikes, who had lost their match against Tony Jacklin and Neil Coles, from the afternoon's matches. It might have been a controversial move, but it seemed to work, as the US once again had the better of the afternoon's matches, winning two and halving two, to level the scores at 8-8 with just the singles to play. Once again tempers had flared though, and the two captains had been forced to speak to their players to calm them down after a rule dispute had threatened to turn into a fist fight.

Although the US won the top two matches in the morning singles, Great Britain won five of the remaining six to take a 13-11 lead into the final session, and a real chance to claim a rare Ryder Cup victory. One of those points had come from Jacklin, who had comfortably beaten Nicklaus 4&3. Playing in his second Ryder Cup, Jacklin was on fine form having won The Open in July, and he had been unbeaten all week, with that singles win meaning he had won 4.5 points out of a maximum of 5. He faced Nicklaus again in the afternoon singles, the pair going out last in a match that always held the possibility of being the one to decide the destination of the trophy.

As the wind got up and the rain started to fall, the USA mounted yet another afternoon comeback. The two teams won two of the top four matches each, moving the score on to 15-13 to Great Britain, but wins for Sikes and for Gene Littler had dragged them level at 15-15. With just two matches left out on the course, the pressure was on. Both were level with just a few holes to play. In the penultimate match Billy Casper tested Brian Huggett's nerve as he chipped in for a birdie on the 17th, but Huggett holed his five-footer to stay level.

As they played the 18th, Jacklin and Nicklaus were themselves negotiating the 17th, with Nicklaus having just won the 16th to go one up with two to play. His approach to the 17th green was good, and he had an opportunity for an eagle. Jacklin in contrast was struggling, and his second shot was wide of the green, but somehow his ball avoided the bushes and made its way onto the green, albeit 50 yards from the hole. Putting first, Jacklin hit an incredible putt under pressure, holing it for an amazing eagle. Nicklaus was unable to respond and missed his eagle putt, and the match was all square going down the 18th.

Ahead of them on the 18th green, Huggett had heard the roar when Jacklin holed his putt, and, not realising that Jacklin had been one down at the time, thought that his team-mate was on the verge of victory. Thinking he needed to sink his four foot putt for a half to win the Ryder Cup he duly did, and for a minute thought he had secured victory. With the score 15.5-15.5 the match now depended on the final hole of the final match. Both men hit solid tee-shots, and were on the green in two. As they walked from the tee the two chatted, and both admitted to being terrified by the situation. Jacklin putted first, reading the line perfectly but leaving it two feet short. Nicklaus went next, with a chance to win the Cup, but with adrenaline surging he hit his ball four foot past. Now needing to hole out to secure at least half, Nicklaus dealt with the nerves to find the middle of the hole. The pressure was now on Jacklin, who needed to hole what would normally be an easy two-footer to tie the Ryder Cup, but with the weight of a nation's expectations on his shoulders, the putt became decidedly miss-able. However, after picking his own ball out of the hole, Nicklaus shocked everyone by picking up Jacklin's marker to concede the putt, giving his opponent a half to tie the match and the Ryder Cup, 16-16.

Jacklin later revealed that Nicklaus had said to him "I didn't think you'd have missed that putt, but in the circumstances, I would never give you the opportunity". It has gone down as one of the most sporting gestures ever seen in a sporting contest, made even more remarkable in light of the bad blood that there had been between the two teams up to that point, but it didn't please his team-mates, who ranged from incredulous to furious, with captain Snead quoted as saying "It was ridiculous to give him that putt. We went over there to win, not to be good ol' boys."

It was the first time the match had been halved, and it has only happened again once since then. The incident became known as "the concession", and the pair, who became friends after the event, designed a golf course together in Florida years later which they named The Concession Golf Club, which opened in 2006.

23rd September 2000
Steve Redgrave wins 5th Olympic gold

In the 1984 Olympics in Los Angeles, one of Great Britain's five gold medals was won in the rowing, in the men's coxed four. Few people would have remembered the names of the victorious crew after the games ended, and no-one could have known that one of them was set to become Britain's greatest ever Olympian.

Steve Redgrave was just 22 when he won his first Olympic gold medal, alongside Richard Budgett, Martin Cross, Andy Holmes and cox Adrian Ellison. Four years later in Seoul he and Holmes had dropped the others and were entered in both the coxed and coxless pairs. They won bronze in the coxed pairs with Patrick Sweeney as cox, but finished first in the coxless pairs to top the podium together for the second time in four years. Their relationship was not good though, and they went their separate ways after the games.

Redgrave's new partner was former Oxford University rower Matthew Pinsent, and he had a new coach too, former East Germany coach Jurgen Grobler. Under Grobler's instruction Redgrave won his third gold medal, in the coxless pairs in the 1992 Barcelona games. They defended their title four years later in Atlanta, Redgrave's fourth gold medal, but it looked as though it would be his last as he told reporters as he gasped for breath at the finish "Anybody who sees me in a boat has my permission to shoot me."

However, after four months away from training, Redgrave was hungry for more, and told Grobler that he wanted to try for a fifth gold. Pinsent had already made it clear that he wanted his third, but that he would prefer to move to a foursome. That gave Grobler just under four years to team them up with two more oarsmen to challenge in Sydney in 2000. He chose Tim Foster, who had won bronze in the coxless four in Atlanta, and James Cracknell, who had missed the 1992 and 1996 Olympics due to injury and illness.

It soon looked as though the German had worked his magic again, as the four became World Champions in 1997, but it was far from plain sailing from there on. First Redgrave was forced to reassess his life and his training after being diagnosed with type-one diabetes, although it didn't stop them winning the Worlds again in 1998. Then Foster injured his hand, then underwent an operation on his back, and he was replaced in the boat by Ed Coode. The new look team won the 1999 World

Championships, but when Foster battled back to fitness he regained his place at Coode's expense in time for Olympic year.

All was not well though, and the four could only manage fourth place in a World Cup event in July, just two months before the Olympic regatta. With work to do to claim an historic fifth gold medal, Redgrave and his team-mates made a good start, winning their heat comfortably ahead of Australia, one of the crews that had beaten them in July. Their semi final was also fairly routine, as they built up an early lead then cruised home to conserve strength.

The Great Britain boat got off to a flying start in the final, opening up a half length lead over Australia by the mid point with a stroke rate of 40 per minute. The Italians weren't going to let them get away though, and put in a brilliant third quarter to put themselves right back into contention, upping their rate to 44 strokes a minute. The British four refused to panic though, and upped their own game, increasing their stroke rate and keeping their noses in front as the two crews edged towards the finish line. There was nothing to separate them, with the Italians gaining inches on the British boat with every stroke, but their monumental efforts kept them just in front to deny Italy and claim a dramatic win.

Utterly spent, the four were unable to celebrate for a few moments, before Foster and Cracknell found the energy to punch the air. Pinsent unstrapped himself and clambered over Foster to embrace Redgrave, before splashing down into the water. They had won by less than four tenths of a second, with Italy taking silver and Australia bronze, themselves little more than a second behind the champions.

This time Redgrave really did say goodbye to Olympic rowing, although he later admitted that he did consider going for a sixth title. He was knighted in 2001 for services to rowing. Pinsent and Cracknell went on to win the title four years later in Athens, with Coode getting his chance along with Steve Williams, in an even closer finish that saw them cross the line eight hundredths of a second ahead of the Canadian crew. It was Pinsent's fourth Olympic gold, an outstanding achievement in itself, but still one short of Britain's greatest ever Olympian.

24th September 1988
Ben Johnson cheats his way to Olympic gold

Whilst Carl Lewis was grabbing the headlines by winning four gold medals at the 1984 LA Olympics, Canadian sprinter Ben Johnson was taking bronze medals behind him in the 100 metres and 4x100 metre relay. Lewis regularly had the beating of Johnson at that time, winning eight of their nine races up until 1985, but then the tide began to turn. Johnson had the upper hand by the 1987 World Championships in Rome, beating his rival four times in a row, and he turned his advantage into gold with a stunning world record time of 9.83 seconds, a tenth of a second faster than the previous record.

His performance shot him to global fame, and meant that he was the favourite for Olympic gold in Seoul the following year. Bidding to become the first Canadian to win 100 metre gold since 1928, Johnson won his heat comfortably in a time of 10.37 seconds. He was beaten into third in the second round however, finishing behind Linford Christie and Dennis Mitchell whilst Lewis broke the ten second barrier in his race. He was back on form in the semi final though, winning it in 10.03 seconds, but Lewis was slightly faster than him again, winning his semi in 9.97 seconds.

Although Lewis had posted the faster times in qualifying, Johnson was confident that he could repeat his World Championship victory in the final. "When the gun go off, the race be over" he told reporters, believing that his superior start would give him the lead he needed to deliver the gold medal. He did make the best start, but not by as much as in Rome the previous year when he had streaked away from Lewis at the gun. At fifty metres he was half a metre clear though, and Lewis never looked like catching him. Johnson crossed the line with one arm held aloft in triumph, claiming the gold medal and also a new world record time of 9.79 seconds, the first man to break 9.8 seconds. Lewis finished in second place for the silver medal with Christie taking bronze. With Calvin Smith finishing fourth in a time of 9.99 seconds it was the first ever race where four men had broken ten seconds.

Johnson was feted as the fastest man in history and one of Canada's greatest ever sportsmen. Canadian Prime Minister Brian Mulroney even rang Johnson on live TV to congratulate him on his achievement. The adulation came to a very abrupt end three days later however, when news broke that shocked the world. Johnson's blood and urine samples were found to contain traces of the banned anabolic steroid stanozolol, and he was stripped of his gold medal and the world record. Lewis was awarded the gold medal instead, with Christie upgraded to silver and Smith to bronze. The IAAF also wiped out his 1987 World Championship gold and world record time, meaning that Lewis was awarded that gold medal as well, plus Lewis' time in Seoul of 9.92 seconds became the new world record.

Johnson quickly turned from hero to villain, especially in Canada, with Canadians feeling a mixture of disappointment, embarrassment and anger. He initially denied cheating however, claiming that a friend of Lewis' who had been hanging around the drug testing room had slipped something into his beer. He later admitted long-term steroid use, but both he and the doctor who had administered his drugs were adamant that he hadn't taken the type of drug that was found in his samples. An enquiry carried out by the Canadian government gave the explanation that his steroids had been wrongly labelled, meaning that he had taken stanozolol by mistake rather than his steroid of choice furzabol. The fact that stanazolol takes longer to clear the system meant that traces were still detectable when he expected them to have gone. But for the mix-up he might well have got away with it.

Johnson was vilified for his deception, but in hindsight he may have been no more culpable than many others competing at the Games, including others who lined up against him in the final. Five of the other finalists failed drug tests at a later date, with Christie failing a test following his 200 metre heat a few days later, only to be reinstated on the grounds that he had ingested the drug in some ginseng tea. It was revealed years later that Lewis had failed a test at the US Olympic trials earlier in the year, and four others who had run that day failed a drugs test at some point in their careers, leading to the final being given the tag "the dirtiest race in history". A Canadian documentary twenty years later suggested that twenty athletes failed tests in Seoul but were allowed to get away with it, and that eighty percent of athletes competing showed signs of having taken steroids at some point in the past.

Nevertheless, Johnson's disqualification remains the highest profile case of drugs cheating in Olympic history, and he never recovered his reputation or his form. Following his two year ban he attempted to make a comeback, but failed to qualify for the 1991 World Championships in Tokyo. He did make it to the 1992 Barcelona Olympics, but finished last in his semi final. He tested positive for high levels of testosterone in 1993, effectively ending his career.

28th September 1996
Frankie Dettori's magnificent seven

Italian born jockey Frankie Dettori was already a firm favourite with punters by 1996, but one afternoon at Ascot was set to catapult him to global fame, making him beloved by race-goers, but far from popular with the bookies.

It was a seven race card at Ascot, with the feature race the Queen Elizabeth II Stakes, and Dettori had rides in all seven, looking to bounce back from a disappointing previous day at Haydock when he had returned no winners from his six rides. It had been an up and down season for him all round, with lots of winners but a period off injured after a heavy fall at Newbury that had made him miss Royal Ascot and Glorious Goodwood.

The first race of the day was the Cumberland Lodge Stakes, and it was no surprise when Dettori's mount Wall Street, the 2 to 1 favourite, finished the mile and a half first to set him on his way.

He was on Diffident for the second race, the Diadem Stakes. This horse was much more of an outsider, having put in a series of disappointing results leading up to the race, which was reflected in his 12 to 1 odds. However, the race was slow, which played into Frankie's hands. The congested field meant that Walter Swinburn on the favourite Lucayan Prince was unable to find space in time, and he just failed to catch Diffident, missing out in a photo finish to make it two wins out of two for Frankie, who later described the win as his luckiest of the year.

Next up was the big race of the day, the Queen Elizabeth II Stakes, in which he was riding Mark of Esteem, a 100 to 30 shot and the winner of the 2,000 Guineas. Although Dettori was on a roll, also fancied was Bosra Sham, the 1,000 Guineas winner ridden by Pat Eddery. Mark of Esteem didn't look to be in the best of condition in the parade ring, sweating profusely, but that didn't seem to affect him once the race started as he went head to head with Bosra Sham. Eddery put Bosra Sham into a lead of almost two lengths in the straight, but an amazing turn of speed saw Mark of Esteem fly past his rival to claim victory number three for Frankie by a length and a half. Dettori said of Mark of Esteem's acceleration "It almost knocked me out of my saddle."

Decorated Hero was his ride for the fourth race, the Tote Festival Handicap. Carrying top weight in a field of twenty six, this was a fairly long shot, reflected by the odds of 7 to 1. Nevertheless, Dettori made it four wins out of four with a comprehensive three and a half length victory.

The Rosemary Stakes was next, with Dettori riding Fatefully. This was a much closer race, and again Dettori had a bit of luck as a gap opened up in front of him when Ninia started to fade a furlong from home. Fatefully finished just ahead of Abeyr to win from a starting price of 7 to 4. There was an anxious wait for the result of a steward's enquiry, but the result stood.

The potential for racing history led the BBC to interrupt its Grandstand schedule to show the race live, and soon it was an amazing six wins from six races, as he won the Blue Seal Stakes onboard Lochangel. It was the first win for the two year old filly, but that hadn't stopped her starting at odds of 5 to 4, probably shortened by money following Dettori on his incredible winning run.

That left just one more race to go, the Gordon Carter Handicap. Dettori was set to ride Fujiyama Crest, which had started the day as a 12 to 1 long shot but had come in to 2 to 1 as the world of racing heard about Dettori's form. Again he was the top weight, and in normal circumstances he would have been seen as a no-hoper. Sir Gordon Richards had once ridden all six winners on a race card, and no-one had ever ridden seven, but the gods seemed to be smiling on the little Italian that day. Fujiyama Crest took the lead at the first bend, and with two furlongs to go it looked like Dettori was going to be the one to do it, with a lead of two lengths, but had the excitement got the better of him, had he gone too soon and would the field be able to close him down? With one furlong to go Northern Fleet made a move, slowly closing in on Fujiyama Crest, cutting the lead to a length then edging closer and closer, but it was too late – Dettori held on to win by a neck and he had done it, a magnificent seven wins out of seven.

A jubilant Frankie treated the raucous crowd to his trademark flying dismount as he returned to the winners enclosure for the seventh time that day. He threw his goggles into the crowd, before soaking the race-goers with champagne. He had incredibly completed a 25,095 to 1 accumulator, which some lucky gamblers had backed at the start of the day, winning themselves more than £500,000 in some cases. In total he is thought to have cost the bookmakers more than £30 million that day.

Five years later Dettori found out that the horse that had sealed his amazing feat was for sale, and bought him, bringing Fujiyama Crest to his home in Newmarket as a family pet. His achievement was almost matched in 2012 when Richard Hughes rode seven winners at Windsor, but that was an eight race card. However, his third place in the sixth race of the day left one small blemish on an otherwise similarly astonishing day.

29th September 1991
The War on the Shore

The USA had dominated the Ryder Cup after the Second World War, having won eighteen of the nineteen contests between 1947 and 1983, but Europe had hit back, winning two in a row in 1985 and '87. A tie in 1989 kept the trophy in Europe, but the US team was determined to win it back when they hosted the event in 1991.

The Ocean Course at Kiawah Island would provide a tough challenge for both sets of players, with steep slopes and challenging rough, as well as strong winds blowing in off the Atlantic Ocean that it bordered. Emotions were already running high in the build up to the match, fuelled by patriotism following the recent Gulf War, and some of the Americans even turned up on the first day wearing camouflage caps.

US preparations had been hampered though by a car crash involving some of the players on the way to a pre-Ryder Cup gala. Worst affected was Steve Pate, who suffered severe bruising that put his participation in doubt, but captain Dave Stockton decided to keep him in the team, although he played little part in the early stages. The Europeans were disrupted in a different way, after a local radio station started phoning them in the middle of the night to wake them up in their team hotel.

The golf finally began with the foursomes on Friday morning, and the American crowd was loud and partisan right from the start. The first of many flashpoints came on the tenth hole of the match between Paul Azinger and Chip Beck for the Americans and Seve Ballesteros and Jose Maria Olazabal, when Olazabal spotted that their opponents were using different balls for each hole, in breach of the rules. A row immediately broke out, the Americans first denying it, then claiming they had been unaware of the rule. The officials ruled that they had to stop doing it, but that there could be no penalty for having done it on the previous holes, but the Spaniards were furious. It worked in their favour though, as they came from behind to win 2&1, with Seve holing a forty foot putt on the 17th to win the match.

The bad feeling between the teams escalated though, especially between Ballesteros and Azinger, the American claiming that his opponent had repeatedly coughed in an attempt to put him off as he was taking his shot. Europe's win in that match had been the only highlight of the morning for them though, as the

Americans opened up a 3-1 lead. The afternoon was better for them though, with the Spanish pair beating Azinger and Beck again in fourballs, which along with a win for Steven Richardson and Mark James and a half for Sam Torrance and David Feherty cut the overnight lead to 4 and a half 3 and a half.

It was no less fiery on the Saturday, and the pattern of the day was the same, with the USA opening up a three point lead by winning the morning session 3-1, Europe's only win again coming from the Ballesteros/Olazabal pairing, only for Europe to fight back in the afternoon. This time it was even better for the Europeans, as they won three of the afternoon fourballs and halved the fourth to level the match at 8-8.

It was all to play for on the Sunday, and tensions escalated still further with the announcement that Pate would not be participating in the singles due to his injuries, despite having played in the fourballs the previous day. This meant that his match, which was to be against the in-form Ballesteros, was automatically halved, which drew heavy criticism from the Europeans. If he had not played the previous day the point would have been given Europe's way, and European captain Bernhard Gallacher questioned how he was fit to play on Saturday and not on Sunday. Under Ryder Cup rules each team has to nominate a player to sit out should an opponent not be able to play, and Europe's was David Gilford, who otherwise would have been playing Wayne Levi, who had struggled all week. Europe felt they had missed out on a good chance for two points as a result.

The drama started when the singles matches got under way. Stockton had tried to send his strongest players out first to try to get the US in front and build some momentum for the rest of the team, but Nick Faldo beat Ray Floyd and Feherty beat Payne Stewart, with Colin Montgomerie halving his match with Mark Calcavecchia, despite having been five shots down at the turn, to give the Europeans the edge. Azinger and Corey Pavin brought the home side level though with victories over Olazabal and Richardson, and the next four matches were shared, Ballesteros and Paul Broadhurst winning for Europe and Beck and Fred Couples for the USA. That left the scores level with two matches left out on the course.

When Lanny Wadkins beat James 3&2 the USA led the Ryder Cup 14-13, and everyone's attention turned to the final match, where Germany's Bernhard Langer was taking on Hale Irwin. The American had held a two shot lead after the 14th, but Langer pulled one back on the 15th. As more matches finished and the players and supporters came to watch the decider, unbelievable pressure started to build on both men. They halved the 16th, meaning that Langer had to win both remaining holes to win the match and level the overall score. The players had found the 17th particularly tough all weekend, and Irwin missed the green with his tee shot, but Langer was on safely. Irwin putted from just off the green, but his ball rolled well past the hole. Langer putted to within four feet, and when Irwin missed with his third shot Langer holed his putt to win the hole and make it all square with one to play.

Irwin's drive at 18 looked to be heading into trouble, but somehow found the fairway after hitting a spectator. His next shot was still thirty feet short though, giving Langer a chance to win the hole. Langer conceded an 18 inch putt to give Irwin a bogey, leaving him a six footer to win the hole with par. The pace was perfect, but he expected it to turn more than it did and it agonisingly missed the hole by millimetres. Langer was in tears as the Americans around him celebrated the tightest of wins by one point.

The bad blood following the contest dubbed "The War on the Shore" continued throughout the next few ties, but reached a head in 1999 at Brookline, where another close match was marred by the celebrations of the American team and their supporters, who ran onto the green to celebrate Justin Leonard's 45 five foot putt against Olazabal when the Spaniard was yet to take his putt that could have won the match.

30th September 2012

The Miracle at Medinah

The Ryder Cup looked to be heading back to the US going into the final day. Trailing 10-6 after the fourballs and foursomes, surely the Europeans, who had been struggling to keep pace with the US side since the opening day, couldn't come back from there. The US just needed 4 and a half points to win, with Europe needing 8 points to retain the trophy and 8 and a half to win it, a feat that would match the greatest ever Ryder Cup comeback. Even the most optimistic Europe supporter doubted it could be done.

The opening session had been level-pegging, with Europe and the USA winning two matches each, but the Americans had started to move ahead in the afternoon four-balls, winning three out of four points to move 5-3 ahead overnight. The Saturday morning foursomes were equally disastrous for Europe, as they again took just one of the four points on offer to trail 8-4. In the process Phil Mickelson and Keegan Bradley had handed out a 7 and 6 thrashing to Lee Westwood and Luke Donald, equalling the biggest ever winning margin in Ryder Cup history and emphasising the gulf between the two teams at that point.

Europe desperately needed to make up ground in the afternoon, but the USA stretched their lead by winning the first two four-balls to lead 10-4. Sergio Garcia and Luke Donald did stop the rot with a win by one hole over Tiger Woods and Steve Stricker, the Europeans just holding on for a one hole win after having led by four at the turn, but that still left them five points behind.

The deficit could have been even worse for Europe but for a late charge at the end of the day by Ian Poulter. Trailing by 2 to Jason Dufner and Zach Johnson with holes running out, the Englishman produced a breathtaking burst of 5 birdies in a row to push himself and his playing partner Rory McIlroy in front. He held his nerve on the 18th to secure the win and restrict the American advantage to 4. The result proved significant, not just in terms of the match score, but it also gave the beleaguered Europeans a vital lift going into the singles on Sunday.

The day started almost as dramatically as it ended, with McIlroy almost missing his tee-time and only arriving at the course ten minutes before he was due to tee-off. The panic didn't seem to affect him though, and he was soon embroiled in an epic battle with the in-form American Keegan Bradley, who was unbeaten all weekend up until then. All over the course the Europeans were starting to get their noses in front, and the nerves were starting to set in for the Americans and their supporters as they watched the scoreboard slowly turn from USA red to Europe blue.

Luke Donald was one of the Europeans who had started well, and it was he who delivered the first point of the day, winning his match against Bubba Watson on the 17th to chip away at the American lead. McIlroy edged a tight match against Bradley on the same green shortly after, and Europe's cheerleader-in-chief Poulter made it 3 points from 3 for the day when he came from behind to beat Webb Simpson. The USA, having started the day 10-6 ahead, suddenly found themselves just 10-9 in front, with the momentum swinging firmly in Europe's favour.

It was now a battle to see who would keep their nerve, and it was the Americans who were making the mistakes having looked imperious during the first two days. Paul Lawrie thrashed Brandt Snedeker, and Justin Rose won a thriller against the experienced Phil Mickelson, producing some brilliant approach play and holing his putts to win the 17th and 18th to pinch it by 1 hole.

It wasn't all one way traffic though, and American wins for Dustin Johnson and Zach Johnson edged them closer to their target, and it looked as if the European challenge might falter. However, Jim Furyk missed crucial putts to go down to Sergio Garcia and Lee Westwood tasted victory against Matt Kuchar to unbelievably put Europe 13-12 ahead.

It was all down to the last two matches out on the course – Martin Kaymer versus Steve Stricker and Francesco Molinari against Tiger Woods – none of whom had won a point all weekend until then. Kaymer had nosed in front of his opponent on the 17th, then found himself with two putts to win his tie and ensure that Europe would at least half the match and retain the trophy. He duly dispatched his ball into the hole to jubilant scenes around the course.

It wasn't all over yet though, as Molinari had a chance for a half against Woods on the 18th, despite going behind on the 17th. Woods had two short putts for the win, but amazingly missed both of them, giving the Italian an unexpected half and outright victory to Europe 14 and a half 13 and a half.

The celebrations were all the more emotional as captain Jose Maria Olazabal dedicated the triumph to he late friend and stalwart of the European team over the years, Seve Ballesteros, who had lost his battle against cancer the previous year. The Europeans had worn his trademark blue and white on the final day. 'Seve will always be present with this team' said Olazabal.

October

1st October 1988
"Where were the Germans? But frankly, who cares?"

For a short while in the Autumn of 1988 you could forget football, rugby and cricket: hockey was the nation's number one sport. A dismal European Football Championships had seen England lose all three group stage matches, and English clubs were still banned from playing in Europe following the Heysel Stadium disaster. England had lost 4-0 in the test series to the West Indies, and only Wales of the four home nations had got further than the quarter finals in the previous year's Rugby World Cup. The country needed new sporting heroes, and Great Britain's men's hockey team stepped up in style.

They had no real track record of Olympic success going into the Seoul Games however. Gold medals in 1908 and 1920 had been followed by years of failure, although things had started looking up in 1984 with a bronze medal after the Soviet Union's boycott of the Los Angeles event had allowed them in as a late replacement. That progress had been followed with a World Cup silver medal on home soil two years later, with the British team losing to Australia in the final. As a result there was cause for optimism in the camp ahead of the Olympic tournament.

Great Britain was seeded two, but they were confident of going one step further and bringing the gold home. They looked to be making a good start in their opening group match against South Korea, going 2-0 up through goals from Paul Barber and Sean Kerly, only for the hosts, spurred on by their home support, to score twice to snatch a draw in a bad tempered match. A comfortable 3-0 win over Canada got their campaign back on track, but then disaster struck as they lost their third match against old rivals West Germany, with a controversial late penalty giving the Germans a 2-1 win despite Barber having scored his third goal in three games.

With just three points taken from a possible six the British men now needed to win all of their remaining matches, but they managed to raise their game with a 3-1 victory over the Soviet Union thanks to another goal for Kerly and a fourth for Barber. They then saw off India 3-0 in a winner-takes-all match, Kerly and Barber again finding the net along with Jon Potter, to secure a semi final place. Here they would face Australia, who had beaten them to the gold at the World Cup.

They got off to a confident start and took the lead thanks to Kerly, and he added a second to go 2-0 up. However, just as they had against South Korea in their opening match they failed to hold onto their advantage and were pegged back to 2-2. This time though they weren't to be denied, and they found something extra to create a winner, Kerly completing his hat-trick and becoming a national hero in the process as he saw his side through to the Olympic final.

With the final scheduled for six o'clock in the morning in the UK millions of people got up early to watch the final against West Germany, who had beaten The Netherlands in their semi final. Having lost to the Germans in the group stage Great Britain needed to try something different, and they decided to attack the Germans from wide to try to get around the back of a well-organised German defence that had only conceded four goals on route to the final. The tactics soon paid dividends, with Imran Sherwani opening the scoring when he cut into the penalty circle from the left to pick up a deflected Sean Kerly pass, took the ball around the keeper and slotted home past a helpless defender.

That gave the whole side confidence, and they threw men forward in search of a second goal. They were open to German counterattacks however, and they were in debt to goalkeeper Ian Taylor for keeping the score at 1-0. Their attacking approach worked though, and twelve minutes into the second half Kerly doubled the British lead, finishing a well-worked short corner routine. Potter fired the ball in, Barber dummied and left the ball for Kerly who swept it home.

As the Germans desperately sought a way back into the match Stephen Batchelor found space on the right wing. He did well to bring the bouncing ball under control, then beat his Horst-Ulrich Hanel to get to the back line, sending in a teasing cross that found Sherwani in the perfect position and unmarked to put the ball into the net. "Where were the Germans," pondered BBC commentator Barry Davies, "But frankly, who cares?"

With the score now 3-0 to Great Britain there was no way back for the Germans, and although they did score a late consolation goal through Heiner Dopp it was too little too late and the victory was Great Britain's. As the players sank to their knees to celebrate, a nation of newly found hockey fans did too.

9th October 1996
"There's only one team in Tallinn"

Scotland had been drawn in a group with Austria, Belarus, Latvia, Sweden and Estonia in their attempts to qualify for the France 98 World Cup Finals. Their campaign had got off to a solid start, with a goalless draw in Austria and a 2-0 victory away to Latvia. For their third game the Scots were again away from home, against Latvia's Baltic neighbours Estonia.

The match was scheduled for a 6.45pm kick-off at the Kadrioru Stadium in the capital Tallinn, but when the Scots trained at the stadium the evening before the match they raised concerns about the standard of the floodlights, which were temporary lights that had been borrowed from Finland. Scottish manager Craig Brown considered them to be too low and the light not suitable for international football, and a complaint was lodged with FIFA. That was the start of the chaos.

FIFA match delegate Jean-Marie Gantenbein had shared their concerns, but had then decided that the game should go ahead as planned. Scotland's complaint was considered by a FIFA committee, which after a late night meeting eventually decreed that the kick-off should be brought forward to 3pm to avoid the need to use the floodlights. Their decision wasn't made until 2.30am on the morning of the match however, and when they found out about it the Estonians were furious with their decision. As the match was being played on a weekday, and most of their team were part-timers with regular jobs, it would be difficult for them to make it to the match, let alone their fans. They would also receive considerably less than the £50,000 they were expecting from the BBC for showing the game due to the unfavourable kick-off time, a big deal for a small footballing nation.

Estonia announced that they would not be changing their plans, and that they would arrive at the stadium ready for the original start time, not the earlier time. Speculation started to mount as to what the consequences would be if Estonia failed to turn up on time. The consensus was that Scotland would be awarded a 3-0 victory by default and would take all three points, and this seemed at the time to have been confirmed by Gantenbein. Chile had been awarded a win in similar circumstances in a play-off for the 1974 World Cup when the Soviet Union had refused to play in a venue they weren't happy with, and it was thought that that decision had set a precedent. The Scots had to be ready to play the match for this to happen though, and with Brown convinced that despite their protestations the Estonians would show up for the new kick-off time he prepared his team for the match as normal, and they took to the pitch ready for the 3pm kick-off.

In a sparsely populated stadium, around six hundred Scottish supporters watched the bizarre sight of their team lining up on their half of the pitch with the other half empty. Referee Miroslav Radoman was determined to do things by the book, and he and his assistants checked the nets, shook hands with Scotland captain John Collins, tossed a coin (Scotland won the toss), and blew his whistle. Billy Dodds, winning what should have been just his second cap, kicked off, passed the ball to Collins, then Radoman blew his whistle again and the match was over. The Scottish players punched the air in mock triumph as their fans sang "One team in Tallinn, there's only one team in Tallinn…"

With the Scottish contingent long gone and on their way back to the airport, the Estonian team arrived at the stadium for the 6.45pm kick-off time. Scotland thought they had earned the three points, but the Estonians were still bitterly unhappy with the way they had been treated, claiming that it had been impossible for them to fulfil the amended fixture.

The incident was referred to FIFA's Executive Committee, who met the following month to give it their consideration. They eventually determined that the match had to replayed at a neutral ground, a decision that some thought was made to favour Sweden, who were also in the group, the country of Lennart Johansson who had chaired the meeting.

The match was eventually replayed the following February in Monaco, and ended in a goalless draw. Despite earning two points less from the tie than they thought they had, Scotland still qualified for France as the highest scoring group runner-up. Estonia finished fifth, and Sweden also failed to qualify. At the Finals Scotland were drawn against another Scandinavian side, Norway, along with defending champions Brazil and Morocco. They lost their opener against Brazil 2-1, Collins equalising Cesar Sampaio's opener from the penalty spot before Tom Boyd's own goal, then Craig Burley's goal gave them a draw against Norway. A win in their final match against Morocco would have seen them through if Norway had failed to beat Brazil, but a disastrous performance saw them lose 3-0, with Norway beating Brazil anyway to go through along with the champions, and Scotland's campaign was over.

10th October 2015
Wales finally qualify for a major tournament

After failing to qualify for a major tournament for 57 years, Wales were on the verge of breaking their hoodoo by qualifying for the 2016 European Championships. No-one in the Principality was counting their chickens yet though, as they had suffered so many heartbreaks in falling just short since their appearance in the 1958 World Cup, when they reached the quarter finals.

Time and time again Wales had appeared to be on the verge of qualification, only to fall at the final hurdle. They had nearly qualified for the 1978 World Cup, needing to beat Scotland to put themselves on the verge of success, but a penalty awarded to Scotland for handball, despite Scottish striker Joe Jordan having handled the ball, turned the tie Scotland's way, and the Scots went through at Wales' expense.

They came close again for the 1982 World Cup, but failed to win a seemingly easy game at home to Iceland, then lost 3-0 in their final match against the Soviet Union to miss out on goal difference. Next it was Mexico '86. A home win against Scotland in the last game would have secured at least a play-off place. Wales took an early lead, but another late Scottish penalty saw Wales miss out on goal difference again.

Eight years later they were bidding for a place at the 1994 World Cup, and yet again their hopes rested on their final game. Needing to beat Romania and with the score at 1-1, Wales were awarded a penalty, but Paul Bodin slammed the ball onto the crossbar. Romania took advantage and won the match 2-1. Finally, Wales made it to a playoff against Russia for a place at the 2004 European Championships. They came away from the first leg in Moscow with the score 0-0, but they fell to a 1-0 defeat at home, agonisingly missing out yet again.

As a result many great Welsh players had never had the chance to show what they could do on the biggest stage: John Toshack, Ian Rush, Mark Hughes, Neville Southall, Kevin Ratcliffe and Ryan Giggs amongst them. One man who was determined not to suffer the same fate was Gareth Bale. The world's most expensive player was determined to see his country qualify, and arguably saved his best form for international matches. This Welsh squad, as well as having star names such as Bale and Arsenal's Aaron Ramsey, had much greater strength in depth, being able to call on a core of Premier League players rather than second and third tier players as previous teams had done. Hopes were high that this time it could be different.

Their campaign had almost floundered at the first hurdle though, with Andorra taking a shock lead in their opening match on a difficult artificial pitch, but two goals from Bale had rescued the win for Wales. They followed that with a goalless draw at home against Bosnia and a 2-1 win with ten men versus Cyprus. From there they gained a highly creditable draw away at Belgium, before an impressive 3-0 victory in Israel as their campaign really started to gain momentum. Then came the best result of the lot, 1-0 against Belgium in front of a raucous Cardiff crowd, then a gritty win by the same scoreline in baking hot Cyprus.

That left them knowing that a victory over third place Israel would guarantee their place in France, but although they dominated the match for long periods, Wales were unable to find a way through the Israeli defence. They could also have clinched qualification later that same day if Belgium had failed to beat Cyprus, but with just four minutes to go Belgium scored a goal that meant that Wales would have to wait a bit longer.

They had another chance to qualify a month later. Playing away in Bosnia they knew that they just needed a draw to seal qualification, but Wales were looking to qualify in style with a win, and started purposefully. They created the better chances of the first half, first Bale's cross just failing to pick out Robson-Kanu, then Neil Taylor unable to control his finish from Ramsey's cross. Bosnia had a chance of their own when Ben Davies slipped and Miralem Pjanic fed Edin Visca only for his shot to fly wide. Ramsey went close with a free kick, then on the stroke of half time should have broken the deadlock when he took too long when through one-on-one with Asmir Begovic in the Bosnian goal.

Bale missed a good chance early in the second half, and Wales were soon made to pay for spurning their opportunities, when out of nothing Bosnia scored from an aimless ball into the Wales box. For once the Welsh defence reacted slowly and Milan Djuric looped a header over Wayne Hennessey. Wales knew they would have a second chance a few days later against Andorra even if they lost, but were keen to seal their qualification without taking it to the wire, and pushed forwards for an equaliser, Chris Coleman bringing on strikers Simon Church and Sam Vokes. They left themselves vulnerable of the break though, and in injury time Djuric found space to lay the ball to Vedad Ibisevic who sealed the win for the home side.

Coleman was initially furious with the result at the final whistle, but then news came through from Jerusalem that Cyprus had beaten Israel, meaning that the

Israelis could no longer catch Wales. His frown turned into a roar of triumph, as he and his side celebrated with the 750 Welsh fans in the stadium something that no Welshmen had done for 58 years - they had qualified for a major tournament.

There was a poignant part to the evening too, as many, including Coleman, paid tribute to former Wales manager Gary Speed, who died in 2011 whilst Wales boss. "Gary Speed played his part and I'm sure he is smiling tonight" said Coleman of his predecessor. Speed, who had started to turn the Welsh side into a winning team during his time in charge, would certainly have been proud of his country's achievements that night.

Wales received a rapturous welcome when they returned to action three days later, beating Andorra 2-0 in front of a Cardiff crowd that celebrated like it hadn't for 58 years. Then, having waited so long to qualify, they made the most of their opportunity and made it through to the semi-finals of the tournament, the best performance by a British side for twenty years, where they lost to eventual winners Portugal.

17th October 1973
"Clown" goalie ends England's World Cup hopes

It was unthinkable that England wouldn't qualify for the 1974 World Cup. Having entered for the first time in 1950 they had been at every World Cup finals since, had won it in 1966 and had been one of the best sides in 1970, pushing Brazil all the way in the group stage but slipping up against West Germany in the quarter finals. Now though they needed to beat Poland at Wembley to make it to West Germany.

England were unused to having to qualify for World Cups though, having qualified by right as the hosts in 1966 and defending champions in 1970, and it was the first time that World Cup winning manager Sir Alf Ramsey had had to lead a qualifying campaign. They got off to a good start in their small, three team group, beating Wales 1-0 in Cardiff, before drawing the return match at Wembley 1-1. Wales then beat Poland before England took on Poland, away in Chorzow.

In a bad tempered match England went a goal down after just seven minutes, Bobby Moore, playing in one of his last matches for his country, failing to clear a free kick to allow Robert Gadocha to pounce to deflect the ball into the net. Moore's day got even worse shortly after half time when he was caught in possession by Wlodzimierz Lubanski who ran on to beat Peter Shilton at his near post. To make matters worse Alan Ball was sent off late in the game, frustration getting the better of him when he lashed out at Leslaw Cmikiewicz following a challenge on Martin Peters.

Poland followed up their victory with a win over Wales, leaving them top of the group with four points, one point ahead of England, with the final match a winner-takes-all showdown at Wembley. England needed to win to qualify, but a draw would be good enough for the Poles. Television pundit Brian Clough, who had resigned as Derby County boss earlier that week, didn't think England had anything to worry about, mainly because of the quality of their goalkeeper, Jan Tomaszewski, who he described as a "circus clown in gloves".

With England having beaten Austria 7-0 in a friendly match a few weeks before the game, England fans were hoping for another goal-fest, and it looked from the off as if the match could go that way, with England's first chance coming after just two minutes when Tomaszewski, seemingly proving Clough right, tried to roll the ball out to a team-mate but gave it straight to Allan Clarke two yards away from him and right in front of goal. The keeper dived at Clarke's feet to make amends, receiving a kick to the hand which he found out later had broken five bones. The adrenaline was flowing though and he was able to carry on to put in a memorable display of saves, some of them inspired, others more luck than judgement, but as the half progressed the game was still goalless. Poland also received some help from the woodwork and their defenders had to clear off the line, but one way or another it was 0-0 at half-time, and was looking as though the breakthrough might never come for England.

Clough wasn't worried though, telling viewers at half time "Keep calm. Put the kettle on mother. Don't worry, the goals are going to come." A goal did indeed come, twelve minutes into the second half, but it was Poland who broke the deadlock. Breaking quickly out of defence they played the ball into the England half where Norman Hunter, brought into the side to replace Moore, came forward to claim the ball. He somehow got the ball stuck under his foot though, gifting possession back to the Poles who charged forwards with Gregorz Lato, who played the ball across to Jan Domarski in space on the edge of the box. Domarski rifled his low shot past Shilton and into the net to give Poland a shock 1-0 lead.

England had to respond quickly, and they thought they had made the perfect response when Mick Channon put the ball in the net, only to see it ruled it out for handball. They finally managed to beat Tomaszewski six minutes after they had fallen behind, but they needed a penalty to do so. Martin Peters ran into the box and was bundled over by Adam Musial. Shilton was unable to watch, but Clarke made no mistake from the spot, sending Tomaszewski the wrong way to level at 1-1.

England now had twenty five minutes to find a winner, and the onslaught continued as they laid siege to the Poland goal. Surely they would be able to find the goal they desperately needed. More goal-line clearances kept the ball out, and Clarke thought he had scored and was turning away to celebrate, only to see his shot somehow kept out by Tomaszewski. With seconds to go a header from substitute Kevin Hector was cleared off the line, and that proved to be England's last chance. Poland had hung on for a famous draw that saw them on their way to the World Cup. Stunned silence filled the ground, the England players in tears and the crowd unable to believe that their team had failed to win despite thirty six efforts on goal to Poland's two. They had had twenty six corners, hit the woodwork twice and had four efforts cleared off the line. It was as one-sided a match as you could expect to see apart from one thing – the scoreline.

It was the end of an era for English football, as Ramsey's eleven year reign as England manager came to an end a few months later. England were not at the

World Cup the following summer, but Poland had a fine tournament, finishing third, with Tomaszewski saving two penalties along the way and being named the best goalkeeper of the competition. He also picked up a silver medal at the Olympics in 1976, and played for his country again at the 1978 World Cup, for which England again failed to qualify. He retired from international football in 1982, his sixty-three caps making him Poland's most capped goalkeeper. He later met Clough, the man who had called him a clown, with Clough apologising for his comments. Tomaszewski went on to become a pundit himself, before turning to a career in politics.

18th October 1968
Bob Beamon shatters the long jump world record

Surely no-one has ever made such an impact on global sport in such a short time as Bob Beamon did at the 1968 Olympics in Mexico City. Competing in his first, and only, Olympic Games, he jumped just twice in the final, taking about six seconds each time, but achieved something that truly shocked sports fans, one of the greatest performances ever seen at the Games.

Since Jesse Owens' twenty five year old world record had been broken by fellow American Ralph Boston in 1960 the record had been edged forward a further seven times, five more times by Boston and twice by the Soviet Union's Igor Ter-Ovansyan, but between them they had added just eight and three quarter inches to Owens' mark from 1935. Despite the presence of both in the 1968 Olympics, plus the 1964 gold medallist, Great Britain's Lynn Davies, Beamon started the event as favourite, having won twenty two of the twenty three competitions he had entered that season. He almost didn't make it through qualifying though, fouling his first two attempts before Boston advised him to play it safe and take off before the board. He re-measured his run-up, took off in front of the board and did enough to qualify.

Although he had stumbled through qualifying, his rivals still saw him as the man to beat. Davies and his coach Ron Pickering both thought he had the talent to jump "out of the pit" and become the first man to break the 28 foot barrier, but they also thought that he was capable of getting it wrong as he almost had in reaching the final. Beamon himself admitted later that he was feeling the pressure, and he found a Mexican bar to down a few tequilas the night before the final, not the recommended method of preparation, but it did the trick in enabling him to get a good night's sleep.

Fourth to jump in the final, Beamon stood stock still on the runway, staring straight ahead at his target, long arms hanging loose and relaxed at his side. He took half a step back, then set off down the track, accelerating quickly, his long strides getting up to his sub ten second 100 yard speed. He hit the board perfectly, reaching an incredible height that allowed him to hang in the air for an eternity before pushing his long legs out in front of him into the pit. As he landed his momentum carried him forward, and he bunny-hopped forward three more times before jogging away. He knew it was a good jump, but he faced a long wait to find out just how good as he had leapt too far for the optical measuring device and the officials had to use their tape measure to record his distance. When they announced it, 8 metres 90, Beamon, not used to metric measurements, still didn't realise what he had done until Boston pointed out that he had not only broken the 28 feet barrier, he had also surpassed 29 feet.

As he realised the enormity of his distance, 29 feet 2 and a half inches to be exact, 1 foot 9 and three quarter inches longer than Ter-Ovansyan's previous record, Beamon collapsed to his knees, literally unable to stand, and he stayed prone on the trackside with his hands over his face. When he was able to celebrate properly his rivals contemplated the effect his jump had had on the competition. They all knew they stood no chance of matching him, and the gold medal had already been decided. "Compared to this, we are children" said Ter-Ovansyan, and Davies added "He's destroyed this event."

Davies was essentially right, the competition stood no chance of reaching a peak like that, especially as a heavy rainstorm hit to make conditions extremely difficult, but it continued as the other jumpers battled for silver and bronze. Beamon himself only jumped once more, jumping 26 feet 4 before passing on his remaining four attempts. West German Klaus Beer managed 26 feet 8 in the second round, more than two feet less than Beamon but enough to give him the silver medal, and Boston's first round effort of 26 feet 7 earned him the bronze, with Ter-Ovansyan in fourth and Davies back in ninth.

Whilst most commentators acknowledged Beamon's famous leap as a wondrous achievement, there were some who pointed out that the jump was at altitude, beneficial to speed events, and that he had a 2 metres per second wind behind him, the maximum permissible for a record to stand. However, those, or similar, conditions were enjoyed by the other athletes that day, and none of them came close to achieving that distance.

Beamon himself never looked like matching or bettering his distance after the Olympics, and he soon signed for the Phoenix Suns basketball team, effectively ending his track and field career. His record however stood for twenty three years until another American jumper, Mike Powell, broke it in a titanic battle with Carl Lewis at the 1991 World Championships in Tokyo. Lewis himself had bettered Beamon's distance in the fourth round, but with an illegally strong tail-wind, before Powell broke it with a legal jump in the fifth. Beamon's remains the second best ever legal jump, and it remains the Olympic record, testament to just how good his jump was.

26th October 1986
Tyre blow-out costs Mansell F1 world title

Podium finishes had been few and far between in the first few years of British Formula One driver Nigel Mansell's career. After a promising third place in just the fifth race of his first full season in 1981, he had achieved just four more thirds by the latter stages of the 1985 season. A fine drive at Brands Hatch saw him pilot his Williams car to the first victory of his Formula one career, and having broken his duck he promptly followed it with his second win, in South Africa. It was back down to earth with a bump in the final race in Australia though as he was forced to retire on the opening lap with transmission problems. It wasn't to be the last time he was beset with bad luck at the Australian Grand Prix.

His performances meant that he was an outside bet for the 1986 Drivers' Championship, but with drivers such as Nelson Piquet, Alain Prost and Ayrton Senna up against him, it was going to be tough. He may have trying too hard in the opening race in Brazil, as he made contact with Senna on the very first lap and span off, forcing him to retire. Senna kept going to finish second behind fellow Brazilian Piquet in a great result for the local fans. It was better news in the next race in Spain though, as he finished second behind Senna.

Both Mansell and Senna failed to finish due to mechanical problems at San Marino, with Prost claiming his first win of the season for McLaren ahead of Piquet in second, leaving the two Brazilians at the top of the Drivers' Championship, with Mansell nine points behind. Prost dominated the weekend in Monaco, claiming pole and his second race win in a row to move to the top of the Championship. It was Mansell's turn at Spa, as he won his first race of the season from fifth on the grid, and he won again in Canada. That put him level on points with Senna, with Prost in the lead two points ahead of them.

An exciting US Grand Prix saw the lead change no fewer than six times, with Senna eventually claiming maximum points, before Mansell again put in two wins in a row. First he topped the podium in France ahead of Prost and Piquet, with Senna losing ground after an accident ended his race. Then he thrilled the crowds at the British Grand Prix, after a dramatic start had led to a restart when a pile-up that saw Frenchman Jacques Laffite break both legs. The eventual race was a battle between Mansell and his team-mate Piquet, which Mansell won despite having to drive the team's spare car. That catapulted him into the Championship lead for the first time, four points clear of Prost.

Two third place finishes followed in Germany and Hungary, both races being won by Piquet, but both men retired in the next race in Austria, with Prost taking his third chequered flag of the year. The Frenchman was disqualified in the next race at Monza though, for changing cars between the parade lap and the race. Piquet and Mansell battled for the victory, with the Brazilian getting the better of his team-mate for a crucial win. Mansell was still leading the Championship, but Piquet was now up to second, just five points behind.

Mansell was second on the grid in Portugal, but led from start to finish for his fifth win of the season, putting himself in pole position to claim the Championship as he opened up a ten point lead over Piquet and eleven over Prost. Austrian Gerhard Berger was a surprise winner of the penultimate race, in Mexico, but more crucially Prost and Piquet were able to cut Mansell's lead by finishing in second and fourth respectively, ahead of the Englishman in fifth.

That meant that with one race to go Mansell was on 70 points, Prost on 64 and Piquet 63, with Senna out of the running on 55. Mansell just needed to finish third or higher on the streets of Adelaide in Australia to secure the Drivers' Championship. If he failed to do so, either Prost or Piquet could pinch the title from him by winning the race. Mansell made the perfect start to the weekend by securing pole position, with Piquet alongside him and Prost on the second row. He made a poor start to the race though, dropping back to fourth on the first lap, with Senna the early pace-setter. Before too long though Piquet took the lead and began to pull away. If it stayed like this, Piquet would be the world champion, but Mansell only needed to move up one place to hold on to the title.

Piquet's lead only last six laps though, as Finn Keke Rosberg overtook him and started to pull away. This was good news for Mansell, and it got even better for him on lap 23 of the 82 lap race, as Piquet spun off the track. He was able to carry on, but dropped back even further. Eleven laps later Prost suffered a puncture, and also lost ground as he limped back to the pits for a tyre change, leaving him in fourth. Piquet had recovered though, and overtook Mansell to retake second.

Mansell was still on course for the title, but the race took another twist on lap 63 when race leader Rosberg was forced to retire after tyre failure. Piquet was now back in the lead, with Prost chasing him hard having passed Mansell, but it still wouldn't be enough to give either of them as long as Mansell could stay in third. On the next lap though, disaster struck the Englishman. Whilst driving at 180 miles per hour down the Brabham Straight his left rear tyre exploded in a burst of sparks and damaged his suspension. He did well to keep control of the car and steer the car off the track safely, but his race, and his championship hopes, were over.

Worried that Piquet would suffer the same fate, Williams brought Piquet in for a precautionary tyre change, handing Prost the lead. Piquet desperately tried to catch the Frenchman, but Prost held on to take the chequered flag and the title, before running out of fuel just metres over the finishing line. He had beaten Mansell to the Championship by just two points, with Piquet one point further behind.

It was a devastating blow for Mansell, and there was further disappointment for him as he finished runner up again in 1987 and 1991 before finally becoming world champion in style in 1992, winning the first five races of the season and securing the title with five races to spare. He promptly quit Formula One at the end of the season following a disagreement with Williams, moving to Indycar and winning that title in 1993, but he did make a short comeback to Formula One, driving for part of the 1994 and 1995 seasons.

30th October 1974
The Rumble in the Jungle

By the end of 1974 Muhammad Ali was 32, and in most peoples minds no longer The Greatest.

In 1967 Ali had been stripped of his world title and banned from boxing for three years having refused to join the US army to fight in Vietnam. He was never quite the same fighter when he returned to the ring in 1970, and he suffered his first ever defeat in 1971, losing to Joe Frazier on points. After winning some more comeback fights he then lost to Ken Norton in 1973, before winning the rematch later that year, and gained revenge against Frazier early in 1974. That earned him a shot at George Foreman for the world title.

Foreman had won eight fights in a row within two rounds, including against Ken Norton and Joe Frazier, the only two men to have beaten Muhammad Ali in his fourteen year career. Foreman had knocked Frazier down no less than six times in the opening two rounds, leaving the referee with no choice but to stop the fight and declare Foreman world champion. He was entering the fight with a professional record of 40 wins and no defeats, 37 of those wins by KO.

Those few who did believe in Ali's chances pointed out that he had beaten big, powerful men like Foreman before, and that his quicker movement and evasive abilities would see him through as they had against Sonny Liston. However, Foreman had himself shown that he was skilled at closing down the ring against opponents who attempted to out-manoeuvre him, homing in on his foe before unleashing his hammer blows. Nevertheless, Ali was happy to go along with the idea that that would be his tactic, telling journalists in his own inimitable style "Float like a butterfly, sting like a bee. His hands can't hit what his eyes can't see. Now you see me, now you don't. George thinks he will, but I know he won't", and "'I'm so fast that last night I turned off the light switch in my hotel room and got into bed before the room was dark.'

The fight was to be staged in Kinshasa in Zaire, for no other reason than the country's dictator Mobuto Sese Seko was keen for the publicity that the fight would generate and had agreed to put up most of the money for the $5 million purse that the two fighters had demanded of promoter Don King. With the venue little more than a clearing in the trees, the fight was dubbed The Rumble in the Jungle.

Whether or not it was all part of his plan to trick Foreman into expecting one style of boxing, then to choose a different tactic or not remains unclear, but Ali was anything but quick and evasive as the fight unfolded. After just one round of "dancing" he chose instead to allow himself to be pinned to the ropes. From there he dodged his head this way and that, leaning back so far that at times it looked as though he would fall out of the ring, and blocking as many of Foreman's violent blows as he could. It looked like a suicidal way to carry on, but as the fight progressed, Ali was still standing and slowly and surely Foreman was running out of steam. Goaded on by Ali with comments like "Hit harder George. That the best you got?" and "Harder sucker, swing harder", Foreman was starting to walk into a series of well placed jabs from Ali.

Many after the fight labelled Ali's tactics "rope-a-dope", but there was more to it than simply letting himself get hit to tire out his opponent. Ali was constantly thinking and moving, even when cornered, throwing Foreman off balance and restricting the power in his attacks by tying him up inside, blocking and denying him the space he needed to land his favourite punches.

Foreman gathered himself for what he hoped would be one final effort, unleashing a furious assault on his opponent, many of his punches this time hitting their target, but Ali survived, and from there on the sting had been taken out of the big man. The tide started to turn in the seventh and eighth rounds, and Ali was on top in the eighth. In the dying seconds of the round Ali put together a combination of punches that Foreman had no answer to. Having been in the corner himself, Ali cleverly manoeuvred his way into the middle of the ring and swapped places with his opponent. Clever footwork kept Foreman turning and off balance, unable to defend himself against a right, left, right, left combination. The final blow landed Foreman on the canvas, visibly dazed and physically spent. He was unable to get back up, and Ali was, against all the odds, champion of the world once more.

Ali went on the defend his title ten times in the next four years, before losing to Leon Spinks in February 1978, only to reclaim it in a rematch in September. He retired from the ring in 1981 with a record of 56 wins and 5 defeats, with most of the boxing world agreeing with him that he was indeed, The Greatest. He developed Parkinsons disease in 1984, but remained in the public eye, and famously lit the Olympic flame during the opening ceremony for the 1996 Games in Atlanta. He died of a respiratory disease in 2016 at the age of 74.

November

2nd November 2008
Lewis Hamilton wins F1 title on final bend

Formula One is sometimes criticised for a lack of excitement and overtaking, but the culmination of the 2008 season had both in abundance, with a dramatic finish to a title race that had never been closer.

One of the favourites at the start of the season was twenty three year old British driver Lewis Hamilton, who had progressed through the ranks of karting and formula racing to make his F1 debut for McLaren in 2007. After a record-breaking debut season he finished the season in joint second place, missing out on the title to Kimi Raikkonen by one point despite having led going into the final race in Brazil. It was one of the closest finishes to a season ever, and hopes were high that the 2008 season could follow suit.

The young Brit got off to the perfect start in his quest to go one better in the opening race of 2008, securing pole position and winning the Australian Grand Prix. Disappointment followed in Malaysia and Bahrain however, Hamilton finishing fifth and thirteenth, and it looked as though Ferrari might dominate the season, with their drivers Raikkonen and Felipe Massa winning both races.

He was back on the podium in Spain, albeit behind the two Ferraris, and he was again behind a Ferrari in Turkey, taking second place behind Massa to keep in touch with the Ferrari pair in the Drivers Championship. Next it was the streets of Monaco, where Hamilton got back to winning ways to take the Championship lead, but his advantage was short-lived, with retirement in Canada and tenth place in France following a ten place grid penalty imposed after an incident in Canada, and with Massa winning in France he took back the Championship lead.

Hamilton was doubly keen to do well in the next race, both to boost his title hopes and because it was the British Grand Prix at Silverstone in front of thousands of British fans. He didn't disappoint, and won the race convincingly with the two Ferraris struggling in the wet conditions. He topped the podium again in Germany and moved back to the top of the standings. All three contenders had disappointing races in Hungary, before Massa won the European and Belgian Grand Prix, the latter after Hamilton had finished first only to be given a penalty and relegated the third, to cut the lead to two points.

Massa and Hamilton could only manage sixth and seventh respectively at Monza, but Hamilton stretched his lead to seven points in Singapore with a third place finish and Massa out of the points despite starting on pole, a mistake in the pit lane costing him valuable time. The race will be most remembered though for an incident that saw Renault's Nelson Piquet Junior deliberately crash his car under team orders in order to bring out the safety car, helping his team-mate Fernando Alonso win the race. Alonso won again in Japan, and the Hamilton/Massa battle continued as the Brazilian cut the gap to just five points with two races to go with a seventh place to Hamilton's twelfth.

The penultimate race was the Chinese Grand Prix, where the year before Hamilton had skidded out of the race whilst in a position to secure the points he needed to secure the World Title, but any bad memories were quickly erased as he produced a perfect weekend, winning the race from pole. With Massa in second though, the World Title was still up for grabs. Hamilton would take a seven point lead over Massa into the final race, on Massa's home track in Brazil. Even if Massa won the race Hamilton only had to finish fifth to secure the crown.

It sounded straightforward, but with memories of falling short on the same track the previous year, it proved to be anything but plain sailing. The drama was heightened by a heavy rain storm shortly before the race was due to begin which delayed the start by ten minutes and made driving conditions treacherous. Massa had given himself every chance of victory, qualifying on pole, and he got off to a good start to lead into the first corner, with Hamilton back in fourth. A couple of spins on the opening lap brought the safety car straight out, but with the track starting to show signs of drying the race became a tactical battle. Massa was the first to come into the pits to change tyres, with Hamilton following suit a couple of laps later. With other drivers doing the same, Massa was back in the lead, with Hamilton now in fifth, enough to give the Englishman the title, but only just.

With further rain expected Hamilton came in again, staying in fifth but now with Sebastian Vettel hot on his heels. Massa also pitted, but managed to keep the lead he desperately needed. With two laps to go disaster struck, as Vettel charged past Hamilton, pushing him back to sixth. It looked as though Massa would be crowned World Champion and Hamilton would lose out in the last race again. As Massa took the chequered flag and the points he needed the Ferrari garage started to celebrate, but with Hamilton still on his final lap it wasn't over yet. With Timo Glock now in fifth place in front of him, struggling on the again wet track on dry tyres, Hamilton made up a monumental amount of time on the final lap. He was still behind him coming into the final bend though, but managed to get past him at the death to claim the fifth spot that secured the World Championship.

It was an unbelievable finish to the season that saw the destination of the World Championship change twice in the final two laps, from Hamilton to Massa and back again, with Hamilton winning by just one point. Hamilton had also become the youngest ever World Champion, and the first black driver to become Champion. He moved to the Mercedes team in 2013, becoming World Champion again in 2014 and 2015.

13th November 1994
Schumacher collides with Hill to claim F1 title

The 1994 Formula One season had it all – drama, controversy, tragedy and a highly contentious finish that decided the destination of the title in the very last race.

It was only the second full season of racing for British driver Damon Hill, although he came with a fine pedigree, his father Graham having been World Champion in 1962 and 1968. Driving for Williams-Renault he finished second in the opening race of the season in Brazil, behind the Benetton-Ford of Germany's Michael Schumacher. The two drivers were destined to be locked together in battle for the rest of the year. Schumacher was the man to set the early pace though, as he followed up his win in Brazil with victories in the Pacific, San Marino and Monaco Grand Prix, with Hill only managing sixth place in San Marino and having retired in the other two.

San Marino will be remembered more for the tragic deaths of two drivers than the race itself however. The weekend had got off to a bad start when Rubens Barrichello crashed during practice and was knocked unconscious, swallowing his tongue and having to be saved by the medical team. Then in qualifying things got much worse, when Roland Ratzenberger crashed into a wall at 180 miles per hour. He later died from the head injuries he sustained. The race went ahead despite the fatality, but after just seven laps three time World Champion and Hill's team-mate Ayrton Senna lost control of his car and left the track at 190 miles per hour. He crashed into an unprotected concrete wall, and despite being quickly airlifted to hospital he was pronounced dead later that day. The Grand Prix Drivers' Association was formed as a result of that weekend to protect the safety of the drivers, leading to several rule changes throughout the rest of the season.

David Coulthard and Nigel Mansell were drafted in to drive for Williams in Senna's absence, and Hill's fortunes started to improve, with a win in Spain, with Schumacher in second, and second places in Canada and France. The German had taken his fifth and sixth wins of the season in those races though, and with six wins and a second place in the first seven races he looked well on track to take the Drivers' Title with a commanding 37 point lead. His luck was about to change at the next race though, the British Grand Prix at Silverstone.

Hill had qualified for the race on pole, but Schumacher had upset the British fans by trying to assert his authority on the parade lap by briefly overtaking Hill.

With Schumacher pushing Hill for the lead when the race began he was given a five second stop-go penalty for his parade lap antics, which his team told him to ignore at first, risking disqualification. He did then take his penalty, dropping down to third. Hill took the chequered flag with Schumacher finishing second, but the German was later disqualified for ignoring instructions, and was also given a two race ban.

He was allowed to race whilst the ban was appealed, but the German fans were left disappointed at Hockenheim as he retired with engine failure. Hill finished eighth and out of the points, leaving Schumacher's lead at 27. Schumacher led Hill home to extend his lead in Hungary, but three wins in a row for the Englishman in Belgium, Italy and Portugal, with Schumacher disqualified in the first then serving his two race ban in the second and third, cut the Championship lead to just one point.

Schumacher marked his return with a win ahead of Hill at the European Grand Prix, but Hill returned the favour in Japan, giving Schumacher a one point lead over his rival going into the final race in Australia. All Hill needed to do was finish ahead of Schumacher to claim the title.

Hill's stand-in team-mate Mansell claimed pole, with Schumacher next to him on the front row and Hill one place behind. Mansell made a poor start though, leaving Schumacher and Hill first and second. They remained in those positions until lap 35, when Schumacher ran wide at a corner and scraped against a wall. This enabled Hill to get right on his tail, with the additional possibility that his car had sustained some damage, although Hill did not know this. Thinking that he might not have a better chance, Hill pulled alongside, but as he did Schumacher turned into him and the cars collided. Schumacher's Benetton was thrown into the air, and he was out of the race. Hill carried on though, and it looked as though he would carry on for the win, but it wasn't to be. His suspension had been damaged by the impact and he too was forced to retire shortly after the incident. With neither man able to score Hill would end the season an agonising one point behind the champion, with many believing that the German had deliberately taken Hill out, realising that he would be unable to complete the race in his damaged car. The FIA took no action against Schumacher however, and Williams made no protest, perhaps as they were still coming to terms with Senna's death, to give Schumacher his first of seven World Titles.

Hill finished second behind Schumacher again in 1995, but finally claimed a World Title of his own in 1996, emulating his father to make them the first father and son to both become Formula One World Champions. Schumacher retired at the end of the 2006 season, but made a comeback in 2010 before retiring for good in 2012. He suffered life-threatening injuries in a skiing accident in 2013.

22nd November 2003
Last gasp Wilkinson drop goal wins World Cup for England

In the 1991 Rugby World Cup final Australia had dashed English hopes as they beat England at their home ground Twickenham. Now, with the two teams meeting in the final again, this time in Sydney, England were out for revenge.

England had disappointed in the 1999 World Cup, beaten comfortably by South Africa at the quarter final stage, but Head Coach Clive Woodward had since turned them into genuine contenders. They had completed the Six Nations Grand Slam earlier in the year, their third championship in four years, and were regularly beating their southern hemisphere rivals. They had comfortably come through their group, scoring 84 and 111 points against Georgia and Uruguay respectively and beating Samoa and South Africa too. The Aussies, aiming to become the first country to retain the trophy, had also had few problems in their group, beating Argentina and Romania before scoring a World Cup record twenty two tries in beating Namibia 142-0. They had been pushed to the wire by Ireland in their final match though, finally triumphing 17-16 in a tight match.

The quarter finals had matched England with old rivals Wales, an encounter they came through 28-17, whilst Australia also faced Home Nations opposition, beating Scotland 33-16. They then met their fierce rivals New Zealand for a place in the final, triumphing 22-10, whilst England beat France 24-7, with all of their points coming from the left boot of outside half Johnny Wilkinson.

The Wallabies got off to a dream start in the final. With just six minutes gone outside half Stephen Larkham put in an inch perfect high kick and winger Lote Tuqiri out jumped England's Jason Robinson to claim the ball and touch down. Elton Flatley was unable to add the conversion, his attempt hitting the post, but Australia had an early 5-0 lead. England hit back five minutes later with a Wilkinson penalty, and two more goals from the England fly half gave them a 9-5 lead after half an hour.

England's pack were starting to dominate, and Ben Kay spurned an excellent chance to score when he knocked on with the try line at his mercy, but moments later they had the try they had been threatening. With just two minutes to go to half time Lawrence Dallaglio made a break in midfield, Wilkinson was on hand to support him and he put the speedy Jason Robinson through to slide home in the corner. For once the metronomic Wilkinson was unsuccessful with his conversion attempt, but England had a crucial 14-5 advantage at half time.

Australia cut England's lead seven minutes into the second half, a Flatley penalty making it 14-8, but the England forwards continued to cause problems for their opponents. They were unable to turn possession into points though, and they were reduced to a number of unsuccessful drop goal attempts from Wilkinson at they tried to increase their lead. Then, with just over an hour played, they were penalised again, and Flatley punished them with his second penalty of the game. With less than twenty minutes to go England led by just three points, and the tension started to build. England tried to find a score to give themselves some breathing space, but handling errors and another Wilkinson drop goal miss put paid to that. Time was running out for the Wallabies though. Going into the final minute Stirling Mortlock and George Smith drove the Aussies into the England half and referee Andre Watson awarded Australia a penalty. Flatley coped with the huge pressure to kick the penalty and bring the scores level at 14-14. It was the last kick of normal time, and the final would have to be settled in extra time.

With England having been so close to winning they had to raise themselves to keep playing, as well as dealing with the tension and battling fatigue, but they managed to do so, and got their noses in front again after just two minutes of the restart through another Wilkinson penalty. Fifteen minutes later, and with only three minutes of extra time to go, the scores were level again though, with Flatley replying for the hosts.

It looked as though sudden death extra time would be needed, but England weren't finished yet. Australian full back Mat Rogers fielded an up field kick, and aimed for touch. He sliced his kick though, and England were gifted a line-out mid way inside the Australia half. From there they began a move that had been years in the planning, drilled by Woodward on the training ground with military precision. Steve Thompson took the crucial line out throw, picking out Lewis Moody at the back of the line. From the resulting ruck scrum half Matt Dawson made a break to gain vital yards, into the 22, catching out the Aussie defence who were expecting the drop goal attempt. Captain Martin Johnson took the ball and drove on, allowing Dawson to get back to his feet for the most important pass of his life. With just twenty six seconds to go Dawson passed the ball came back to Wilkinson, who took the ball at shoulder height. He aimed his drop goal at the posts, kicking with his right foot rather than his usual left, and the crowd held its breath. It wasn't his best ever strike, but it was good enough, between the posts, and the men in white were 20-17 ahead with time virtually up.

This time the Wallabies had almost no time to respond. All England had to do was to hold on to the restart, which Trevor Woodman did. The extra time clock ticked past twenty minutes, and the ball was thumped out of play by Mike Catt. England had done it – the first northern hemisphere team to be crowned world champions in the most dramatic style imaginable.

The side was given a hero's welcome when they arrived back at Heathrow Airport, with thousands of ecstatic fans there to cheer their heroes and sing *Swing Low Sweet Chariot.* An open top bus tour through the streets of London followed a few days later, where hundreds of thousands of fans turned out to celebrate English rugby's greatest moment.

AFTERWORD

Thanks for reading Incredible Moments in Sport – I hope you enjoyed it.

If you did, could you do me a big, big favour? I would be massively grateful if you could take a second to post a short review on Amazon/Goodreads or wherever you review books. It might sound like nothing, but ratings can make a huge difference to whether other readers choose to read books by indie authors like me.

I truly appreciate all of your reviews and make sure I read them all.

To find out more about me and my other books please visit www.ianslatter.com.

Printed in Great Britain
by Amazon